The Book of Books

A Brief Introduction to the Bible

(Revised Edition)

John Schaller

NORTHWESTERN PUBLISHING HOUSE
Milwaukee, Wisconsin

Second edition,   2002

Cover art by Frank Ordaz.

Covers of first edition volumes and certain second edition volumes feature illustrations by James Tissot (1836–1902).

Library of Congress Card 90-60998
Northwestern Publishing House
1250 N. 113th St., Milwaukee, WI 53226-3284
© 1990 Northwestern Publishing House
Published 1990
Printed in the United States of America
ISBN 978-0-8100-1270-7
ISBN 978-0-8100-2533-2 (e-book)

23 24 25 26 27 28   12 11 10 9 8 7 6 5 4

CONTENTS

Editor's Preface

The People's Bible is just what the name implies—a Bible for the people. It includes the complete text of the Holy Scriptures in the popular New International Version. The commentary following the Scripture sections contains personal applications as well as historical background and explanations of the text.

The authors of The People's Bible are men of scholarship and practical insight, gained from years of experience in the teaching and preaching ministries. They have tried to avoid the technical jargon that limits so many commentary series to professional Bible scholars.

The most important feature of these books is that they are Christ-centered. Speaking of the Old Testament Scriptures, Jesus himself declared, "These are the Scriptures that testify about me" (John 5:39). Each volume of The People's Bible directs our attention to Jesus Christ. He is the center of the entire Bible. He is our only Savior.

The commentaries also have maps, illustrations, and archaeological information when appropriate. All the books include running heads to direct the reader to the passage he is looking for.

This commentary series was initiated by the Commission on Christian Literature of the Wisconsin Evangelical Lutheran Synod.

It is our prayer that this endeavor may continue as it began. We dedicate these volumes to the glory of God and to the good of his people.

FOREWORD

As God's Word is timeless, so what is written true to God's Word shares that timeless quality. With that thought in place, Northwestern Publishing House determined to publish this revised version of *The Book of Books* by Pastor John Schaller. From the time that his English edition was first published in 1924 until now, the truths expressed in it have not changed. It is still a "fundamental truth that all Scripture is given by divine inspiration, the holy men of God having verily and truly written the words which the Holy Ghost taught them." It is still rewarding to read John Schaller's introduction to the inspired Scriptures.

In making this treasured book available to today's readers, the editors were careful to retain his thought without further comment while bringing his style and some information up-to-date. For example, the preface that follows is reproduced as Pastor Schaller wrote it, but in the rest of the text, outdated expressions such as "twelvemonth" and "Holy Writ" have been modernized. Also, the dating of the prophets has been made to coincide as closely as possible to Edwin R. Thiele's more recent chronology of the Hebrew kings. Finally, some highly technical pages on textual criticism and some dated material on the church year have been omitted.

Appropriately, the first editorial hand to help create this revision belonged to Pastor Loren A. Schaller, grandson of the author. Following further revision, we are pleased to offer *The Book of Books* as a fitting companion volume to The People's Bible and as a volume of interest to all who treasure the Book of books, the Bible.

The Publisher

AUTHOR'S PREFACE

Nearly 20 years ago, it became my privilege to present my *Kurze Bibelkunde* to those whose special calling or personal desire demanded certain information concerning the Scriptures in their historical aspect. The edition of the German book having become exhausted since about a twelvemonth, the question was raised whether a new edition would find a market of profitable extent. A survey of present-day conditions in the Lutheran church of our country, especially in regard to the rapid growth of the English work among Lutherans of German descent, suggested the advisability of reissuing the *Bibelkunde* in the American language, in order that the needs of the greater number might be met or, if so be, anticipated. It was therefore decided not to print a second edition of the German book but to put forth the volume herewith offered to the Christian reader.

No one who recognizes the urgent need for more and better Bible study among our people will deny that those who are to be the leaders in this desirable endeavor should have at hand, in compact form, what every reader of the Bible should know concerning its history as a book. Who were the writers of the various parts of the Scriptures; under what circumstances each book was written; what we know of the special purpose of each book; how the various books came to be assembled in the volume which we now call Holy Writ; how this volume was handed down to us—these and kindred questions in great number must on occasion be answered not only by our pastors but also by those who are called upon to aid in the Christian education of our children and young people. It is the special hope of the author that his effort may prove of some value to the ever-increasing army of young men and women who are put in charge of parochial schools or of classes in our Sunday schools. At the same time, the information herewith presented should prove both interesting and suggestive to Christian men and women generally who take real pleasure in reading and studying the Bible for their own edification.

It was not my intention to offer a treatise that might be considered exhaustive in any respect. The numerous questions that come up for discussion here have been debated for many centuries, both by the friends and by the enemies of the Holy Book. Hundreds of pens have been busy producing a voluminous literature in which the results of much laborious and minute research have been recorded. Add to this that we come in touch with all branches of theological study as we proceed along our way, and it will be plain that our short sketch is no more than a summary of results. It should be stated at once, however, that we are hopelessly at variance with all those alleged results of modern biblical criticism that rest upon the false premises of rationalism in any guise. Whatever faults may otherwise be found to disfigure this book, it is confidently asserted that every statement it contains was written with sincere faith in the fundamental truth that all Scripture is given by divine inspiration, the holy men of God having verily and truly written the words the Holy Spirit taught them. This position may be sneered at as old-fashioned and unprogressive, but an experience of many years has proved it to be the only safe and sane one for a Christian to maintain, since it rests upon the Scripture's own witness of itself.

No defense is offered for the selection of the material discussed in this book. Since no attempt was made to discuss all sides of every question, the choice of items to be enlarged upon was necessarily governed by the personal judgment of the writer concerning the requirements of the readers whom he had in view. As those who have used his German book have abundantly testified to its helpfulness, there seemed to be no reason why this English volume should differ from it materially in scope and content. But while the same general scheme of arrangement was also retained, every paragraph was recast into what is hoped to prove a more pleasing and readable form. The continuous numeration of the paragraphs throughout the book is a minor change, introduced to facilitate reference.

Should it please the Lord our Savior to grant to the readers of this book but a portion of the spiritual enjoyment that went with the work of its composition, the chief desire of the writer will be gratified.

Wauwatosa, Wis. J. Schaller

PART ONE

The Old Testament

Chapter 1
The Holy Book

1. Name

The most wonderful book in the world is called the Bible. The name is derived from the Greek word *biblia,* which means "books." So this name of the Bible suggests that what we look upon as *one* book really consists of quite a number of single books, written by many human authors. The line of writers who contributed to the Bible begins with Moses, 1,500 years before Christ, and ends with the apostle John, about one hundred years after Christ.

Though so many different men in so many ages became authors of biblical books, the contents of the Bible are nevertheless so homogeneous throughout that every attentive reader finds its teachings to be altogether uniform from first to last. This feature, among others, makes the Bible a unique book and points to its supernatural origin.

Another name for the Bible is the Scriptures, or Scripture, from the Latin word meaning "to write."

2. Origin

Though written by men and in the language of men, the Bible is of divine origin, because it was written by the inspiration of God. According to the testimony of the holy

1

writers, they were not only told by God *what* to write but were given *the very words* that they were to record. Thus Moses declares a hundred times that "the Lord said to Moses." Every reader of the Bible has seen similar assertions made by the prophets. The same claim is implied in many statements of the apostles; read 1 Corinthians 11:23; 15:3; and Galatians 1:11,12 as examples.

The Christian church has never challenged, and cannot challenge, this claim of the holy men. In fact, the church has always understood the human writers of the biblical books as declaring that they received from God not only the thoughts to be expressed but also the words to be used in their expression. This is called the verbal inspiration of the Scriptures, a doctrine that is unmistakably enunciated in such texts as John 14:26; 2 Peter 1:20,21; and 1 Corinthians 2:13 ("expressing spiritual truths in spiritual words").

This truth does not change the fact that every human writer thus inspired wrote the divine revelation in his own particular style. The Holy Spirit employed the minds of his human instruments as they were and yet spoke his own words through them. Again, it does not affect the reality of inspiration that some of the holy writers certainly made use of previous written records or of human tradition. As the Holy Spirit directed their attention to such sources of information and guided them in the choice of material and of words, all that they wrote became part of the inspired Word of God.

Upon this truth Paul based his assertion that the gospel is the power of God for salvation (Romans 1:16). Were it not for divine inspiration, it would be impossible that the Word as written could effect a total change of human nature (2 Timothy 3:16,17). It alone explains the so-called civilizing influence of the Bible.

Furthermore, verbal inspiration guarantees the inerrancy of the Scriptures. Because every word of the Bible is given by the inspiration of God, the Holy Book is altogether without error, even when it makes statements concerning minor facts of history or science. Wherever its statements may seem to contradict one another or to vary from facts otherwise known to us, the reason for this disagreement is to be sought not in the Scriptures, as though they were at fault, but in our own imperfect, fallible knowledge and understanding. In this way verbal inspiration confirms the authenticity of the Scriptures, which depends upon its divine origin.

Verbal inspiration, however, is an article of faith. It cannot be demonstrated or understood by reasoning. The unbelief of all ages, but especially that unbelief which determines the character of "modern theology," agrees in denying that the Scriptures were given by God. When it admits that the Bible contains erroneous statements, "theological science" of our day gives up the firm foundation of faith and widely opens the door to all manner of false doctrine.

3. Content

Summarizing the witness of the Bible itself as to its content, we declare that it is the Word of God. It would be hazardous to say that the Bible *contains* the Word of God. This phrase is freely used by those who declare that, though the Bible offers divine truth, it presents the truth with an inextricable mix of erroneous human statements. If this were true, the Bible would obviously cease to be the Word of God.

All the wealth of information contained in the Bible centers in two distinct and utterly diverse doctrines, the law and the gospel. Every divine command requiring definite acts by humans and every threat directed against sin and sinners is law. Every statement declaring to sinners the free grace of God in Christ Jesus is gospel. Whatever statements do not answer either of these descriptions will always be found to serve as a guide to the better understanding and appreciation of either the law or the gospel.

Though both law and gospel come from God and are revealed in the Bible, yet it should be remembered that the gospel, and not the law, is the most important doctrine of the Bible. The Holy Book was written because of the gospel and not because of the law. Had there been no gospel to proclaim, no further revelation beyond man's natural knowledge of the law would have been needed. Though necessary for diverse reasons, the preaching of the law in the Bible is always incidental and subordinate to the teaching of the gospel. Thus it happens that the gospel is frequently designated as the Word of God, especially in the New Testament (Luke 8:11; 11:28; John 17:14,18).

Remember the important rule of interpretation: Every statement of the Bible has only one meaning intended by the Holy Spirit. At the same time, law and gospel may be so closely joined in the same text that the Bible teaches either, if rightly understood and applied. The story of the sufferings of Christ, endured for our sake, is sweetest gospel, yet nothing shows the wrath of God against sin more poignantly than this very story. The genealogies of the Old Testament are really a part of the gospel, since they all point forward to the coming Savior, yet in each section of Genesis chapter 5 the addition of the words "and died" is a sharp reminder of the curse pronounced by God after the fall.

4. Greater divisions

Although the Bible is divided into the Old and New Testaments, the doctrines in these two divisions do not differ in essence. The division happened because the two parts of the Holy Book were written in two distinct periods. All books written by inspiration before the birth of Christ belong to the Old Testament, while those written since that time compose the New Testament.

The word *testament* is often used in the Scriptures to denote a covenant, which God made with his people on earth, as in Romans 11:27; 1 Corinthians 11:25; and Hebrews 8:9,10. So we often speak of the books of the Old and the New Covenants. This does not mean, however, that either group of biblical books declares one of the great covenants of God to the exclusion of the other. The old covenant, or testament, that of the law, was established in the creation of man, while the new covenant, or testament, that of the gospel, was established immediately after the fall of man. As a result, both of these divine covenants are preached side by side in the books that we call the Old Testament, just as they are both taught in what we call the New Testament. Therefore we are using the word *testament* in a wider sense when we use it to designate the two great divisions of the Bible. We should therefore avoid the serious error that the doctrine prevailing among the people of God before Christ was of a different nature from the doctrine preached after Christ. Both divisions of the Bible preach the same law and the same gospel, and these fundamental doctrines of the Scriptures produce the same results in the hearts of men at all times.

But there is a difference in the manner of presenting the divine truth in the two great sections of the Bible. The historical books of the Old Testament describe the people of God as they lived under a taskmaster, the Mosaic Law, while the New Testament depicts them as enjoying the full liberty of the gospel. Again, in the Old Testament the gospel of Christ is naturally couched in terms of prophecy, while the New Testament proclaims the fulfillment, in Christ, of all promises of God. Finally, in the Old Testament the preaching of the law preponderates in the sense that the number of texts containing law are more numerous than those containing gospel, while the reverse is true of the New Testament.

The entire body of the Bible is frequently called the canon of the Scripture. It consists of the canonical books of the Old and the New Testaments. The Greek word *canon* signifies a "standard" or "guide," and is properly used here because the Bible is the only true standard, or guide, of faith and life. The fact that the canonical books of the Bible were given by inspiration of God distinguishes them from the Apocrypha (apocryphal books), which owes its origin to human authorship alone.

Chapter 2
The Old Testament

5. Books and general character

The canonical books of the Old Testament number 39. They record the history of God's people and the teachings of God's prophets during the age of prophecy preceding the advent of the Savior. Originally, the two books of Samuel, the two books of Kings, and the two books of Chronicles were each an undivided volume, so that even today only 36 books are counted in the Hebrew Bible. The very first translators of the Old Testament, however, cut each of these books into two parts, in order to make it easier to find references. This example has been imitated by all subsequent translators.

6. Language

All canonical books of the Old Testament were written in the Hebrew language, with Aramaic used in a small number of instances. Like Arabic, Syriac, and Chaldean (Aramean), the Hebrew tongue belongs to the great Semitic family of languages, but it was spoken by the descendants of Abraham alone. In its way this peculiarity served to keep Israel a distinct and separate people among the idolatrous nations surrounding it, according to the plan of God. Thus, also, the sacred books became a treasure entrusted to the Jews alone (Romans 3:2).

7. Groups of books

In our Bibles the books of the Old Testament are arranged in three large groups, the first containing historical books; the second, poetical books; and the third, prophetical books.

The Hebrew Bible exhibits a different arrangement, which had become definitely fixed before the time of Christ. To this day the Jews divide the Old Testament into the parts named by Jesus: the Law, the Prophets, and the Psalms (Luke 24:44). The Law distinguishes the books of Moses. The division called the Prophets includes all historical and prophetical writings except Lamentations, Ruth, Chronicles, Ezra, Nehemiah, and Daniel. The third section is called the Psalms, because the book of Psalms stands there in first place. It contains all poetical books, together with the historical and prophetical books excluded from the second division. This last section is also known by the Greek name *Hagiographa,* which means "sacred writings."

The poetical books in today's designation are sometimes denoted as doctrinal books, but this name appears misleading in the face of Paul's assertion that "everything that was written in the past was written to teach us" (Romans 15:4). The writings of Moses and the other prophets are doctrinal books in the fullest sense of the word and were always used as such by the Israelites. On the other hand, we must admit that the divisions suggested in our Bibles are not entirely adequate either, since the prophets often speak in highly poetical language and the Mosaic writings contain many portions that are distinctly prophetical. Yet these terms probably serve better than any others as general descriptions of the several groups. The three groups follow:

A. Historical books	
(The five books of Moses—The Pentateuch)	
1. Genesis	4. Numbers
2. Exodus	5. Deuteronomy
3. Leviticus	
(The remaining historical books)	
6. Joshua	12. Second Kings
7. Judges	13. First Chronicles
8. Ruth	14. Second Chronicles
9. First Samuel	15. Ezra
10. Second Samuel	16. Nehemiah
11. First Kings	17. Esther
B. Poetical books	
18. Job	21. Ecclesiastes
19. Psalms	22. Song of Solomon
20. Proverbs	
C. Prophetical books	
23. Isaiah	32. Jonah
24. Jeremiah	33. Micah
25. Lamentations of Jeremiah	34. Nahum
26. Ezekiel	35. Habakkuk
27. Daniel	36. Zephaniah
28. Hosea	37. Haggai
29. Joel	38. Zechariah
30. Amos	39. Malachi
31. Obadiah	

8. When assembled

The Scriptures naturally contain no information about when the inspired books of the Old Testament were assembled to form the canon. Though we are told that Moses wrote down the Law and delivered it to the Levites (Deuteronomy 31:9,26) and that Joshua followed this example (Joshua 24:26), we are not told when the other books were collected. The Jews, however, have an ancient tradition that Ezra or some other prophet established the canon after the return from the Babylonian exile. Regardless of that, we are sure that the Old Testament as we now have it has been preserved by the Jews since that period. Various remarks in the books of the Prophets indicate that copies of the sacred books were widely distributed among the Jews. Otherwise the people could not have understood and appreciated the many allusions to the older historical and poetical writings to which the prophets constantly refer. As the Psalms were continuously used in the temple worship, they surely were copied extensively.

The Jewish tale concerning the establishment of the canon by Ezra contains so many incredible statements that the reader is tempted to reject it as a mere legend of no historical value. Yet it may be based on fact, for it is not at all improbable that Ezra recognized the urgent need of collecting the sacred books of his people to preserve them. At any rate, prophecy ceased in the days of Nehemiah, when Malachi died, and it's likely that Israel had the inspired writings all assembled by that time.

The Jews held the canon of the Old Testament sacred even outwardly, and their jealous care of it only increased as their religion gradually degenerated into a system of outward observance. Manuscript copies of the sacred books, especially those that were to be used in the public worship of the synagogue, were written under strict rules, in order to ensure perfect exactness. For this reason there are comparatively few variant readings in the Hebrew text. At first the lines were written without any separation of words or marks of punctuation, and it was necessary to have special lectors, who were trained to read the lessons appointed for each Sabbath. Centuries passed before it became customary to set off each word and each sentence or verse in the manuscripts.

Chapter 3
The Historical Books

A. *The Pentateuch*

9. *Name and purpose*

The five books of Moses tell us how the theocracy and its code of law were established among the people of Israel. *Theocracy* means "government by God" and denotes that form of government in which God controls all civic activities by his laws and institutions. To establish the theocracy in Israel, God not only renewed the revelation of the moral law on Mount Sinai and gave his people a complete system of religious forms, but he also added all the statutes necessary for their civil and social intercourse. This pure theocracy came to an end when the people of Israel later demanded, and were given, a king as a visible head and ruler of their state.

The Greek name Pentateuch signifies that the writings of Moses are contained in a book of five volumes. In the Scriptures the Pentateuch is often referred to as the book of the Law (as in Deuteronomy 31:26) or briefly as the Law (*Thora,* as in Nehemiah 8:2,7; Luke 24:44). We note in passing that the Jews followed the custom of most ancient peoples by usually naming the single books of the Pentateuch from their first words, for example, Genesis, "In the beginning," and Exodus, "These are the names."

10. *Authenticity*

The authenticity of a biblical book is related to whether the writer whose name it bears is really its author. Investigators belonging to the modern school of negative criticism have for many years labored diligently to destroy all faith in the historical reliability of the Bible and have succeeded only too well in spreading doubt and unbelief. In particular, they have directed much concerted effort against the Pentateuch and have tried to prove that this magnificent work was certainly not written by Moses but consists of a great number of fragments assembled by various unskillful editors and put into its present shape during the period of the prophets.

To appreciate how serious such destructive efforts are, we must remember that the Christian faith becomes a baseless fancy if it could be proved that the writings ascribed to Moses are not genuine. Fortunately, only those who wish to be deceived fail to observe how vain and arbitrary the processes are by which the "critics" arrive at their conclusions. That their reasoning is purely arbitrary may be seen in that hardly ever do two of the eminent "critics" agree as to the size and number of fragments from which the Pentateuch is supposed to have been pieced together. Since their testimony disagrees except in the underlying hostility against God's revelation, these critics are thereby shown to be false witnesses against God.

The trustworthy testimony of the prophets of the Old Testament, as well as that of Jesus and his apostles in the New Testament, is unanimous in declaring that Moses truly wrote the five books that bear his name. For the Christian believer the authenticity of the Pentateuch is definitely established by such statements as Luke 2:22; 24:44; John 5:46,47; Acts 13:39; 15:5; and 1 Corinthians 9:9.

B. Genesis

11. Name

Genesis, a Greek word, signifies "origin," or "beginning," and is an apt name for that book. It not only contains the only reliable account of the creation of all things but also describes the beginning of sin, the first preaching of the gospel, the first judgment of God upon a sinful world, and the beginnings of the chosen people of God. It may be divided into two chief parts, the first recording the beginnings of all history and the second showing how God paved the way for the establishment of the theocracy.

12. Period

The first period of human history, beginning with the creation of man and ending with the flood, lasted some 1,700 years. Though we have no reason to assume that the art of writing could not have been developed by the men of that age, they had no urgent need to record the Word of God, because men then lived to a very great age and were able to pass on from generation to generation by word of mouth what God had revealed. The record shows, for instance, that Adam lived 56 years after Lamech, the father of Noah, had been born. This providential arrangement continued for some time after the flood, for Abraham was born 150 years before the death of Shem and surely profited by Shem's instruction.

The period of the patriarchs begins with the deliverance of Noah from the ark and ends with the death of Joseph, covering a space of some six hundred years. At its close the chosen family of Abraham had multiplied into a numerous people.

13. Prophecy

Besides the remarkable prophecy of Noah (Genesis 9:25-27), which revealed a definite plan of God covering the future of all mankind, Genesis contains several distinct messianic promises of God. The first, couched in very general terms, designates the Savior as the offspring (seed) of the woman and as the future conqueror of the serpent (3:15). This is rightly called the *protevangel*, that is, the first gospel. As far as we know, this one promise sufficed to sustain and continue the people of God in the saving faith throughout the long period preceding the flood.

To the patriarchs the promise was made more definite. God declared that the Savior should come from the posterity of Abraham, Isaac, and Jacob. In this form, repeatedly pronounced by God (to Abraham, 12:3; 18:18; 22:18; to Isaac, 26:4; to Jacob, 28:14), the gospel comforted those holy men, until the further knowledge was granted to Jacob that the Promised One should spring from the tribe of Judah (49:10-12; KJV, *Shiloh*).

Summary of contents

   I. The beginnings of history, chapters 1–11.

      A. Creation; fall of man; first promise of the Savior; expulsion from Paradise; birth of Cain and Abel; the crime of Cain, chapters 1–4.

      B. Genealogy of the patriarchs before the flood, chapter 5.

      C. Noah and the flood, chapters 6–9.

      D. The patriarchs from Noah to Abraham, chapters 10,11.

   II. History of the patriarchs, chapters 12–50.

      A. Abraham, chapters 12:1–25:10. The call and the departure from Chaldea to Canaan; stay in Egypt; separation from Lot; defeat of the five kings and the blessing of Melchizedek; Abraham's faith; birth of Ishmael; seal of the promise by the sacrament of circumcision; further confirmation through the Son of God in person; destruction of Sodom; Abimelech; birth of Isaac and expulsion of Ishmael; sacrifice of Isaac and renewal of promise; death of Sarah; marriage of Isaac; second marriage of Abraham; his death at age 175 .

B. Isaac, chapters 24–35. Marriage with Rebekah; birth of Esau and Jacob; renewal of the promise; wanderings and troubles in Canaan; blessing of Jacob and Esau; sending of Jacob to Mesopotamia; after Jacob's return, Isaac's death at age 180 .

C. Jacob and his sons, chapters 25–50. Twin brother of Esau; blessing; flight and vision of God; service and marriage in Mesopotamia; his family and wealth; escape from Laban; prayer and wrestling; reconciliation with Esau; massacre of Shechem; death of Rachel; Joseph sold; sin of Judah; Joseph's temptation, sufferings, and exaltation; Joseph visited by his brothers, revealing himself to them; Jacob removes to Egypt; a good home; blessings for his sons; prophecies concerning Christ; Jacob's death at age 147; burial in Canaan; Joseph's death at age 110, after he enjoined that his bones should be carried to Canaan on that future day when his people would be led to the Promised Land.

C. Exodus

14. Purpose of the book

Exodus means "departure," an apt name for the book, which begins with the story of the departure of the people of Israel from the land of bondage and the beginning of their journey to the Promised Land. This remarkable occurrence was foretold by God many times as a promise (Genesis 15:13-16; 35:11,12), the fulfillment of which the children of God looked forward to in firm faith (Genesis 48:21,22; 50:25).

But the chief purpose of the book is to relate how the theocracy was established among the people of Israel by the solemn giving of the Law on Mount Sinai. Thus that covenant was made and confirmed which God had graciously planned for his people.

15. *Mosaic Law*

To understand the purpose of God in giving his Law through Moses, the following important facts must be considered: (a) This Law was not meant for all nations in all ages of the world but for the people of Israel alone, and only for the period of waiting for the Messiah. (b) It was not meant to instruct men how to earn salvation through their works, as it was sadly misinterpreted by the Jews in later days, but it was based upon the promises given to the fathers (Galatians 3:16-18) and presupposed that God had chosen Israel to be his people (Genesis 19:5,6). (c) This Law begins with a gospel declaration (Exodus 20:2). The Hebrew word for Lord is *Jehovah* (or *Yahweh*), the name describing God as the God of promise and salvation. Moreover, the entire Law is permeated with continuous references to the promise of the salvation through Christ.

The Mosaic code contains three distinct kinds of law. It begins with a formal pronouncement of the moral law but includes detailed instructions concerning divine worship (ceremonial law) and also a very extensive code of civil law.

The moral law, of which the Ten Commandments are a brief summary, is also called the natural law, because it is known in part to all men by nature, without special revelation, and is binding upon them all without exception. Of this law in particular Jesus said that he did not come to destroy it (Matthew 5:17).

The ceremonial law, also called Levitical law, defined and ordained all forms of divine worship that were to be observed by the people of God in the centuries before the coming of Christ. It includes all ordinances concerning the Sabbath and other holy days, the designated place of worship, the priesthood, and the sacrifices. This law has been abolished by Christ and is no longer binding upon the people of God (Colossians 2:16,17).

The civil law was given to the people of Israel as a separate people among the nations of the earth. It became void when God finally destroyed the nationality of the Jews and dispersed them over the whole earth.

16. Messianic prophecy

Exodus contains no direct promises concerning Christ and his salvation, unless the words in 19:6 and 34:6,7 are put under this heading. Yet the book is replete with messianic prophecy in that it describes many types of which Christ is the antitype and the fulfillment. Paul calls these types "a shadow of the things that were to come" (Colossians 2:17), the shadow disappearing when the body came.

These types are designated and explained by the writers of the New Testament. Thus Hebrews 8:5,6 explains the typical character of the tabernacle that Moses constructed in the wilderness as a place of worship for his people. Having been built according to a design revealed by God, it afterward became the pattern for the temple of Solomon. It consisted of three chief sections, the Court, the Holy Place, and the Most Holy Place. The people were admitted only to the court; the priests entered the Holy Place; the high priest alone was permitted to enter the Most Holy Place, and he but once every year. In the court stood the great altar of burnt offering, with the perpetual fire. In the Holy Place were placed the table with the showbread, the altar of incense, and the candlestick with seven arms. The mysterious darkness of the Most Holy Place concealed the ark of the covenant. The whole sanctuary measured about 150 feet in length and 75 feet in width. As the structure was built of light wooden scaffolding, which was hung with furs and woven materials, it could be carried easily from place to place. Other types mentioned in Exodus and referred to in the New Testament are the cover of the ark, known as the mercy seat (Romans 3:25; Hebrews 4:16), the Sabbath-rest (Hebrews 4:9,10), the high priest (Hebrews 5), and others.

Summary of contents

I. Preparations for the exodus, chapters 1:1–12:28. Increase and oppression of the Israelites; birth and education of Moses; his flight and call; negotiations with Pharaoh; the ten plagues; institution of the Passover.

II. Journey of Israel out of Egypt and to Sinai, chapters 12:29–19:25. The exodus; passage through the Red Sea; destruction of Pharaoh; songs of Moses and Miriam; bitter waters of Marah; quail; manna; water from the rock; battle with Amalek; Jethro's advice; preparations for the giving of the Law.

III. The solemn legislation, chapters 19–40. The Ten Commandments and the fundamental ordinances of the people; building of the tabernacle ordered; Aaron and the people sin but are restored to grace upon the intercession of Moses; the tabernacle is built.

D. Leviticus

17. Name and purpose

Leviticus received its name because it contains detailed ordinances describing the Levitical worship as it was to be observed in the tabernacle and afterward in the temple. Certain supplements to this Levitical law were added in the book of Numbers. Though this book contains no direct messianic promise whatever, it is, really and by the intention of God, one continuous sermon of the salvation in Jesus Christ. As the New Testament shows conclusively, the entire magnificent system of sacrifices was nothing less than a type of the vicarious sacrifice of Jesus Christ, which was foreshadowed by every bloody offering on the sacred altars.

18. Review of Jewish festivals

The Sabbath, the seventh day of every week, was to be observed as a day of rest, in memory of the Sabbath of the Lord that followed the work of creation.

The Passover was to preserve the memory of the divine deliverance from Egypt and to symbolize the substitutionary death of the Lamb of God through the killing of the Passover lamb. It was observed on the 14th day of the first month, called Abib, or Nisan (corresponding to the latter half of our month of March and the first half of April). The Feast of the Passover introduced the Feast of Unleavened Bread, which lasted seven days.

The Harvest Festival was set for the 50th day after the Passover; hence it was later called Pentecost, that is, the 50th day. On this occasion the firstfruits of the harvest were offered to the Lord.

New Year's Day *(rosh ha-shannah* in Hebrew) for the Jews was the first day of the seventh month, Tisri, or Ethanim (our month of October).

The Day of Atonement was observed on the tenth day of the month of Tisri. It was a day of penance, on which the people were to mortify their bodies by fasting.

The Feast of Tabernacles began on the 15th day of Tisri and continued for seven days. It was to remind the Jews that their fathers dwelt in tents at the time when the Lord delivered them from Egypt. "Choice fruit from the trees, and palm fronds, leafy branches and poplars" were to be used for decorations (Leviticus 23:40).

Besides these feasts, which were to be observed with sacrifices and religious worship, the Lord also ordained that the land should not be seeded every seventh year (the Sabbath Year) and that every 50th year should be a Year of Jubilee (Leviticus 25:8-55). The beginning of the jubilee was announced by the sounding of trumpets on the first day of Tisri. During that year the land rested, as during the Sabbath Year. Every Jewish servant was freed, and every parcel of land that had been sold was returned to its original owner, so that every family might retain its inheritance.

The Feast of Purim (Esther 9:32) and the Feast of the Dedication (1 Maccabees 4:53; John 10:22) were not of divine appointment but were instituted later by men.

19. Levitical sacrifices

The most important sacrifices were those in which the life of some beast was offered upon the altar. All these bloody sacrifices were of special significance, inasmuch as they were intended and understood to foreshadow the sacrifice of Christ's life for our propitiation. By laying his hand upon the offered beast, the priest accepted and designated it as a sacrifice unto the Lord. All beasts thus offered were required to be altogether without fault or blemish; in many cases the required age was also specified. Cattle, sheep, and goats, together with turtledoves and young doves, comprised the list of sacrificial animals.

There were four classes of bloody sacrifices.

The burnt offerings were performed every morning and every evening upon the great altar in the court of the sanctuary. At stated times each Israelite was also required to bring a burnt offering. The beasts were slain and burned; the blood was either sprinkled or poured against the altar.

21

Thank offerings were brought in token of thanksgiving to God for special favors. The blood of the animal was sprinkled against the altar, and the fat was burned. The flesh was to be eaten within two days.

Sin offerings were to be made by those who had transgressed a divine commandment in ignorance or weakness. A sin of the whole people was also required to be reconciled in this manner. The blood of the sacrifice was partly sprinkled upon the altar and partly poured out before it. All parts of such offerings were burned before the camp, the fat upon the altar and the other portions of the body outside.

On the Day of Atonement, the sacrifice consisted of a young ox, which the high priest offered for himself, and of a goat, which was offered on behalf of the people. A second goat, upon which the sins of the people were laid in solemn ceremony, was driven into the desert. Only with the blood of the ox and the goat slain on this one day of the year did the high priest enter the Most Holy Place, in order to sprinkle the blood upon the cover of the ark of the covenant.

Special guilt offerings were prescribed for minor offenses. The rites of these sacrifices were similar to the above, except that the flesh of the slain beasts belonged to the priests as part of their sustenance.

Of bloodless sacrifices there were two kinds, meat offerings and drink offerings. The gifts here consisted of meal, cakes, grain, oil, incense, salt, or wine, according to the circumstances. A portion of the offering was burned; what remained belonged to the priests.

Summary of contents

first sacrifice; strange fire causing the deaths of Nadab and Abihu.

III. Levitical purity, chapters 11–22. Clean and unclean beasts; purification of mothers; general purification of the whole people through the great sacrifice of atonement; forbidden marriages; various ordinances.

IV. The great festivals, chapters 23–27. Ordinances concerning the festivals; stoning of the blasphemer; promise of blessing and threat of curse; vows; tithes.

E. Numbers

20. Book

Numbers received its name because the first chapter tells of the numbering of the people. According to chapter 26, the numbering was repeated at a later period.

The narrative of the book summarizes the experiences of the people of Israel in the wilderness during the 39 years following their departure from Mount Sinai. It is merely a sketch, which mentions only those occurrences of vital significance for the people. They had remained at the foot of Mount Sinai, at the southern extremity of the Sinai peninsula, for an entire year. On their way to the Promised Land, they encamped for unknown periods at various places, which we can no longer locate.

In the second year of their wanderings, they reached Kadesh Barnea, which must have been close to the boundary of Palestine. From there the 12 spies were dispatched to visit the Promised Land and to report on its character and the character of its population. The tale that they told on their return terrified the Israelites and caused them to rebel against the guidance of the Lord. He punished them by condemning them to a total of 40 years of wandering in the desert. Then a portion of the people attempted to force an entrance into the Promised Land, but the attempt failed most disastrously, and the people then bowed humbly to the decree of God.

Turning away from the desired goal of their journey, they sadly began many years of weary plodding. The Scriptures are almost silent as to their adventures during the remaining 38 years; we know hardly more than the names of their chief camps, the locations of which remain uncertain. The book ends with the story of the second arrival of the Israelites at Kadesh Barnea.

Interspersed among the various parts of the narrative, we find additional legislation, most of the ordinances referring to the civil life of the people, together with some further instructions concerning the religious ceremonies.

A notable messianic prophecy, given through the mouth of Balaam, is recorded in 24:17 (the Star of Jacob). Note also the gospel significance of the Aaronic blessing in 6:24-26.

Summary of contents

I. Preparations for the departure from Sinai, chapters 1–10. Numbering and reviewing of the tribes; the order of encampment; ordinances to secure cleanliness in camp; the Passover and ordinances concerning its observation; the trumpets for signaling.

II. Journey of the people up to the beginning of the 40th year, chapters 10–19. The departure from Sinai; second year of the journey; fire from God; quail from God; God's anger against Miriam and Aaron; the 12 spies; rebellion and condemnation of the people; laws concerning meat offerings; the Sabbath breaker; Korah and his band; laws for purification after touching a corpse.

III. The first ten months of the 40th year, chapters 20–36. The water of separation; message to Edom;

death of Aaron; victory over King Arad; fiery ser-
pents; from Hor to Pisgah; defeat of Sihon and Og;
Balaam and his prophecies; idolatry and its punishment; second numbering; ordinances concerning
inheritances; installation of Joshua; laws concerning
feast offerings and vows; victory over the Midianites;
two and a half tribes settle in the land east of Jordan;
list of encampments; ordinances respecting the
expulsion of the Canaanites, the boundaries and distribution of the conquered land, the cities of the
Levites, the free cities, and the marriage of daughters
inheriting land.

F. Deuteronomy

21. Purpose

The Latin name *Deuteronomium,* from which the English
name Deuteronomy is derived, may be translated "the second
giving of the Law." It describes the book as essentially a
review of all the commandments and statutes that the Lord
had given to his people.

The book contains the last discourses of Moses, the man
of God, addressed to the people of Israel. Before taking
leave from this earth, Moses once more reminds the people
of all the mercies, ordinances, and promises of God. The
time is the 11th month of the 40th year after the exodus
from Egypt. The place is the encampment of Israel east of
the Jordan and opposite Jericho, in the land of Moab. The
last three sections of the book, which contain the announcement of the death of Moses, his last blessing, and the narrative of his death, may have been added to Deuteronomy by
the inspired author of the book of Joshua.

Among these last utterances of Moses we find a great
messianic prophecy concerning the prophetical office of
Christ (18:15,18,19).

22. Authenticity

Modern critics insist that Deuteronomy was not written earlier than the period of the Jewish kings. They flout the idea that Moses is its author. Their arguments and alleged proofs, being based entirely on hypothesis and presumption, are not worth serious attention by those who believe the inspiration of the Bible, since Moses is unmistakably designated as the writer of Deuteronomy in 31:24-26.

As to the appendix, which tells of the departure and death of Moses, we may admit that it was written by some other person, provided that the authorship be ascribed to some inspired prophet. Yet it must not be considered impossible that Moses himself may have recorded what the Lord had told him concerning his approaching demise and how he gave his final blessing to the people. This is true even of the last chapter, of which Luther says, "Moses did not write this chapter, but Joshua or Eleazar, unless you would choose to say that Moses, knowing his death before, did actually describe it in this manner."

Summary of contents

   I. Three discourses of Moses, addressed to Israel, chapters 1–30. The first discourse is a brief review of the journey through the desert and warns against apostasy. In the second discourse, the laws and ordinances of God are summarized with some explanations and many urgent, fatherly admonitions to keep the Law. In the third discourse, Moses declares most impressively both the blessing and the curse of the Law.

  II. Moses delivers the book of the Law to the Levites and sings a song of praise, 31:1–32:47.

 III. Three supplements, 32:48–34. Announcement of Moses' death; Moses' blessing of the people; narrative of Moses' death and burial.

G. Authors of other historical books

23. No names given

It is remarkable that all historical books of the Old Testament, except those of Moses, Ezra, and Nehemiah, are anonymous, the names of their authors not being mentioned anywhere in the Scriptures. It has also been found impossible to make any acceptable guesses at their identity. The fathers of our Lutheran church do indeed sometimes ascribe a book to a definite author, but this amounts to no more than a personal assumption and is not based upon unanswerable arguments. As we discuss the single books, it will appear that frequently we can only show who is not the author.

This, however, does not affect the canonical value of these books. When speaking of them, Christ adopted the popular classification of the books of the Old Testament without correcting it. According to his veracious testimony, these books belonged either to the class called the Prophets or to the class headed by the book of Psalms (read Luke 24:44 and compare section 7). We are assured, therefore, that these books were without exception written by inspired prophetical men during that period when God gave prophets to his people.

It should also be noted that the prophets generally considered it a part of their work to chronicle current events (1 Chronicles 29:29; 2 Chronicles 12:15; 32:32). These particular records have not been preserved, presumably because their contents were not religious. But they would not have been mentioned in the manner indicated if they had not served as sources of information for the writers of the inspired books that we possess.

24. Purpose

These books were not written merely for recording the varying fortunes of the people who had descended from

Abraham but for the religious purpose of showing how God faithfully kept the covenant made with his chosen people, though they often turned from him in unfaithfulness. Thus every affliction befalling them was indeed due to their sin, while their salvation was ever the work of God, their Savior. This is the point of view indicated by God himself, speaking through Hosea (13:4,9).

So it happens that these records often fail to furnish information that would be interesting to a student of secular history. Rather, they always discuss such persons, facts, and happenings in which either the gracious providence of God or the rebellious spirit of the people and their leaders becomes singularly apparent. Again, we rarely are told how other people and external, political considerations influenced the chosen people, but we are always told at great length how God controlled the development of all occurrences in his own wonderful way. This unity of purpose also explains why these books are so similar in style and literary character, though they surely were written by many different people and at different times.

H. Joshua

25. Book

The story presented in Joshua is a continuation of the history recorded by Moses. It was written to show how Canaan was occupied under the guidance of God and how the land was distributed among the tribes of Israel in accordance with divine instructions.

The author also takes pains to make it clear that Joshua, to the day of his death, never grew weary in his efforts to preserve the true worship of God. Instead, he ever urged the Israelites to remain faithful to the covenant that God had made with them. Thus the author gives a detailed account of Joshua's meeting with those tribes from east of the Jordan before they returned from the conquest of Canaan and erected an altar in their territory. In the story of the last great assembly of all the tribes, held shortly before his death, Joshua appears in the same light.

26. Author

It is certain that this book was written by an eyewitness of the occurrences. In 5:1 we read the words "until we had crossed over" and in verse 6, "The LORD had sworn to them that they would not see the land that he had solemnly promised their fathers to give us." Even though a carping critic might insist that the latter words may have been written by a person of a later date, the words quoted from verse 1 could not have been so written except by an eyewitness. On the other hand, it is just as plain that Joshua was not the author. To be sure, we are told in 24:26 that "Joshua recorded these things in the Book of the Law of God." This, however, obviously was no more than a record of the proceedings of the great assembly that Joshua had called together. On the other hand, the book of Joshua mentions several occurrences from a period long after the death of the great leader. Thus we learn from 19:47 that the people of Dan captured the city of Leshem. But this happened quite a number of years after Joshua's death, as we know from Judges chapter 18. Again, Joshua 15:13-19 relates how Caleb took possession of his inheritance. But this also took place after Joshua's death, as we know from Judges 1:12. These and other parallel statements in the two books make it fairly certain that the book of Joshua was written by an eyewitness but after Joshua's death. It follows that the story of 24:29-33 was not added by a later hand but is a part of the original book.

Summary of contents

I. The conquest of Canaan, chapters 1–12. Call of Joshua; passage through the Jordan River; circumcision of the people and the Passover; Jericho; Ai; Achan's sacrilege; the blessing and the curse on Gerizim and Ebal; the Gibeonites; conquest of Southern Canaan; list of the conquered kings.

II. The distribution of the land, chapters 13–24. Preparations; the distribution; cities of refuge and of the Levites; dismissal of the three and a half tribes; last assembly of Joshua; deaths of Joshua and Eleazar.

For a description of Canaan, see the addendum.

I. Judges

27. Chronology

There is some uncertainty as to the length of the period covered by the book of Judges. While the most important deeds of some judges are described with much interesting detail, everything else is only briefly summarized. We are told, however, that when Jephthah became a judge, three hundred years had passed since the people had occupied their assigned portions of Canaan after the exodus (11:26). Then followed 40 years in which Israel groaned under the oppression of the Philistines (13:1), from which Samson began to deliver them, while Samuel completed the task. Thus it appears that we may safely figure the period of the judges at about 350 years.

28. Character of the period

On taking leave of the people, Joshua had once more exacted from them the sacred promise never to run after false gods but to remain faithful to the God of the covenant. But they failed to destroy the Canaanites as they had been instructed to do, and thus the idolatry of these heathen became a swift snare for the people of God, who began to practice the abominations of their neighbors. Because the people would not turn their hearts to true wisdom, although God chastised them at various times, God finally decreed that those remnants of the original inhabitants should remain, to be a constant test for the faith of Israel (2:19-23). But whenever the people turned to their God in their affliction and repented, the Lord would send them a heroic leader to deliver them. Hence the judges are referred to as "deliverers" ("saviors, " KJV) by Nehemiah (Nehemiah 9:27).

In view of the perverseness of the people and their many saddening experiences under the chastising hand of God, it seems improper to call this period the golden age of Jewish history. Yet such it should have been, for God had intended that his people should live quietly and peacefully under his direct guidance, observing the laws that he had given them. At any rate, it is foolish and unscriptural to say that the people of the covenant needed a monarch for their proper and happy development. Surely the theocratic government, as God had intended it to be, would have left nothing to desire. In fact, God himself declares that the people rejected him when they demanded a human ruler (1 Samuel 8:7).

Because commentators are not agreed whether Deborah and Abimelech should figure in the series, the list of judges varies. The people to be considered are Othniel, Ehud, Shamgar, Deborah and Barak, Gideon, Abimelech, Jephthah, Ibzan, Elon, Abdon, and Samson. Samuel is usually named as the last of the judges, but his work is not described in this book.

29. Author

The writer of the book of Judges does not give his name, nor is it mentioned anywhere in the Scriptures. But the book itself furnishes certain clues. From 13:1 we learn that the book was written after Samuel had broken the yoke of the Philistines. It would also seem certain that the author lived to see the beginnings of the kingdom (17:6; 18:1; 19:1; 21:25). Moreover, when the author says that "to this day the Jebusites live there" (in Jerusalem, 1:21), we know he completed the writing before David destroyed the Jebusites (2 Samuel 5:6-10). We know of no person living in the period circumscribed by these statements who was better fitted than Samuel to write the book of Judges. Probably for the same reasons, the Jewish Talmud names him directly as the author.

Summary of contents

I. Introduction, chapters 1,2. The intercourse arising between Israel and the remnants of the heathen tribes; the continuous alternation of guilt and punishment, repentance and deliverance.

II. Certain occurrences described at length to prove the general thought expressed in the introduction, chapters 3–16.

III. Two supplements (the idolatry of the Danites, chapters 17,18, and the sacrilege of the Gibeites, together with the destruction of Benjamin, chapters 19–21) refer to matters occurring shortly after the death of Joshua and are not directly connected with the body of the book.

J. Ruth

30. Purpose, date, and author

The charming story told in this short book introduces us to some of the ancestors of David and thus becomes an important supplement to the books of Samuel, which contain no detailed genealogy of the great king. This information gains in significance if we remember that the genealogy of David is at the same time that of Jesus Christ. The story therefore shows how Ruth the Moabitess, by birth an alien to Israel, was chosen to become an ancestress of the Savior. Her reception into the communion of Israel also testified that even in the days before Christ, Gentiles were admitted to the kingdom of God when they received the promises of the covenant in true faith.

As the genealogy here ends with David's name, it is improbable that the book was written before David had become a person of influence and renown among the people of the covenant. We find an additional reason for this assumption in 4:7, where the author explains a peculiar custom, which had fallen into disuse in his days.

The author remains unknown to us, but it has been suggested that David himself might well have penned this account of a significant episode in his family history.

K. Samuel

31. Name and purpose

The record contained in the two books of Samuel is really one continuous story and forms one book in the Hebrew original. The division into two books was introduced by the authors of the ancient Greek version (see section 142).

These books are named after the man whose powerful personality was an important factor in the young monarchy of Israel. The influence of Samuel, who had called and anointed both Saul and David, was felt in Israel throughout the reign of Saul and must have been a decisive factor in the training of David for his future task. Beginning with a biographical sketch of Samuel's life before he became the last judge of Israel, the author takes up the thread of history at the point where the book of Judges drops it, after the death of Samson, and carries it forward to the close of David's reign.

These books, however, were not merely written to be a record of the lives of three great men whom God gave to his people, although their stories are full of human interest. The Christian reader will retain the proper point of view that this account sets forth the providential control that God exercised over the affairs of his people, achieving his purposes without fail. Note, for example, the messianic prophecy in 2 Samuel 7:12,13.

32. Date of writing

Since the occurrences here related cover a period of more than a century, extending far beyond the death of Samuel, that prophet surely did not write the books that bear his name. Indeed, it is fairly certain that the author wrote after the separation of the two kingdoms. Not only does he find it needful to explain words and customs current in the days of Samuel and David (as in 1 Samuel 9:9; 2 Samuel 13:18), but he also specifies "kings of Judah." Probably he was a prophet who lived shortly after the death of Solomon.

We also learn that he made use of the writings of older prophets, for 2 Samuel 1:18 refers to "the book of Jashar." Furthermore, chapters 8 to 25 of 2 Samuel are similar to chapters 11 to 20 of 1 Chronicles, whose author declares that he drew from the books of Samuel the seer, Nathan the prophet, and Gad the seer (1 Chronicles 29:29). These sources, therefore, must also have been available to the author of the books of Samuel.

Summary of contents

I. Samuel, the last judge over Israel, 1 Samuel 1–12. His birth; the call; loss of the ark of the covenant and its recovery; victory over the Philistines; the people demand a king; Saul is anointed, chosen, and installed as king; Samuel takes leave of the people.

II. Saul's reign up to his rejection, 1 Samuel 13–15. Saul's first campaign against the Philistines and Jonathan's victory; other wars and successes of Saul; his disobedience in the war against Amalek; his rejection.

III. History of Saul from his rejection to his death, 1 Samuel 16–31. David's anointing; David becomes musician to Saul; David's victory over Goliath; David flees from Saul; David's stay and experiences among the Philistines; Saul's last war against the Philistines; the witch of Endor; Saul's death.

IV. David as king, 2 Samuel 1–4. David's lament over Saul and Jonathan; his return to the land of Israel; his anointing as king over Judah; struggle between David and the house of Saul; David wins out and is anointed king over Israel; his reign, with Hebron as capital.

V. Increasing power and glory of David, 2 Samuel 5–9. Jerusalem made the capital city; defeat of the Philistines; regulation of public worship; victory over all external enemies; Mephibosheth.

VI. Adverse experiences of David, 2 Samuel 10–20. David's adultery with Bathsheba; Amnon's incest; revolt of Absalom; Sheba's rebellion.

VII. End of David's reign, 2 Samuel 21–24. Famine; wars with the Philistines; David's song of praise and last words; list of his heroes; census of the people; pestilence.

L. Kings

33. Purpose

Like the books of Samuel, the books of Kings originally were a single volume, which was cut into two parts by the earliest translators (see section 142). The books relate the history of the people of God under their kings, from the beginning of Solomon's reign to the destruction of the kingdom of Judah and the Babylonian captivity.

Like all historical books of the Bible, they are not intended merely as a source of historical information but were written chiefly for religious purposes. Therefore they do not give all the details of the reigns of the several kings but relate only such acts by which their faith or disbelief is revealed. The writer shows, moreover, that God always kept a man from the seed of David upon the throne, according to his promise. He also demonstrates that the division of the monarchy, the destruction of Israel, and the Babylonian captivity of Judah were the proper consequence and punishment of the sins of the people. The labors of the prophets are set forth in great detail, and the acts of the kings are always judged according to the standard of divine law. This is called the theocratic character of these books, which is common to all historical writings of the Old Testament. For examples of this peculiarity, read such passages as 1 Kings 11:33,38; 14:8-10; and 2 Kings 23:3,21,24.

34. Sources

The author repeatedly refers to the sources from which he derived his information and where further details might be sought by those who desired additional historical knowledge of the period. He names "the book of the annals of Solomon" (1 Kings 11:41), "the book of the annals of the kings of Judah" (14:29), and "the book of the annals of the kings of Israel" (14:19).

Some commentators believe that these annals were written by officers of the kings as official records of their reign, which then were used as sources by the author of the books of Kings. But this view is hardly tenable. Most of the kings of Israel and many kings of Judah were at least indifferent and often distinctly hostile toward the Word of God and his true worship. It cannot be supposed, therefore, that their official recorders were God-fearing men, who would dare to measure all acts of those kings by the divine standard. It is rather to be assumed that such chronicles were written in the schools for prophets, which had been begun first by Samuel and seem to have flourished long thereafter (1 Samuel 19:19-24; 2 Kings 2:3,5). From the complete records thus made, the writer of the books of Kings, being guided by the Holy Spirit, chose such details of information as suited his particular purpose.

35. Author

The style in which the books of Kings are written is so entirely uniform throughout as to leave no room for the supposition that several writers united their labors to produce this record. It is the work of a single author.

From the last date quoted (in 2 Kings 25:27) it appears that this work was written after the death of Jehoiachin, in the second half of the Babylonian exile. Furthermore, since Evil-Merodach, whose reign was very brief, is mentioned without any reference to his demise, the date of these books seems to be defined quite closely. They must have been written about 570 B.C.

At that time, Jeremiah the prophet was still living in Egypt, and the Jewish teachers of the Talmud were the first to suggest that he may have been the author of these books. Many Christian theologians have adopted this theory and have endeavored to show that the book of Jeremiah and the books of Kings exhibit a striking similarity in diction and other peculiarities. Their arguments, however, are not convincing, chiefly because the statements contained in 2 Kings 25:27-29 seem to indicate that the author lived among the exiled Jews in Babylon.

Summary of contents

I. The reign of Solomon, 1 Kings 1–11. Solomon's enthronement; his marriage, court, wealth, and wisdom; building of the temple and the royal palace; dedication of the temple; the queen of Sheba; Solomon's polygamy; idolatry and its consequences; Solomon's death.

II. Contemporaneous history of the two kingdoms up to the destruction of Israel, 1 Kings 12–2 Kings 17. The kingdom is divided according to prophecy; hostility between the two kingdoms under Rehoboam, Abijam, and Asa of Judah and Jeroboam I, Nadab, Baasha, Elah, Zimri, and Omri of Israel; Ahab of Israel establishes the worship of Baal, calling forth the powerful witness of the prophets Elijah and Elisha; Jehoshaphat of Judah and Ahab of Israel combine and become entangled in fateful troubles with the Syrians; deaths of Ahab and Jezebel; ascension of Elijah; miraculous works of Elisha; Jehu slays Ahaziah of Judah and Jehoram of Israel; renewed hostility of the two kingdoms, until Israel is destroyed by Shalmaneser during the reign of Hezekiah in Judah.

III. History of the kings of Judah until the Babylonian exile, 2 Kings 18–25. The kings Hezekiah, Manasseh, Amon, Josiah, Jehoahaz, Jehoiakim, Jehoiachin, and Zedekiah; Sennacherib's attack and defeat; Hezekiah's illness, restoration, ambition, and punishment; the book of the Law is found under Josiah; beginning of the exile, 605 B.C.; Jehoiachin taken to Babylon; destruction of Jerusalem, 586 B.C.

M. Chronicles

36. Name

The Hebrew Bible called this important work Words of Days, a name suggesting the translations "day book," "journal," or "annals." Jerome, the reviser of the ancient Latin version, introduced the name of Chronicles, which naturally passed into our modern languages because of the exclusive use of the Latin Bible during the Middle Ages.

The Greek translators named this work Paralipomena, signifying things "passed by" (by the writers of the other historical books) or things "left over," omitted in the other books. This name is not happily chosen, however, for this work is quite independent of the other historical books and is written according to a definite plan, surveying in a summary manner the entire history of the people of God up to the days of the Babylonian exile.

Like the books of Samuel and Kings, Chronicles was written as one volume, the division into two books being introduced by the Greek translators (see section 142).

37. Purpose

Though Chronicles discusses largely the same period as the books of Samuel and Kings, it treats the subject matter in a distinctive way, selecting the material and handling it according to a purposeful plan. While the other books tell their story to prove that God made good both his promises and his threats with a powerful hand during the rule of the kings, the author of Chronicles tells the story of Levitical worship among the Jews. Therefore, he relates many occurrences that had not been mentioned in the preceding works and omits many little stories that had been told there in great detail.

Whatever pertains to the priesthood and to the worship of the sanctuary is sure to find a place in this record. Thus the author speaks at length of David's persistent efforts to introduce and establish a permanent order of divine services and of his preparations for the erection of a temple, but he refers to David's other achievements in quite a summary manner. Solomon, the wise king, is to be remembered chiefly as the builder of the magnificent temple. In the history of the kings of Judah, the writer emphasizes the labors of Josiah to make the knowledge of the Law common property among the people. He gives a full account of the celebrations of the Passover arranged by Hezekiah and Josiah and winds up his story with an account of the order of Cyrus authorizing the rebuilding of the temple.

As the Psalms demonstrate that the Law of Moses really became a living force among the people of Israel and a schoolmaster unto Christ, so Chronicles on its part sets before our eyes the actual history of the forms of public worship among the people. Here we may learn that for all the sinful waywardness of Israel and Judah, Jerusalem remained a place where the worship of the true God was maintained, on the whole, in accordance with Moses' ordinances. This characteristic of Chronicles explains the omission of such interesting stories as those relating to David's fall and repentance, to his many afflictions, to Solomon's magnificence and sins, and even to the entire history of the kingdom of the ten tribes.

38. Date and author

The story of Chronicles ends with the statement that King Cyrus of Persia permitted the Jews to return to Jerusalem after the 70 years had elapsed, according to prophecy (2 Chronicles 36:21-23). This is sufficient reason to assume that this work was written after the exile and in Jerusalem. That it must not be dated later is amply proved by the fact that the author speaks of darics (1 Chronicles 29:7), which were Persian gold coins bearing the image of Darius. It was only under the Persian dominion that the Jews used such coins.

As Ezra was the dominating figure among the people in those days and was endowed with the spirit of prophecy, it is probable that he wrote Chronicles. This conjecture is strengthened by the observation that the last two verses of 2 Chronicles are almost literally identical with the opening statement of the book of Ezra, that in both books the Law is referred to with the same set formula (for example, 1 Chronicles 23:31; Ezra 3:4), and that both books contain similar and quite unusual expressions in the original Hebrew text. This argument is so convincing that some expositors have suggested that Chronicles and the book of Ezra were written as one work. This, however, is not correct, because Chronicles is brought to a definite close by a statement that corresponds exactly with the character of the entire work.

39. Authenticity

The gifted man who wrote Chronicles in a spirit of deepest reverence for the ancient religion and worship of his people surely must have been well versed in the older historical literature of the Jews. It is just as certain that he did not simply copy from others what he wrote under the inspiration of the Holy Spirit. Not only does he furnish much information that is not found anywhere else, but when he speaks of the same occurrences, his presentation is altogether independent. He also takes pains to inform the readers what documents were at his disposal. His most frequent reference, couched in varying but essentially identical terms, is to "the book of the kings of Judah and Israel" (2 Chronicles 16:11). He also had a biography of King Uzziah, written by Isaiah the prophet (2 Chronicles 26:22); a history written by Iddo the prophet (2 Chronicles 13:22); a book of Jehu (2 Chronicles 20:34); a vision of Isaiah, recorded in the book of the kings of Judah and Israel (2 Chronicles 32:32); and certain words of the seers (2 Chronicles 33:18).

While an unbiased reader of Chronicles will discover no real reason to doubt the reliability of the author or the early date of his writing, no book of the Old Testament, outside the books of Moses, has suffered so many violent attacks concerning its veracity and age.

Such destructive criticism begins, it seems, because Chronicles contains some statements that do not seem to agree with history as we know it from the other historical books. But the viciousness and persistence of the attacks have a far deeper reason. This has been admitted by DeWette, a leader in this field of higher criticism, who explained that the critic gets rid of a great number of vexatious and irrefutable proofs of an early date for the books of Moses once he can show that Chronicles is a forgery, dating from the days of the Maccabees or later. In order to deny with some show of right that Moses wrote the books that bear his name, it is necessary first to set aside the testimony of Chronicles!

A Bible believer who is aware of this confession will hardly be upset by any suspicions impugning the truth of Chronicles. It is true that some numbers and names given in Chronicles are not easy to reconcile with statements of other historical books referring to the same matters. The difficulty, however, lies not in the inspired records but in the deficiency of our information on those points. Those who lived in the days of Ezra surely did not see any of these discrepancies, because for them they did not exist. In some cases the apparent discrepancies disappear at once upon closer inspection, as a single example will show. According to 1 Chronicles 21:25, David paid Araunah six hundred shekels of gold. The same payment is apparently given as amounting to only 50 shekels of silver in 2 Samuel 24:24, but in the latter case, the price is distinctly described as a payment for the threshing floor and the oxen, while the greater sum mentioned in Chronicles was paid for the whole place, which was Mount Moriah. Thus the two statements supplement each other.

Summary of contents

   I. Genealogy from Adam to the grandsons of Zerubbabel, together with some historical notes and geographical lists, 1 Chronicles 1–10.
  II. History of David's reign, 1 Chronicles 11–30. Detailed information concerning David's plans for the temple and his last decrees.
 III. History of Solomon and the kings of Judah up to the exile, 2 Chronicles 1–36. Building and dedication of the temple; the queen of Sheba; deeds and experiences of the kings of Judah, many of which are not mentioned in the books of Kings.

N. Ezra

40. Author

Ezra himself indicates that he wrote the book of Ezra, for he tells his story in the first person, beginning at the eighth chapter. Hence the Christian church has always maintained his authorship, as has the Jewish tradition. The objections raised against this view by rationalistic critics are not worthy of serious consideration.

Under God's providential guidance Ezra became the leader of the second company of the Jews who returned from the land of their exile. This and his untiring efforts to reestablish the true worship of God in its appointed forms have earned for him the name Second Moses. The Jewish rabbis have preserved the tradition that Ezra also assembled the historical books of the Old Testament and that he first began to establish synagogues throughout the land, in which the Word of God was read on the Sabbath Day, as we know from the story of the life of Christ.

As Ezra surely was not a young man when he first came to Jerusalem and as he worked at the side of Nehemiah for 12 years (Nehemiah 8:2), he must have attained a great age. Nevertheless, the Jewish legend that says he lived to the age of 120 years is probably exaggerated. We have no information regarding the end of his life.

41. Period

After the people of Israel had returned to their land from the Babylonian exile, Ezra wrote this book as an account of Jewish history in the first 80 years after the return. He tells how the first company of returning exiles, led by Zerubbabel, rebuilt the temple under great difficulties, and how he himself, 70 years later, reached Jerusalem at the head of a second company and immediately instituted a much-needed reformation.

The whole account is arranged chronologically, according to the reigns of the Persian kings. Because we know from secular history when Cyrus, the Persian king, captured the city of Babylon and thus became the ruler of the exiled Jews, Ezra's statement in the first chapter fixes the year 536 B.C. as the date of the return from the exile. Thus the captivity lasted for 70 years (606–536 B.C.), in literal fulfillment of the prophecy of Jeremiah (Jeremiah 25:11). Ezra mentions four other Persian rulers besides Cyrus, but the investigators do not agree in their identification of these kings with those known from secular historians.

42. Language

Though the body of the book of Ezra is written in Hebrew, the sacred language of the Old Testament, its first part contains a section of considerable length written in Chaldee, or Aramaic (4:8–6:18). This peculiarity does not, of course, justify any doubt as to the inspiration of the book. During the 70 years of their exile, the Jews had acquired a thorough knowledge of the Aramaic tongue and thus could readily read what Ezra had recorded in this language. Moreover, the section in question contains an account of a negotiation that was carried on through the medium of the Aramaic language, and Ezra naturally incorporated the original record into his book without translating it. From 5:4 it appears that the entire account was transcribed from some older document, because the writer there speaks in the first person, but Ezra was not an eyewitness of the occurrence.

Summary of contents

    I. Return of the first company of exiles under Zerubbabel, chapters 1–6. The edict of Cyrus; list of those who returned; the foundations for the temple are laid; hostility of the Samaritans; completion and dedication of the temple.

    II. Return of the second company under Ezra, chapters 7–10. Artaxerxes authorizes Ezra, who gathers a company of the Jews; laden with rich gifts for the temple, they reach Jerusalem; there Ezra carries out a needed reformation by expelling the heathen women whom Jews had married.

O. Nehemiah

43. Author

Because the book of Nehemiah continues the narrative of Ezra, who also is a person of great importance in the story there related, the book of Nehemiah is called by many the Second Book of Ezra. This misleading name, based upon a superficial impression, does not decide the question

45

of authorship. It has, however, been eagerly seized upon as an argument by the champions of destructive criticism, who strive laboriously, though quite unsuccessfully, to prove that the books of Chronicles, Ezra, and Nehemiah are forgeries that were written at a very late time, hardly predating the birth of Christ.

The unbiased reader finds no reason to believe that this book ever formed a part of the book of Ezra. All real evidence also goes to show that Nehemiah is the author, because the first seven chapters, together with chapters 12 and 13, are written by him in the first person. In the intervening chapters, the person of Ezra is in the foreground, but this is easily explained by the nature of the occurrences there related and cannot justly be quoted as a reason for doubting the authorship of Nehemiah.

44. Importance

Nehemiah contains the last of the inspired records of Jewish history that we possess. The book of Esther tells of an occurrence that took place under King Xerxes, in the days of Ezra and Nehemiah. It must have been written before the book of Nehemiah. The books of the Maccabees, being apocryphal, are not inspired narratives but owe their existence purely to human endeavor. Their historical reliability may be questioned occasionally without offense to the Christian mind.

Thus the book of Nehemiah brings to a close the canonical history of God's people in the Old Testament. All later documents rank no higher than secular histories. After Nehemiah and Malachi, all special revelations of God ceased, and the pious believers looked forward to the fulfillment of all those great and beautiful messianic promises given to them through the prophets (Luke 2:38).

45. *Purpose*

Nehemiah was a person of exalted rank at the court of the Persian king Artaxerxes, being the monarch's cup-bearer, with the special title of Tirshatha (10:1, KJV), which probably signifies a governor (12:26). It is not certain whether the remark in 10:8 indicates that Nehemiah was a priest.

Though highly honored and enjoying the confidence of the great ruler, Nehemiah was seized with a desire to return to Jerusalem, the city of his fathers, because he was deeply moved by reports of the conditions existing there. His humble request, laid before Artaxerxes at a favorable moment, was willingly granted. Clothed with high authority, he proceeded to Jerusalem and soon succeeded in stopping the intrigues of the Samaritans. But the most important result of his labors was the complete restoration of the appointed worship, in which he was supported by Ezra.

The Scriptures tell us nothing of the death of Nehemiah.

Summary of contents

  I. Efforts of Nehemiah for the benefit of Jerusalem, chapters 1–7. Nehemiah's prayer for Jerusalem; arrival in the city; building of walls and gates; hostility of the neighbors and their repulse; list of returned families.

 II. The solemn restoration of divine worship, chapters 8–10. Reading of the book of the Law; repentance of the people; sealing of the covenant.

III. Various lists; remaining labors of Nehemiah, chapters 11–13. List of the inhabitants of Jerusalem and its environs; list of priests; dedication of the city; improvements introduced by Nehemiah.

P. Esther

46. Purpose

The book of Esther, written in a lively and even dramatic style, tells the remarkable story of Esther, a Jewess, who was made a Persian queen by the favor of King Xerxes. As such, she became the instrument of God for preventing a massacre of the captive Jews, which Haman had wickedly planned.

It is plain, however, that the real purpose of the author was not primarily to add one more to the many proofs of that unfailing divine providence which watched over the Jews but, rather, to record, for the information of posterity, how the Feast of Purim came to be observed among the Jews. The Persian word *pur* (plural, *purim*) signifies a "lot." This feast was to be a reminder of how Haman had cast lots to determine the day for the massacre (3:7; 9:26).

It is worth noting that the name of God is never mentioned in this book and that neither Esther nor Mordecai seem to exhibit any longing for the land of their fathers. This peculiarity, however, is due to the purpose of the book and to the circumstances under which it was written. Since it relates a story of the royal court and was intended to set forth the historical reason for a festival appointed by men, it was not necessary to mention the name of God. To be sure, all the acts of Mordecai and Esther are plainly controlled by the true fear of the God of Israel. Furthermore, the author probably did not consider it necessary to voice a desire for the homeland, because the return of the people had already begun.

47. Date of the story

To decide the date of the story, it would be necessary to determine which Persian king is here called Xerxes (or

Ahasuerus, 1:1, NIV footnote). All investigations and discussions have so far failed to clear up this point to the satisfaction of everybody. However, the most commonly accepted view, as reflected in the NIV translation, seems to be that this Ahasuerus is none other than the redoubtable King Xerxes, who achieved doubtful renown in history by his mighty, but unsuccessful, campaign of vengeance against Greece, 480 B.C. In point of character, Ahasuerus is the speaking likeness of Xerxes, as the Greeks knew him. Both are described as men of most capricious moods and heartless cruelty, delighting in the most sensual luxuriousness. To this must be added the historical coincidences. The realm of Xerxes, like that of Ahasuerus, extended from India to Ethiopia (1:1). In the third year of his reign, Xerxes assembled all dignitaries of his vast domain and took counsel with them concerning the plan of attacking Greece. This great council was marked by a succession of voluptuous carousels, which lasted for 180 days (1:3,4). The choice is only strengthened by the statement that Esther was not chosen until the *seventh* year of Ahasuerus' reign (2:16). The intervening four years would have been spent by Xerxes upon the great campaign into Greece.

48. Historical truth

From the date of the story, it immediately appears that the story of the book of Esther is not fiction but relates an actual occurrence. This is further established by other considerations. The Feast of Purim is not only celebrated to this day by the Jews in the beginning of the month of March of every year, but it had come to be observed even in the days of the Maccabees (2 Maccabees 15:37). It would be difficult to show that any such popular festival has ever come to be observed without some good historical reason.

We know, moreover, that the Jews thought very highly of the book of Esther, so much so that their poets could not refrain from embellishing its story with various additions. We still possess some of these, which Luther translated separately. Though these apocryphal additions are valueless in themselves, they do show that the narrative of the book of Esther is based upon a wonderful occurrence, which served to inspire succeeding generations with intense patriotism.

The author is unknown, although some have suggested that it may have been Mordecai. It is certain, however, that the writer was a contemporary of Ezra and Nehemiah and that he issued the book soon after the story had happened. The book itself offers not the slightest reason for the hypothesis that its existence dates from the periods after Nehemiah.

Summary of contents

   I. Esther is made queen, chapters 1,2. Feast of Xerxes; rejection of Vashti; Esther chosen queen; Mordecai saves the king's life.

  II. Rise of Haman; his murderous plan against the Jews, chapters 3–5. Haman, having been insulted by Mordecai, causes the king to issue a bloody edict against the Jews; Mordecai reports this to Esther; she devises a plan to prevent the massacre.

 III. Deliverance of the Jews, chapters 6–10. Xerxes remembers the service of Mordecai; Esther accuses Haman; the fall of Haman and the rise of Mordecai; the king countermands the first edict; the Jews take vengeance upon their enemies; the Feast of Purim instituted.

Chapter 4
The Poetical Books

A. Hebrew poetry

49. Character

Since the life of the Jewish people in all its aspects was pervaded and controlled by religious thought, there was little opportunity and inspiration for the development of nonreligious poetry. It would seem, however, that songs and poems of a worldly character were not entirely unknown in the days of the earlier prophets. Thus we read of the "Book of the Wars of the LORD" (Numbers 21:14), the "Book of Jasher" (Joshua 10:13), and a book of the same title but of a later date (2 Samuel 1:18), which seem to have been collections of songs. If the lamentation of David over Saul quoted in the last passage is a fair sample, the songs certainly were not of a religious character. This may also be the reason why such collections were not preserved. At the same time, the example just referred to suggests that among the Jews even secular poetry usually exhibited traces of religious thought.

Epic poetry was not developed among the people of Israel. They lacked the myths concerning gods and heroes that furnished the material for the great narrative poems among the ancient heathen peoples. Pious reverence for the details of God's guidance effectively prevented any attempts to convert them into poetry.

For similar reasons the drama is unknown in ancient Jewish literature. To be sure, we find certain passages in the poems of the Bible that exhibit a certain dramatic character, because of the rapid change of the people introduced as speaking (Psalm 2). But nowhere do we find any attempt at anything similar to the Greek and Roman drama.

Since the efforts of prophets and poets among the Jews were directed toward the preservation and increase of spiritual life and power, the writers of biblical poetry seem to have confined themselves to lyrical and didactic (instructive) efforts. Where the inspired poets describe the emotional effects produced in their hearts by the divine promises, the lyric character predominates. Where they use divine truths as subjects for instruction, the result is a didactic poem. But just as the lyric poems contain a great wealth of instruction, so the didactic poems are frequently embellished with lyrical strains. In the Hebrew language, these two kinds of poetry are distinguished by different names; the lyric poem is called *sheer,* "song," while the didactic poem is known as *mashal,* "proverb" or "adage."

50. Development

The most ancient piece of Hebrew poetry is the song of praise by Moses after the miraculous deliverance of the people of Israel from the hands of the Egyptians (Exodus 15). Another song of that period has been preserved as Psalm 90, which is titled "A prayer of Moses the man of God."

From that time to the end of the prophetic period, the making of religious poetry never ceased altogether. In the historical and prophetical books, we find a number of songs from the pens of inspired men of God (compare the song of Deborah and Barak, Judges 5; the last words of David, 2 Samuel 23; the prophecy of Balaam, Numbers 23,24; and also Hannah's song of thanksgiving, 1 Samuel 2). In the books of the prophets, we find not only numerous passages of unsurpassed poetic beauty but also sermons clothed in true poetic form (as Habakkuk 3).

In this connection, however, we confine our remarks to those biblical books written entirely in poetry, namely, the book of Job, the book of Psalms, Proverbs, Ecclesiastes, and the Song of Solomon. The Lamentations of Jeremiah, though truly poetic in character, figure among the books of the prophets because of the arrangement adopted in our Bibles. Of these poetic writings, all psalms, the Song of Songs, and Lamentations belong to the class of *sheerim,* or songs, while Proverbs, Ecclesiastes, and the book of Job, being largely didactic, must be classed as *meshalim,* proverbs, or adages.

51. Peculiarities

Hebrew poetry, as we know it from the Bible, makes no use of either rhyme or meter, though the language itself is not unrhythmical and the word forms offer much opportunity for rhyming. This is a trait common to many Oriental languages. It was only after the establishment of the biblical canon that Jewish poets began to adapt the rhyme and the meter to their productions.

For poetic effect the Hebrew writer of songs and proverbs depended upon the grandeur of words and the skillful use of figures of speech. The main external characteristic of poetic form observable in Hebrew literature is parallelism, which simply means that every verse consists of two or more members that stand in some definite relation to one another. In synonymous parallelism the members of the verse express about the same thought. In antithetic parallelism the thoughts expressed in the two members are opposed to one another. In synthetic parallelism the thought expressed in the first member is developed or amplified in the subsequent members. Examples: The members are synonymous in Psalms 2:1; 17:5; 22:3;

53

antithetic in Psalm 18:41; and synthetic in Psalms 31:5; 16:1; 22:13,14.

Verses of only one member (as in Psalms 18:1; 25:1; 29:7) are rare. By far the greatest number of verses are distichs, having two members. Then there are some tristichs, having three members (as in Psalm 7:6); tetrastichs, of four members (as in Psalm 5:9); pentastichs, of five members (as in Psalm 39:12); and even hexastichs, of six members (as in Song of Songs 4:8). But note that the members are not always distinct in the translation, whereas in the Hebrew text, the marks of punctuation set them off very precisely.

Frequently a certain number of verses are found to form a stanza. This is indicated in various ways. Psalm 62, for instance, consists of three stanzas with four verses each; in the Hebrew each stanza begins with the same word. In Psalm 39 we find two stanzas ending in the same words, in verses 5 and 11. In Psalm 42, verses 5 and 11 close the stanzas in the form of a refrain.

Didactic poems sometimes exhibit an alphabetic structure. Each verse or even member begins with a different letter, in the order of the alphabet, so that the number of verses, or members of verses, agrees with the number of letters in the Hebrew alphabet. This structure cannot, of course, be recognized in a translation. To this class belong Psalms 25, 34, and 145; also Proverbs 31:10-31; and Lamentations. In Psalms 111 and 112 each half of every verse begins with the proper letter. The most elaborate structure of this kind is Psalm 119, in which a stanza of eight verses (an octonary) belongs to each letter and each verse of the stanza begins with the stanza letter. In the English Bible, this arrangement is indicated by the placing of the name of each Hebrew letter above the appropriate section.

B. Job

52. Purpose

The book of Job is an imposing poetical narrative, in which the author discusses the serious question of how one reconciles the sufferings of righteous men with the justice of God. Job, a righteous and pious man who had been blessed with great wealth and happiness, lost all his possessions, and finally his health, through the wickedness of Satan but under the permission of God. Nevertheless, Job remained steadfast to his trust in God until provoked by the behavior of his three friends, who had come to comfort him and sat with him in utter silence for seven days.

In his dejection Job cursed the day of his birth and thus challenged the justice of God's providential guidance. Then the friends opened their mouths in defense of God's righteousness. They argued that the question of a man's righteousness must be answered according to the measure of good or evil fortune that he experiences. While Job took issue with their accusations, they gradually unfolded their opinion that his present sufferings must be a just punishment for his sins. Though they were silenced at last by Job's vehement defense, the sufferer himself could not solve the serious problem and even involved himself in error.

Then Elihu, a fourth friend, entered the discussion, rebuked both the friends and Job, and demonstrated that God remains just under all circumstances and delivers the righteous man from evil. Finally God himself addressed Job, extolling his omnipotence, glory, and wisdom. Thus Job was convinced of his error, and God showed his kindness by bestowing a double blessing upon the afflicted man.

53. Historical value

Though the book of Job is a poem, its story is surely not fiction but records an actual occurrence. There is no reason to doubt that Job was a man of renown in his day, probably before the deliverance of Israel from Egypt. He may have lived somewhere in Arabia and surely was subjected to the experience that the poet describes. The free invention of such a character and such a plot is not only without a parallel in Hebrew literature but must be denied on account of Ezekiel 14:14,20 and James 5:11, where Job is referred to as a historical person.

54. Poetic structure

The inspired author has shaped the materials at his command into a work of art of surpassing beauty. Aside from the masterful diction, the poetic form is emphasized in the arrangement and treatment of the material. The reader should note the elaborate and dramatic dialogue between Job and his three friends, a sharp lingual contest of three rounds, in which the friends arise to speak in succession, each being at once answered by Job.

The many bold figures of speech, which delight Oriental ears, offer extreme difficulties to any Occidental translator. Luther declared that even with the aid of Melanchthon and Aurogallus, he barely succeeded at times in translating three lines within four days. In a letter addressed to Spalatin, dated February 23, 1524, he wrote, "In translating Job we had much trouble because of the loftiness of the grandiose diction, so that he would seem to be much less willing to suffer our translation than the consolation of his friends."

Note that Job's confession of faith, in 19:25-27, is an utterance of messianic hope.

55. *Author and date*

As the name of the author has not been recorded, there is wide disagreement among scholars as to the date of this wonderful poem. Some older commentators have suggested that either Job himself or Moses wrote it. It would seem, indeed, that Job lived in the days of Moses, and this prophet may have met Job in the course of his sojourn in Midian, before the exodus. But this does not make it necessary that the book should have been written at that early date. The polished language and the skillful arrangement of the poem rather suggest that it was written in the period of Solomon, when Hebrew poetry attained the height of its development. In the psalms and in the books of the prophets, we may discover many indisputable allusions to the book of Job. Compare Psalm 39:13 and Job 10:20; Psalm 58:8 and Job 3:16; Isaiah 19:5 and Job 14:11; Jeremiah 20:14-18 and Job 3:1-26; Amos 5:8 and Job 9:9. Note that the passages from the prophets referred to show definitely that the book of Job existed at the time and was known to the prophets as well as to their listeners.

Summary of contents

    I. Prologue: Job's blessed state, his affliction, and his sinful despondency, chapters 1–3.

    II. Dispute between Job and his three friends concerning the cause of his affliction, chapters 4–31. First round, chapters 4–14; second round, chapters 15–21; third round, chapters 22–31.

    III. Elihu defends the justice of God, rebuking both Job and his three friends, chapters 32–37.

    IV. God himself extols his omnipotence and glory, chapters 38–41.

    V. Epilogue: Job confesses his sinful error; receives twofold blessing, chapter 42.

C. Psalms

56. General character

This section of the Bible is a collection of 150 spiritual songs, in which the inspired poets of the Old Testament declared the great truth of the gospel and expressed the thoughts and emotions that the Holy Spirit effected in their souls. Since every believing heart here finds the best expression for its own spiritual experiences, the church of God has always held the book of Psalms in high esteem and has made constant use of the psalms for its own edification. We have no space here for even a few of the many testimonials written about the edifying power of the psalms. It suffices, however, to point out that the Scriptures themselves contain evidence of the constant use made of the psalms by pious men and women. Thus Mary's hymn of praise, the Magnificat, consists almost entirely of quotations from the psalms, and Zacharias likewise makes free use of them (Luke 1:46-55,68-79). Furthermore, a great number of our best church hymns are psalms put into metrical form.

57. Date of collection

Though we are not informed who gathered the psalms into one book, a careful examination will show that they are arranged according to a definite plan. It's clear they did not accumulate by chance but were assembled by one man into their final order. As it is certain that Psalm 137 was written in Babylon, the same being probably true of Psalms 102 and 126, it is very likely that the book of Psalms was put into its present form by Ezra after the return from the exile. There is no convincing evidence whatever that some of the psalms originated in the Maccabean period, as rationalistic critics maintain.

58. Arrangement

The entire collection is divided into five sections, or books, the end of each being marked by a doxology, as follows: Book 1, Psalms 1–41 (doxology, 41:13); Book 2, Psalms 42–72 (doxology, 72:18,19); Book 3, Psalms 73–89 (doxology, 89:52); Book 4, Psalms 90–106 (doxology 106:48); Book 5, Psalms 107–150, (doxology, Psalm 150). The collector appears to have imitated the number of the books of Moses. It is also plain that the doxologies do not properly belong to the psalms to which they happen to be attached.

59. Authors

Most of the information concerning the men who wrote the psalms is obtained from the superscriptions, which are integral parts of these sacred songs, added by the authors. It is quite in keeping with the practice of Hebrew and Arabic writers that an author places his name over a poem, instead of under it, as is our custom. Hence there is no reason to challenge the truth of the statements contained in these superscriptions.

There are 49 psalms that do not bear the names of their authors; two of these, however, are definitely ascribed to David elsewhere (Psalm 2 in Acts 4:25; Psalm 95 in Hebrews 4:7), so that really only 47 psalms are anonymous. Sometimes such a psalm may be dated approximately from its contents (Psalm 57), but as a rule, this test brings no result. Of the named psalms, David wrote 75, Asaph 12, the sons of Korah (one of whom was Heman, Psalm 88) 11, Solomon 2, and Moses and Ethan 1 each.

60. Classification

The psalms are usually classified as (1) songs of praise and thanksgiving, (2) songs of sorrow, repentance, or prayer, and (3) didactic psalms. It is not always easy, however, to decide on the class to which a psalm belongs, because the character of the song often changes. A song of praise turns into a solemn prayer, or a penitential prayer ends in a hymn of jubilation. Special mention must be made of the seven penitential psalms (Psalms 6,32,38,51,102,130,143), which are assigned as Scripture lessons for appointed fasting days in many old liturgies.

In all the three classes described above, we find messianic psalms. Many of these are designated as such by the Holy Spirit in the New Testament. In others the contents are unmistakably prophetical of the salvation that was to come in Christ. In this important group, we find the following psalms: 2 (Acts 4:25); 8 (Hebrews 2:6-9); 16 (Acts 2:25-31); 22 (verse 1!)–24, 40 (Hebrews 10:7); 45 (Hebrews 1:8,9); 47 (ascension!), 68 (Ephesians 4:8-10); 69 (John 2:17); 72, 89, 93, 97 (Hebrews 1:6); 110 (Matthew 22:44,45); 118 (Matthew 21:42). Furthermore, it should be observed that all psalms that extol the Word of God or the glory of the church must be understood as referring to the gospel of Jesus Christ and its successes in the New Testament. Hence they all are messianic prophecies. Modern critics here betray their utter unbelief and ignorance of the gospel by denying that any psalm was originally meant to be a prophecy of Christ.

61. Various notes

Besides the names of the authors, many superscriptions contain interesting bits of information. Some tell of the date and purpose of the poem (as in Psalms 18,30,38,51,52,54,56, 57,59,63, etc.); others of the chief musician, the leader of the temple choirs (one of these was Jeduthun, 1 Chronicles 16:41); and still others of the instruments to be used (as in

Psalms 4,54,67, etc.). Certain expressions found in some superscriptions are extremely puzzling and have exercised the imagination of older commentators.

Luther, who attempted to translate them, was inclined to regard them as symbolic references to the contents of the particular psalm. Thus, in Psalm 22:1 he translates the words *ajeleth ha-sha-har* as "the doe which is hunted down at dawn," thinking that the words might be meant as an allusion to the sufferings of Christ, which are described in the psalm. His example was followed by other Lutheran commentators. This theory, however, is quite untenable, because many of the remarks seem to have no relation to the contents of the psalms, yet all are of the same kind, for they are introduced in the same way.

The English translators sometimes simply retain the Hebrew words (as in Psalm 46, *alamoth*). Probably all these expressions referred to melodies or tunes, according to which the psalms were to be sung. This is the meaning of the words "according to" which the NIV uses with the terms. This explanation also disposes of the word *gittith* (as in Psalm 8, etc.), which Luther believed to be the name of an instrument.

The puzzling title "A song of ascents," given to Psalms 120–134, has never been satisfactorily explained. Probably, however, the term signifies a particular poetical form (similar to our sonnet). All the psalms so inscribed seem to be built up according to definite rules affecting the arrangement of thoughts and words.

The word *selah* also remains unexplained to this day. It may be taken as certain, however, that it was not part of the text. It is supposed to be a musical term, probably conveying some instruction concerning the use of musical instruments, perhaps marking an instrumental interlude.

61

D. Proverbs

62. Author

Solomon "spoke three thousand proverbs and his songs numbered a thousand and five" (1 Kings 4:32). In the book of Proverbs, we have a collection of some of these proverbs of Solomon, which, as the introduction declares, serve "for attaining wisdom and discipline; for understanding words of insight; for acquiring a disciplined and prudent life, doing what is right and just and fair; for giving prudence to the simple, knowledge and discretion to the young" (Proverbs 1:2-4).

That the three chief sections of this book are from the pen of Solomon cannot reasonably be doubted, although some other person, or persons, may have selected and arranged the proverbs. This is surely true of the third section, for we read in 25:1 that "these are more proverbs of Solomon, copied by the men of Hezekiah king of Judah." These were undoubtedly men of prophetical authority, and the statement renders it highly probable that the two preceding sections of the book were assembled in the same way.

The only real doubt as to Solomon's authorship involves the two appendices, contained in chapters 30 and 31, the superscriptions of which contain some puzzling statements. In 30:1 we read, "The sayings of Agur son of Jakeh—an oracle: This man declared to Ithiel, to Ithiel and to Ucal . . ." The enigmatic names, which occur nowhere else in the Scriptures, have led many expositors to assume that chapter 30 is not from the pen of Solomon. The verse also contains certain terms that otherwise are used only as designations for the sayings of prophets. Hence the commentators of Luther's Weimar Bible say, "It is safest to assume that Agur was a prophet in the days of Solomon, who handed these words to his men as a divine utterance, and that the men of Hezekiah thereafter added them to Solomon's proverbs under divine guidance."

Furthermore, the last part of the chapter contains many ingenious similes, which may well have been taken from among the three thousand proverbs of Solomon. It is not a violation of historical propriety, therefore, to include the chapter among those ascribed to Solomon, without attempting to solve the puzzle of the superscription. The same may be said of chapter 31, which is described as containing "the sayings of King Lemuel—an oracle his mother taught him" (verse 1). Here, as in chapter 30, we find it possible to assume Solomon's authorship, although one cannot insist on it.

63. Arrangement and contents

The first section of the book (chapters 1–9) contains a series of connected sayings, praising the wisdom of the true fear of God and exposing the folly of a sinful life. In the two other sections (chapters 10–24 and 25–29), the proverbs are strung together loosely, though they are clearly assembled according to topics. Of the two appendices (chapters 30,31), the second is most notable for the beautiful eulogy upon the virtues of a good wife.

E. Ecclesiastes

64. General character

The Greek name by which Ecclesiastes is subtitled in some English translations means "a preacher," an appropriate title for the solemn discourse here presented to the reader. Luther characterizes this book as follows: "Sum and substance of this book is the word of Christ (Matthew 6:34): 'Do not worry about tomorrow, for tomorrow will worry about itself. Each day has enough trouble of its own.'"

The Preacher demonstrates that while all earthly things are indeed meaningless and transitory, yet the blessings of this earthly life may well be enjoyed without detriment to the soul, provided the true fear of God is the supreme and controlling influence. Hence he summarizes his teachings at the end as follows: "Now all has been heard; here is the conclusion of the matter: Fear God and keep his commandments, for this is the whole duty of man. For God will bring every deed into judgment, including every hidden thing, whether it is good or evil" (12:13,14).

65. Author

Most modern critics agree that for various reasons Solomon cannot be the author of this book. All their arguments, however, whether based upon the style or upon the contents of the book, are so inconclusive that they fail to shake the statement of the title, which unmistakably names Solomon as the author. It has been suggested that some unknown writer may have ascribed his product to the great king, in order to give it the weight of exalted authority. This theory, however, can be acceptable only to those who deny divine inspiration. If Ecclesiastes is truly the Word of God, the superscription must surely not only be trustworthy but must also be taken as literally true.

The author gives us to understand that he has personally experienced not only the vanity of all earthly pleasures and, particularly, of all sinful enjoyments but also the peculiar troubles of advancing years. It would appear, therefore, that Solomon wrote this book in his old age, after he had come to know and truly repent of his grievous sins. Thus we may consider this book as a counterpart of the confession that David penned under similar circumstances in Psalm 51 for our warning and instruction.

Summary of contents

I. First Discourse, on the meaninglessness of human wisdom and earthly pleasures, chapters 1,2.

II. Second Discourse, on the proper use of earthly goods and pleasures, chapters 3–5.

III. Third Discourse, on the meaninglessness of riches and the achievement of true wisdom, chapters 6–8.

IV. Fourth Discourse, on the proper rules of conduct, as based upon true wisdom, chapters 9–12.

F. Song of Songs

66. Character and purpose

The title of the Song of Songs (1:1) testifies to Solomon's authorship and calls this beautiful poem "Solomon's Song of Songs." The exquisite loveliness of the song alone would not justify the poet's claim that it is excellent above all songs if it were meant for anything else than an allegory of most sublime things. This has been the understanding of the church at all times. A mere love song would surely not have been found worthy of a place among the sacred writings of the Old Testament.

Every reader of the Bible is aware that the wonderful and intimate relationship existing between Christ and his church is frequently symbolized by the simile of the bride-groom and his bride. A very fine application of this thought is found in Hosea 2:19,20. That also is the meaning of the Song of Songs. Its dramatic scenes depict the longing of the church for her heavenly bridegroom, as well as the Savior's divine love for her. This understanding is fully established by the words of John the Baptist in John 3:29 and by Christ himself in Matthew 9:15. Both speak of the Savior as the bridegroom and of the church as his bride, with the assurance that this comparison was altogether familiar to their hearers from the Old Testament. They likely referred to Solomon's song and thus have given us the proper key to its true meaning.

Chapter 5
The Books of the Prophets

A. The prophets and their ministries

67. Peculiar position

Besides the priests and Levites, who were appointed to instruct the people of God in the Law (Leviticus 10:11; Deuteronomy 17:11; 33:10; Malachi 2:7), God raised up among the people of Israel numerous prophets as special teachers, endowed with special gifts of the Spirit for the exercise of their extraordinary functions. The distinction between these two classes of ministers of God was quite the same as that between the apostles in the New Testament and the ministers of the gospel who followed after them. Like our ministers the sons of Levi performed the work allotted to them without a special endowment of spiritual gifts and were bound to conform their teachings strictly to the written Word of God. The prophets, on the other hand, like the apostles, were blessed with an extraordinary measure of the gifts of the Spirit. They were not merely teachers and expositors of the sacred books then in the hands of the people, but they also were the messengers of new revelations, given to them by divine inspiration.

In exceptional cases the divine spirit of prophecy descended even upon ungodly persons, making them true witnesses of God's truth for that occasion. Thus Balaam, the heathen soothsayer (Numbers 22–24), and Caiaphas, the high priest (John 11:49-52), were compelled, against their own intentions, to testify concerning the saving work of Christ.

Occasionally, holy women were inspired to speak words of prophecy. The title of prophetess is conferred in the

Bible upon Miriam (Exodus 15:20), Deborah (Judges 4:4), Huldah (2 Chronicles 34:22), and Anna (Luke 2:36).

68. History of prophecy

Moses is the first person named in the Scriptures who claims the title of a prophet. He also declared that in this capacity he was a type of Christ (Deuteronomy 18:15-18).

As for the period of the judges, the biblical record does not mention any prophetical activity. It would appear, then, that the period of prophecy, properly speaking, began with Samuel, who is again styled a prophet (1 Samuel 9:9,11,19). He probably was also the founder of schools in which young men seem to have been instructed and trained, similar to the practice in our theological seminary. The first trace of the existence of such institutions is found in 1 Samuel 10:5,10,11. At the same time, this story seems to say that the "procession of prophets" was frequently seized with the spirit of prophecy. The same fact is disclosed in the words spoken to Elisha by the "company of the prophets" (2 Kings 2:3,5).

At times the number of students in these schools must have been considerable, since the school at Jericho could send forth 50 men to seek Elijah (2 Kings 2:16,17), and Elisha had assembled a hundred men in the school at Gilgal (4:43). We have no means of ascertaining how many of these students were afterwards made prophets by the direct call of God, but we do know that the prophets known to us were not all educated in such schools.

Of the prophets who lived and preached in the days of David and Solomon, we know Nathan, Gad, Ahijah, and Iddo by name (2 Samuel 12:1-25; 24:11-19; 2 Chronicles 9:29). In the kingdom of the ten tribes, a burdensome and dangerous task was assigned to the powerful prophets Elijah and Elisha. In the very days when the Jewish people had become utterly corrupt, the prophetic messengers of God seem to have been most numerous. In 1 Kings 18:4, for example, we are told that Obadiah, a servant of Ahab, hid a hundred prophets in two caves to save them from the wrath of Jezebel. It is rather probable, furthermore, that many others died in that persecution.

This brief sketch will serve to show that the 16 prophetical books of the Old Testament contain only a small fraction of the instruction extended to the Jewish people by God through his inspired prophets. It is to be assumed, however, that the discourses of most prophets referred to particular circumstances and were not of general importance to the kingdom of God. Only those sermons of the prophets have been preserved that are profitable for instruction and comfort of the church at all times.

69. 16 prophets

The prophets whose writings have been preserved in the Bible are Isaiah, Jeremiah, Ezekiel, Daniel, Hosea, Joel, Amos, Obadiah, Jonah, Micah, Nahum, Habakkuk, Zephaniah, Haggai, Zechariah, and Malachi. The first four mentioned are called the major prophets, because their books are notable for their volume and wealth of content. The other 12 are called the minor prophets.

We possess no information whatever concerning the dates of some of the minor prophets, so it is impossible to determine their historical order. It is assumed, however, that Obadiah is the oldest of the 16 prophets and that he preached between 853 and 841 B.C. or possibly earlier. Since Malachi, the last of the prophets, delivered the sermons recorded in his book in the years between 433 and 424 B.C., it follows that the activity of our 16 prophets extended for a period of over four hundred years. But this does not mean that they followed one another in regular succession. At various times two or three of them worked simultaneously.

Only 2 of the 16, Hosea and Amos, preached in the Northern Kingdom. Judah and Jerusalem heard the words of Isaiah, Jeremiah (who afterward preached in Egypt among the Jewish refugees), Joel, Obadiah, Micah, Nahum, Habakkuk, Zephaniah, Haggai, Zechariah, and Malachi. Ezekiel and Daniel performed their ministries among the exiled Jews in Babylon. Jonah was sent on a mission to the city of Nineveh.

In the Hebrew Bible, the arrangement of the prophetical books differs from that with which we are familiar. The Lamentations of Jeremiah, placed immediately after his prophecies in our Bibles, are really songs of lamentation, belonging to the same class of literature as the psalms, with which they are grouped in the Hebrew Bible. The Jews assigned the book of Daniel to the same group, briefly called the Psalms, because the book of Psalms stands first. But the prophetic character of this book is so unmistakable that the very first Greek translation, made about 150 years before Christ, placed Daniel among the prophets, an example followed by all versions thereafter.

70. Chronological order

The order in which the minor prophets are arranged is hardly based on their succession in time. It would seem that similarity of contents helped to decide the position of each book. Thus we know nothing whatever concerning the date of Joel, but because Amos begins his prophecy (1:2) with one of the closing statements of Joel (3:21), Amos was placed after Joel. We also do not know definitely when Obadiah, Jonah, Nahum, Habakkuk, and Malachi delivered the discourses that we read in the Bible, but the contents of their writings (for Jonah adds the remark in 2 Kings 14:25) permit certain fairly satisfactory conclusions as to their various dates.

In the following table, which shows the probable historical sequence of the prophets, contemporaries are indicated by brackets joining the names:

1. Obadiah, under King Jehoram, between 853 and 841 B.C.
2. Joel, under King Joash, between 835 and 800 B.C.
{ 3. Jonah, under King Jeroboam II, between 793 and 753 B.C.
  4. Amos, under Kings Jeroboam II and Uzziah, between 770 and 750 B.C.
{ 5. Hosea, under Kings Uzziah to Hezekiah, between 750 and 686 B.C.
  6. Isaiah, under Kings Uzziah to Hezekiah, between 740 and 686 B.C.
  7. Micah, under Kings Jotham, Ahaz, Hezekiah, between 740 and 686 B.C.
8. Nahum, under King Manasseh, between 660 and 650 B.C.
{ 9. Habakkuk, under King Josiah, between 640 and 609 B.C.
  10. Zephaniah, under King Josiah, between 640 and 625 B.C.
{ 11. Jeremiah, under Kings Josiah to Zedekiah, between 627 and 586 B.C.
  12. Ezekiel, in the Babylonian exile, between 593 and 571 B.C.
13. Daniel, in the Babylonian exile, between 606 and 530 B.C.
{ 14. Haggai, after the return from exile, from 520 B.C.
  15. Zechariah, after the return from exile, from 520 B.C.
16. Malachi, after the return from exile, between 433 and 424 B.C.

71. Manner of teaching

The various titles by which the prophets are known in the Bible indicate their special tasks. They were called prophets, that is, speakers, because they declared unto the people the supernatural, divine revelations God gave them. Furthermore, we may safely assume that they publicly expounded the sacred writings then available, especially the prophecies concerning the coming Christ. They were also called seers because of their peculiar gift of foreseeing the future and proclaiming their visions to the people in the form of prophecies, to warn the unbelievers and to comfort the faithful.

They received their revelations partly by direct inspiration and partly in visions, during which they were in a state of ecstasy, without, however, losing consciousness. (Read Paul's declaration in 2 Corinthians 12:4.) Thus Isaiah was called in a vision (Isaiah 6); Ezekiel received visions concerning the future spread of the gospel (chapter 1) and concerning the future glory of God's kingdom (chapters 40–48, the most elaborate prophetic vision recorded in the Old Testament!). In a vision at night, in a dream, Daniel saw the four great world monarchies that were to be followed by the kingdom of Christ (chapters 7,8,10,11).

As a rule, the prophets proclaimed their revelations in public discourse. Sometimes, however, they were instructed to employ symbolical actions, in which even the person of the prophet was employed as an illustration. The most remarkable symbolical act of any prophet was the marriage of Hosea, whose very family life served as a sermon to the people (chapter 1). In a similar way, a son of Isaiah had to be a living representation of a prophecy (Isaiah 7:2-4; 8:1-4). A great number of symbolical actions are described by Jeremiah: the linen belt (Jeremiah 13), the broken jar (chapter 19), the yoke (chapter 27), the purchased field (chapter 32).

72. Authority

The prophets unmistakably claimed not only that they spoke with divine authority but that their very words were the words of God. This is the only reasonable and correct understanding of the expression "This is what the Lord says," with which the prophets customarily prefaced their statements. By so insisting that they received their message through the Spirit of God, they have furnished one of the strongest proofs for the doctrine of verbal inspiration.

In this connection the testimony of Balaam is noteworthy. He certainly would have profited in a material way if he had concealed what God had revealed to him, but he resisted the strongest temptations, declaring that he could not speak but what the Lord had told him. In the same way, the holy prophets likewise knew that the Spirit of God spoke through them and gave them the words that they were to speak.

This also is the only explanation for the indisputable fact that the prophets were able to foretell certain circumstances that were entirely beyond human computation or guessing, such as the virginity of the Lord's mother (Isaiah 7:14); the place of Jesus' birth (Micah 5:2); his sufferings and resurrection (Isaiah 53); the sequence of the four world monarchies (Daniel 7–11); the 70 weeks (9:24); the 70 years of the exile (Jeremiah 25:11); and even the name of the future deliverer of the Jews (Isaiah 45:1).

These overwhelming proofs of the divine origin of the Bible are so utterly unpalatable to unbelieving critics that they brazenly make the claim that such prophecies are impossible. Having thus prejudged the matter in spite of all evidence, they either deny that the prophets intended to foretell the future or take a cheap shot at inspiration by claiming that the alleged prophecies were written after the events had occurred, thus branding the holy writers as willful deceivers. By resorting to such unreasonable and violent measures, modern criticism betrays its unscientific and unholy character.

In conclusion, it should be noted that the prophets knew no more of the future than what had been revealed to them. The veil of futurity was never lifted altogether from before their eyes. Hence we are told that they even studied their own prophecies for more enlightenment (1 Peter 1:10,11) and found much cause to meditate upon the writings of other men of God (Daniel 9:2).

B. Isaiah

73. Prophet

Of the family connections of Isaiah, we know no more than that his father was named Amoz (1:1, not to be confused with the prophet Amos!). Isaiah tells us that he was called by God in a glorious vision during the last year of Uzziah's reign (6:1). His ministry, therefore, began about the year 740 B.C. According to chapters 36 to 39, he was still active in the 15th year of Hezekiah, about 700 B.C. Thus he completed at least 40 years of prophetic service.

Concerning his death we have no reliable information. A rabbinical legend relates that when King Manasseh, the successor of Hezekiah, began to persecute believers, he also sought the life of Isaiah. The prophet hid in the trunk of a cedar, which had opened to receive him but closed at once after he had slipped in. Manasseh ordered the tree to be sawed in two, and when the saw reached the mouth of the prophet, he died.

74. Rank

It is not only the size of Isaiah's book that entitles it to its place at the head of the prophetical group. We may easily observe that those whom God called to be his apostles or prophets differed greatly among themselves in temperament and gifts of the mind and that the Holy Spirit used those natural gifts. In Isaiah's case, his gifts excel those of all other prophets, just as Paul ranks first among the apostles. Isaiah's elegant style, together with the abounding evidences of poetic imagination, mark Isaiah as one of the most highly gifted persons known in history. This is acknowledged even by those who reject the message of Isaiah altogether.

But a higher measure of excellence must be noted. No other prophet was chosen by the Holy Spirit to proclaim so many and such remarkable prophecies concerning Christ and the church of the New Testament. For this reason Isaiah is justly called the evangelist of the Old Testament, after the suggestion of Jerome, one of the so-called fathers of the church, who says, "It would be proper to call him, not so much a prophet, but rather an evangelist; for he displays before our eyes the mysteries of Christ and the Church so clearly that one might think he were not writing prophecies of future events, but were telling the story of past occurrences."

Note this prophet's references to Christ in 4:2 (the Branch of the Lord); 7:14 (born of the virgin); 9:6,7 (a child born who is God); 11:1 (the Branch from Jesse); 28:16 (the cornerstone); 40:11 (the Good Shepherd); 42:1-3 (the Servant of the Lord in whom he delights); 49:6 (the light of the Gentiles); 50:6; and 53:1-12 (the sufferings of Christ); 61:1,2 (explained by Christ himself, Luke 4:18,19); 63:1-6 (he who treads the winepress). Add to these the many passages in which Isaiah sets forth the glories of the kingdom of grace in the New Testament.

75. Period

The days of Isaiah lie midway between those of Moses and of Christ. His work had to be done at a time when the punishment of unfaithfulness, as had been foretold by Moses, was rapidly approaching. And though Isaiah is outspoken in his denouncements of Jewish apostasy, yet it was his most precious task to comfort the remaining believers, the true Israel, with the assurance that God's promises of salvation would surely be fulfilled.

Though Isaiah did not live to see his people carried away to Babylon, he was enlightened by God to recognize as the forerunners of the threatening catastrophe the tribulations that he witnessed. When Ahaz, spurning the faithful warning of the prophet, allied himself with Assyria against his insolent neighbors Rezin and Pekah, Isaiah announced that Assyria was to be brought low in due time, which shattered the earthly hopes of the Jewish people. When Hezekiah became filled with sinful pride after his deliverance from the hands of Sennacherib and from his deathly sickness, Isaiah rebuked him by foretelling the Babylonian exile. But he always added words of comfort for those who continued to put their trust in the Lord, declaring the sure mercies of David and the firm covenant of God, who had prepared an everlasting salvation for his people in the Messiah, who was to come.

76. Authenticity

Although we cannot show that the various discourses contained in the book of Isaiah were assembled in the order in which they were first delivered, the unity of the entire book is apparent to every careful reader.

It is quite natural, however, that the magnificent prophecies proclaimed by Isaiah are challenged by modern rationalistic critics, whose favorite theories fall to the ground if such wonderful statements are true. Accordingly, they have gone to work to tear the prophet's book to pieces, even as they did the books of Moses. They are fully agreed that chapters 40 to 66 cannot possibly have been written by Isaiah but were added to the canon much later under the name of the prophet by some imposter.

But there is no reason whatever why a faithful believer in the divine origin of the Bible should become disturbed by the impudent and baseless claims of such enemies of the gospel. It happens that the Holy Spirit, speaking in the New Testament, has quoted various passages precisely from the second part of the book of Isaiah, declaring in so many words that they were written by the prophet. Compare Isaiah 61:1,2 and Luke 4:17-21; Isaiah 53:1 and Romans 10:16; Isaiah 65:1 and Romans 10:20; Isaiah 40:3 and John 1:23; and many others. It would be rank blasphemy to say that the Holy Spirit chose to tell a deliberate lie by ascribing to Isaiah a document that falsely bears his name.

Summary of contents

I. First group of Isaiah's discourses, chapters 1–27, having for its historical background the disobedience of Ahaz when he was beset by Pekah and Rezin.

II. Second group of discourses, chapters 28–66, the historical background being the deliverance of Hezekiah and his miraculous recovery from a fatal disease.

C. Jeremiah

77. Prophet

In the 13th year of King Josiah (627 B.C.), Jeremiah, then still a youth, was called as a prophet. He was of priestly descent, having been born in the city of Anathoth, situated only a few miles from Jerusalem in the land of Benjamin. Hilkiah, his father, must not be confused with the high priest of the same name who lived in the days of Jeremiah. He was called when he considered himself still a "child" (Jeremiah 1:6), about 70 years after the voice of Isaiah had been stilled in death.

From 32:8-15 and 37:12, it appears that Jeremiah possessed an estate outside of the city, but he dwelt at Jerusalem and probably delivered most of his discourses in the temple (7:2). He lived to see the destruction of Jerusalem but was not carried into captivity. By special favor of Nebuchadnezzar, he was permitted to remain in the devastated land, to minister to the needs of the poor remnants of the people (39:11-14).

Shortly thereafter, however, Gedaliah, whom the Babylonian king had appointed governor of Judea, was treacherously killed by one of the Jews. Fearing the vengeance of the Babylonians, the Jews then decided to flee to Egypt. Jeremiah accompanied them and continued to teach in their midst. Thus he rounded out about 41 years of prophetical activity. According to a legend, he was at last stoned to death by the Jews in Egypt—a sorry return for his faithful labors.

78. Period

In the turbulent years that immediately preceded the exile, the work of the prophet was both arduous and dangerous. While the prophets had still been respected in the days of Isaiah, the leaders of the people to whom Jeremiah preached had lost all reverence for the messengers of God. False prophets were heard willingly, and they deceived the people. As a result, the threatening announcements of Jeremiah were rejected, at first with contempt, then with bitter hatred.

Of the five kings under whom Jeremiah lived and worked, only the first one, Josiah, is described as a God-fearing man. In his days the Law of Moses was read to the people, and he not only put away the abominations of heathen idolatry but also reestablished the true worship of God. But his successors, Jehoahaz, Jehoiakim, Jehoiachin, and Zedekiah, spurned all warnings of Jeremiah and other true prophets, turned their hearts from God, put their faith in the lies of false prophets, and were haughty and tyrannical rulers.

Whoever dared to preach against Jerusalem, that is to say, to proclaim the wrath of God against the wicked city, was denounced as a traitor. In this manner the prophet Uriah lost his life (Jeremiah 26:20-23). In the same chapter, Jeremiah records that he also was in danger of death on account of his preaching (26:14,15,24). Even in the city of his birth, deadly hatred threatened him (11:21).

No other prophet was so often in imminent danger of losing his life as Jeremiah. When he had written his prophecies in a book at the command of God, the wicked King Jehoiakim, to whom the book had been delivered by treachery, cut it to pieces and burned it. Then he sought to imprison both the prophet and Baruch, his scribe, but the Lord hid them (36:21-26).

Under Zedekiah, Jeremiah was actually confined in the court of the prison. At length the cowardly king delivered the prophet into the hands of his enemies, who, not daring to murder him outright, threw him into an empty cistern, expecting him to perish there from thirst and starvation. Jeremiah did not regain his liberty before the city was captured. Then, however, he was treated with great consideration, because the Babylonians knew very well that he had denounced Zedekiah's breach of faith (chapters 37–40).

In all his trying experiences, Jeremiah remained faithful and true to his calling. To be sure, he had his hours of weakness and days of despondency, so that he complained loudly over his afflictions (20:7-18). But the Lord always calmed him and renewed his strength, according to the promise given when Jeremiah was called: "'Today I have made you a fortified city, an iron pillar and a bronze wall to stand against the whole land—against the kings of Judah, its officials, its priests and the people of the land. They will fight against you but will not overcome you, for I am with you and will rescue you,' declares the LORD" (1:18,19).

After his book had been destroyed, Jeremiah was instructed by God to rewrite it for an everlasting witness against the people who had hardened themselves against their God.

79. *Character*

While the speech of Jeremiah is not so rhetorically and poetically resplendent as that of Isaiah, his witness is, nevertheless, a most powerful arraignment of the Jewish people. His discourses mirror the distracting character of the developments that unfolded before his eyes. Lamentations over the sins of his people alternate with threats of impending disaster. But because God had some of his elect even among that stiff-necked generation, the sweet strains of messianic promise frequently sound amid the thunders of approaching doom. These gospel messages mostly appear in the form of general promises of spiritual salvation, as in 3:12,13 and 31:3. But the distinct references to the Savior occurring in 23:6 and throughout chapter 33 must have been priceless words of comfort for the true children of God, just as the Christian church of today counts them among its treasures.

One of the most notable features of the revelation given to Jeremiah is the great number of predictions regarding specific dates, all of which were gloriously justified by the outcome. We mention especially the announcement that the Babylonian supremacy, and with it the exile of the Jews, was to endure 70 years (25:11,12; 29:10).

80. Authenticity

That the book of Jeremiah is a genuine product of the prophet's pen is hardly questioned even by the most rabid rationalists. What timid objections they see fit to raise we confidently set aside because of the endorsement given to the book of Jeremiah by Christ and his apostles, who quote it as genuine (Matthew 2:18; 21:13; Luke 19:46; 1 Corinthians 1:31).

81. Arrangement

As Luther notes in his preface to this book, the discourses of Jeremiah do not seem to have been arranged according to a definite plan. Still, we may separate the chapters into the following groups:

Summary of contents

    I. The calling of the prophet and his denouncements of Judah and Jerusalem, chapters 1–35.

    II. Historical notes concerning the experiences of the prophet, the siege and capture of Jerusalem, and the flight of the Jews who had remained, chapters 36–45.

    III. Discourses of the prophet concerning heathen peoples, chapters 46–51.

    IV. Addendum: Detailed description of the destruction of Jerusalem and the fate of the royal house, chapter 52.

D. Lamentations

82. Book

Viewing the dreadful ruin that had replaced the former beauty and glory of Jerusalem, Jeremiah sat, mourning amidst the desolation, and wrote five songs of lamentation. This reminds us of the Jewish custom, derived from distant antiquity, to raise the voice of lament at the tomb of some beloved or revered person. (Genesis 50:10; 2 Samuel 1:17-27; 3:33-35; the lamentation of Jeremiah over Josiah, referred to in 2 Chronicles 35:25, has not been preserved.) Seated at the "tomb" of the city of Zion, in whose service he had spent his days and his strength, Jeremiah laments its deplorable fate. He pours out the deep sorrow of his heart, which is tempered, however, by an unfailing hope of future restoration (Lamentations 3:22-24).

Like several psalms, four of these lamentations are alphabetical songs. Each of chapters 1, 2, and 4 has 22 verses, after the number of letters in the Hebrew alphabet, and each verse begins with a different letter. Chapter 3, however, is divided into stanzas of three verses each, and each verse of a stanza begins with the same letter. This chapter, therefore, has 66 verses. Chapter 5 has the usual 22 verses, but the arrangement is not alphabetical.

Summary of contents

I. First Song: The captivity of the people and the pitiful fate of the city.

II. Second Song: The horrors of destruction.

III. Third Song: The soul-sufferings of believers and their hope of deliverance.

IV. Fourth Song: The catastrophe as a revelation of the righteousness of God.

V. Fifth Song: Prayer for deliverance from the great affliction.

E. Ezekiel

83. Prophet

Among the ten thousand prominent Jews whom Nebuchadnezzar carried to Babylon in the year 597 B.C., together with King Jehoiachin, was Ezekiel, the son of Buzi, the priest. In the fifth year of this captivity, Ezekiel was called as a prophet, and he served in this ministry for at least 22 years thereafter among the exiled Jews.

Of his personal history, we know only what Ezekiel himself has recorded. With the other exiles, he dwelt in the northern part of Mesopotamia, at Tel Abib, on the Kebar River. There he owned a house (8:1) and was married (24:18). He must have been highly respected among his companions in adversity, for their elders often gathered in his house (8:1; 14:1; 20:1). Nevertheless, he shared the fate of other true prophets in that his word was not believed (3:7; 33:32). When Ezekiel's wife died, God demanded that he repress his own sorrow, while explaining to the people that the sad occurrence was to be for them a portent of the destruction of Jerusalem (24:15-27).

We do not know how long Ezekiel continued his work after the destruction of Jerusalem. The last date that he mentions (29:17) carries us only to the 27th year of the captivity. The Jews have a tale, which is altogether unauthenticated, that Ezekiel was finally murdered by a prominent man from among his own people, whom he had taken to task for idolatrous practices.

84. Circumstances

As long as Jerusalem still stood unharmed, the Jews in Babylon kept constantly in touch with their old home. Thus they learned that those who had remained behind were left in peaceful possession of their homes. This information caused false prophets to arise, who tried to show that Jeremiah had deceived the people when he admonished everyone to submit unresistingly to the control of Nebuchadnezzar (Jeremiah 27:11).

At the suggestion of Shemaiah, one of the false prophets, the Jews of Babylon even dispatched a letter to the priests at Jerusalem, declaring their convictions and demanding that Jeremiah be put to death (Jeremiah 29:24-28). Jeremiah answered this attack with a powerful message (29:1-23,29-32), and shortly thereafter Ezekiel was called to denounce the false prophets to their faces. At first it was his task to convince the Jews at Babylon by untiring reiteration of the message, in words and symbols, that Jerusalem would surely be destroyed, in inescapable retribution for the faithlessness of the people. He received the last revelation in this matter on the very day when Nebuchadnezzar began the attack upon Jerusalem (Ezekiel 24).

In order to show, however, that the fall of Jerusalem was not due to the superior strength of the heathen nations but directly to the righteous judgment of God, Ezekiel also prophesied against seven heathen peoples, foretelling their destruction. After the fall of Jerusalem, his prophecy was designed to strengthen the faith and hope of the exiles. Speaking of the restoration of the Holy City and the entire land of Judea as an assured fact, Ezekiel foreshadowed the rise and glorious development of the church in the days of the New Testament.

85. Character of the prophecy

In the first two parts of the book, the prevailing tone is that of rebuke. Nevertheless, Ezekiel finds opportunity for gospel allusions. He certainly preaches Christ in such passages as 17:22-24; 34:11-23; and 37:24. Beginning with chapter 40, Ezekiel records a series of magnificent revelations, which must be understood as prophecies concerning the church of the New Testament. Although he refers, in terms, to Jerusalem and the temple and speaks of their restoration, his descriptions do not bear a literal interpretation.

If they had been meant as promises to the Jewish people as such, prophecy would have failed, because outwardly these promises were never fulfilled. In fact, they could never have been so fulfilled, because all the measurements given of the temple and the city as described do not agree with physical possibilities.

Hence this section has always been understood by the church as a vast allegory, foreshadowing future events. In his preface to the book of Ezekiel, Luther says:

> The altar is described as being eleven cubits high [1 cubit equals 1½ feet], measuring fourteen cubits across the top, so that a priest, though he were to use a stairway, must needs have an arm seven cubits long in order to reach to the middle of the altar to perform the sacrifice. A sizable little priest that would be who would measure fifteen or sixteen good large cubits in length or height! Therefore this structure of Ezekiel must not be understood as referring to some new material building, but, like the chariot in the first part (chapter 1), that structure described at the end is nothing less than the kingdom of Christ, the holy church or christendom on earth, until the Last Day.

86. Difficulty

Commentators have found no prophetical book quite so difficult to explain as that of Ezekiel. This is due in part because Ezekiel employs many symbolical acts to convey his messages, ranking next to Jeremiah in this respect. The most perplexing features of this book, however, are found in the magnificent allegories and bewildering metaphors with which Ezekiel's discourses abound. This was recognized even by early Jewish expositors; in fact, as Jerome has noted, no person among the Jews was permitted to read the book of Ezekiel before attaining the age of 30 years—this applied also to the first chapters of Genesis and the Song of Solomon.

Luther, who had found the true gospel key leading to the understanding of the wonderful visions of this prophet, nevertheless expresses the opinion that their full understanding would hardly be achieved by anyone in this life. It should be noted that the mysterious descriptions of the third part of the book have suffered greatly at the hands of misguided interpreters, who have read into the words of the prophet a meaning that is utterly at variance with other unmistakable teachings of the Scriptures. Some of them, while adopting Luther's understanding of the purpose of this prophecy, have tried to show that Ezekiel promises a future of external, material welfare and glory for the kingdom of God on earth (millennialism, or chiliasm). As the idea of a millennium of glory on earth is altogether at variance with the Scriptures, it is necessary to avoid this error even in its most subtle forms.

Summary of contents

85

the return from the exile, which prove that this part was written after the fall of Jerusalem, chapters 25–39.

III. Prophecy concerning the future glory of Christ's kingdom, chapters 40–48.

F. Daniel

87. Prophet

In the third year of King Jehoiakim (606 B.C.), Nebuchadnezzar deported to Babylon a number of young men from distinguished Jewish families. Among them was Daniel, a youth whose faith in the God of Israel was so strong that he resisted all contamination of the abominable practices of heathenism. By the grace of God, he found favor with the king, and being instructed in all the wisdom of the Chaldeans, he became singularly proficient in knowledge. He acquired the Aramaic language, so that it became as familiar to him as his native tongue. It is not strange, therefore, that a large portion of his book (2:4–7:28) should have been written in that language. As the Jews doubtless learned this language in the long years of the exile, they were well able to read and understand Daniel's book.

When Daniel was called upon to interpret a dream of the king, it became known that he had the gift of prophecy. The king honored him by appointing him chief of governors over all wise men of Babylon, as well as ruler of the whole province of Babylon. His authority over the wise men, or magi, may not have sufficed to convert them from all their error of superstition, but we may well conclude from the visit of the magi at Bethlehem and their worship of the child Jesus that the gospel preached by Daniel did not fail to produce spiritual results among his heathen associates.

During the life of Nebuchadnezzar, Daniel remained a man of great importance at court, and it was due to his

influence that Nebuchadnezzar at length publicly acknowledged the glory of the God of Israel. Under the following
kings, Daniel seems to have withdrawn from public life.
Twenty-five years after the death of Nebuchadnezzar, it was
necessary to make Daniel's gift of prophecy known to King
Belshazzar. Darius, however, once more appreciated the sin-
gular spiritual endowment of the prophet, appointing him to
a ruler's office and favoring him in many ways. His influence continued at the court of Cyrus, so that the determination of this king to return the Jews to their home may well
have been suggested and fostered by Daniel.

The last prophetical utterance of Daniel is dated in the
year 534 B.C., the third year of Cyrus. Thus it appears that
his ministry extended over a period of at least 73 years, and
if he was 16 or 17 years old when he came to Babylon, he
reached an age of more than 90 years. Concerning the end
of his life, we know nothing more than that he departed in
the blessed hope of the resurrection (12:13).

88. Character

Of all the other prophets, we know definitely that they
moved and preached among their own people. But nothing
of the kind is recorded concerning Daniel. Thus it seems
that the royal court was his appointed sphere of work.
While his contemporary Ezekiel labored among the Jews,
Daniel preached the name of the God of the vanquished
people before the throne of the victorious monarch. The
worldly honors that he received undoubtedly served to
make his message more impressive to his heathen audience.

It happened, however, that the prophecies of Daniel,
which were given under such unusual circumstances,
assumed a style quite different from that of the writings of
the other prophets. This was noted by those who assem-

bled the books of the Old Testament, who accordingly thought it proper to place the book of Daniel not among the prophets but among the hagiographa (see section 7) in the third part of the canon.

This fact does not mean, however, that the Jews thought less highly of Daniel than of the other prophets. They accorded the same reverence to all books of the Old Testament alike, as being without exception given by God. In fact, they must have held Daniel in particular esteem, for we know that some writers thought it worthwhile to embellish the statements of Daniel with various apocryphal additions. Luther translated these fancies for the German Bible, and we will refer to them when speaking of the Apocrypha.

89. Main features

The revelations that were granted to Daniel are of so exalted a character and his presentation bears the stamp of divine inspiration so distinctly that his book justly belongs with the books of the other major prophets.

In the first six chapters, Daniel furnishes historical information tending to show how the Lord God of Israel displayed his truth at the court of the Babylonian ruler through the services of Daniel and his friends. As a result, not Nebuchadnezzar alone but also Darius and Cyrus after him acknowledged the power of Israel's God. Nebuchadnezzar declared at various times that he was greatly moved by the words of Daniel (2:47; 3:29; 4:33,34), and Darius spoke in a similar vein (6:26,27). In Ezra 1:2-11 we are told how the message of the prophet affected Cyrus.

This does not imply, however, that those great monarchs became true believers of the gospel. History shows that they did not experience a real change of heart. When Daniel interpreted the first dream of Nebuchadnezzar, he set forth a powerful and clear prophecy of the four great world powers that were to succeed one another. The last one was destined to give way to the kingdom of Christ.

The second part of the book is a record of magnificent visions, in which the prophet received further revelations of the four monarchies, of the advent of the Messiah after 70 weeks, of the antichrist, and of the resurrection of the dead on the Last Day. Note the messianic prophecies in chapters 2:44; 7:13-28 (from this passage Christ adopted for himself the title of the Son of Man); and 9:24-27 (which foretells the advent of the Anointed One; Christ alludes to this passage in Matthew 24:15). The statements contained in 11:36-45 have been understood by some expositors as referring to Antiochus Epiphanes, the Syrian ruler, but Luther and Lutheran commentators feel sure that Daniel is here fore-telling the Antichrist, concerning whom the Holy Spirit also prophesied in the New Testament.

90. Authenticity

As this book contains so many definite predictions of future events, it could not fail to become a target of violent attack at the hands of unbelieving critics. It must be admitted that various statements of Daniel present unusual difficulties to the Christian scholar. But this happens because the Babylonian exile belongs to a period of history of which we know very little except from the Scriptures. The difficulty, therefore, is not due to any fault of the prophet, but to the incompleteness of our information.

On the other hand, all debatable points admit of some satisfactory explanation, based upon permissible conjectures, as Christian expositors have often demonstrated. It is also true that all definite information newly discovered by historical research bears witness to the reliability of Daniel's statements. Whatever debatable points may remain, the authorship of Daniel is distinctly attested by our Lord, who quotes from this book and declares that it was written by the prophet whose name it bears (Matthew 24:15).

Summary of contents

I. Historical part, chapters 1–6. Education and faithfulness of Daniel; interpretation of the dream concerning the four monarchies; the three men in the fiery furnace; second dream of Nebuchadnezzar and its fulfillment; Belshazzar's feast and destruction; Daniel in the lions' den.

II. Visions of the coming monarchies and of the eternal kingdom of Christ, chapters 7–12.

G. Hosea

91. Prophet

The ministry of Hosea, son of Beeri, coincides in time with that of Isaiah. But while Isaiah preached in Jerusalem, Hosea was a prophet in the Northern Kingdom. Apparently he was a native of that kingdom, because elsewhere it is considered an unusual occurrence for a native of Judah to be sent as a prophet to Israel (1 Kings 13:1; Amos 7:10-17).

We know nothing more either of Beeri or of the personal history of Hosea. He was called to his ministry in the days of Jeroboam II of Israel (about 750 B.C.), and he informs us that he labored until the days of King Hezekiah of Judah (1:1). Consequently, he must have borne the burden of his office for nearly 65 years (to 686 B.C.).

Since his book is addressed to the people of the Northern Kingdom exclusively, it would seem that he dwelt and preached in that part of the country throughout those long years, though he incidentally directs words of warning or consolation to the people of Judah (1:7; 4:15; 5:5,10,14; etc.). It is remarkable that Hosea names all the kings of Judah who ruled during his time but mentions only Jeroboam II among the rulers of his own people. This probably happened because after the death of Jeroboam II, the rulers of Israel followed one another at such short intervals that it was difficult to fix a date by referring to their administrations. At any rate, the book was to become part of the record of that revelation which God entrusted to Judah after the ten tribes had disappeared.

92. Book

While in many prophetical books the different sections are distinguished not only according to their contents but also according to their dates, the book of Hosea has no distinct parts, dated or otherwise. If it were not noticeable that the first three chapters are a composition in prose, while the remainder of the book is written in somewhat poetical style, it would be difficult to decide how to divide the contents. This form of the book seems to suggest that the prophet composed it near the end of his life as a summary, so to say, of all his discourses, presenting the gist of his particular message.

The obvious unity of the book has also prevented any serious attempt to demonstrate that it is not authentic. In the first three chapters, the prophet denounces the spiritual adultery of the northern tribes, who had deserted their God to follow all manner of false gods. The prophet, at the command of God, emphasized this rebuke by performing a very peculiar symbolical act, namely, marrying an adulterous wife, Gomer. The remaining chapters of the book are a connected discourse, preaching first the wrath of God, then his merciful grace.

Though we find no direct messianic references in Hosea, he nevertheless penned several precious gospel sayings, which are treasured by the church of God. Thus he speaks clearly of the inability of sinful man to contribute anything whatever toward his salvation (2:19,20; 13:9). Chapter 13:14 was obviously in Paul's mind when he wrote 1 Corinthians 15:54,55; and in Romans 9:25,26 the apostle quotes directly from Hosea 1:10 and 2:23.

Summary of contents

I. Rebuke of spiritual adultery, chapters 1–3. Hosea's marriage to symbolize the relation existing between God and the people; compare also the significant names of Hosea's children.

II. Reproof of Israel, coupled with promises of grace for those who would convert to the Lord, chapters 4–14.

H. Joel

93. Prophet

Because Joel never even mentions the kingdom of Israel but does name Judah and Jerusalem, it is considered certain that his mission was to the Southern Kingdom.

As to the date of his prophetic activity, however, we are entirely in the dark. It may be that the arrangement of the prophetical books is an indication that the ancient scribes believed Joel lived at some time between Hosea and Amos. But other investigators give some good reasons why he belongs to a much earlier date. They note that Joel does not mention the Syrians and Assyrians as enemies of the Jews, but only the Philistines, the Egyptians, and the Edomites (3:4,19). Since the first recorded attack of the Syrians, led by Hazael of Damascus, cost King Joash his life (2 Kings 12:17-21), it is assumed that Joel preached no later than the last years preceding this occurrence (between 835 and 800 B.C.).

94. Book

Unlike Hosea, Joel does not begin his discourse with an argument against the sins of the people but with the description of a judgment of God under which Judah was then groaning. The plague of which he speaks, however, is held up as a portent of future and greater afflictions, which were sure to come unless the people repented. Finally he gives comfort by foretelling that not only the present chastisement was to come to an end but that after these afflictions, the blessed time of salvation in the New Testament was to arrive.

This understanding of the prophecy of Joel is verified by the sermon that the apostle Peter preached on the occasion of Pentecost, when the Holy Spirit was poured out upon the apostles (Acts 2:16-21). He declares that this wonderful occurrence had been foretold by Joel and thus leads us to understand that everything Joel says in that connection refers to matters pertaining to the New Testament. Paul also quotes from Joel, but without naming him (Romans 10:13; Joel 2:32).

Summary of contents

I. Lament over the affliction of the people; call to repentance, chapters 1:1–2:14.

II. Promise of divine mercy to those who repent, chapters 2:15–3:21.

I. Amos

95. Prophet

The date of the prophet Amos is indicated in the superscription of his book. He preached in the days of King Uzziah of Judah and King Jeroboam II of Israel, shortly before the time of Hosea. Because he introduces his own discourse with a quotation from the prophecies of Joel, using it as a text, so to speak, it would seem that he had the book of Joel before him (1:2; Joel 3:16).

Amos declares that he had not been trained for the ministry in one of the schools of prophets and therefore did not belong to the generally known class of prophets. He had been a herdsman until God called him away from the flock, giving him a message to the people (1:1; 7:14,15). In this respect Amos reminds one of Elisha (1 Kings 19:19), whom he also resembles in natural gifts of the mind, which were enhanced by the additional gift of the prophetical spirit. His discourses abound in pleasing and vivid metaphors taken from nature and from a shepherd's life.

Tekoah, Amos' birthplace, was a fortified town (Jeremiah 6:1) lying at the edge of the desert, about 11 miles south of Jerusalem, in a district given over entirely to the grazing of flocks. He was sent by God to preach in the kingdom of the ten tribes, but his efforts were unsuccessful (Amos 7:12,13). A Jewish legend says that Amos was often maltreated, that on one occasion his teeth were knocked out, and that the king finally had a nail driven into Amos' temple, so that he was carried to his old home mortally wounded.

96. Book

It is plain that Amos, like Hosea, did not write all his discourses as he delivered them. His book must have been written as a summary of his message. Hence it was probably composed toward the end of his life.

His message as written is harsh and threatening throughout. The only word of gospel import is found in 9:11, the deep meaning of which is disclosed by the apostle James (Acts 15:16). Luther says of this prophet, "He is violent, rebuking the people of Israel fairly throughout the whole book, up to the end of the last chapter, where he foretells Christ and his kingdom and thus brings his book to a close."

Summary of contents

I. Introduction; warnings addressed to some neighbors of the Jews and to Judah and Israel, chapters 1,2.

II. Three calls to repentance addressed to Israel, each beginning "Hear this word," chapters 3–6.

III. Three discourses upon visions, chapters 7–9.

J. Obadiah

97. Book

Obadiah is the shortest of all prophetical books. Of its author we know nothing but what may be deduced from his own statements. Although the Scriptures mention several God-fearing men who bore the name Obadiah (1 Kings 18:3; 2 Chronicles 17:7; 34:12), none of these can be identified with the prophet.

Apparently Jeremiah quotes from the book of Obadiah (Jeremiah 49:17-22; Obadiah verses 2-4), so the latter must have preceded Jeremiah. This assumption is strengthened by the observation that Obadiah has nothing to say of the impending fall of Jerusalem, which is the constant burden of Jeremiah's message. The allusion to a misfortune that had befallen Jerusalem (verses 11,12) may refer to the capture of the city in the days of Jehoram (2 Chronicles 21:16,17), the king under whom Obadiah is supposed by many to have lived.

The prophecy of Obadiah is directed against Edom, foretelling the destruction of this people and the preservation of the people of Israel.

Summary of contents

I. Certainty of Edom's destruction, verses 1-9.

II. Edom's fate due to its enmity against God's chosen people, verses 10-16.

III. The certain deliverance of the people of Israel, verses 17-21.

K. Jonah

98. Prophet

An extraordinary call of God sent Jonah, son of Amittai, to the great heathen city of Nineveh with a message urging instant repentance. There is no good reason why we should not identify this prophet with the prophet of the same name mentioned in 2 Kings 14:25. Jonah, accordingly, was a native of Gath Hepher, of the tribe of Zebulun, situated midway between the Sea of Galilee and the Mediterranean Sea. He lived in the days of Jeroboam II of Israel (between 793 and 753 B.C.) and received a revelation, the import of which is merely suggested in the passage referred to above. This view of the date of Jonah is further strengthened because certain Greek historians describe the Nineveh of that day almost in the very terms used by the prophet. The Jewish legend that Jonah was the son of the widow of Zarephath whom Elijah raised from the dead cannot be true, because Zarephath was a town of Phoenicia.

99. Historical character

The remarkable experiences and difficulties accompanying the flight of Jonah and his stay at Nineveh have always been welcome to unbelievers and blasphemers. They have centered their attacks on these events in Jonah's life, hoping to raise doubts concerning the truth of the entire story and arouse venomous ridicule. Their arguments cannot affect those who believe that all things are possible to God, whom it pleased to corroborate the message of his prophets and apostles by miracles of many kinds.

In the case of Jonah, we derive additional assurance from the words of our Lord, who quotes Jonah by name and title, refers to his story as to actual history, uses it for important instruction, and even designates the prophet as a type of himself (Matthew 12:40; 16:4). This divine testimony also disposes of the laborious arguments of critics, who try to show at least that Jonah was not the author of the book that bears his name.

The historical truth of the narrative is, moreover, impressed upon the reader by its very character. No writer of fiction would have discredited his hero by ascribing to him such moral defects as come to the surface in Jonah's flight and in his inexcusable behavior following the remarkable result of his message.

100. Purpose

The story of Jonah was told to the Jews to impress upon their minds the gospel fact that God will have all men, including the Gentiles, to be saved and to come to the knowledge of the truth. In this sense the book is prophetical of the days of the New Testament. Yes, Jonah personally, and without being aware of it, was chosen to be a type of the future Messiah, as Jesus himself declares.

Summary of contents

I. The mission, flight, and chastisement of Jonah, chapter 1.

II. Jonah's prayer of repentance, chapter 2.

III. Jonah's message to Nineveh and its result, chapter 3.

IV. Jonah's envious impatience and God's rebuke, chapter 4.

L. Micah

101. Prophet

Micah did the work of his prophetical ministry under Jotham, Ahaz, and Hezekiah, kings of Judah (between 740 and 686 B.C.). Thus he was a contemporary of Isaiah and probably a fellow laborer of that great prophet in the city of Jerusalem (1:9). As the Hebrew text of Jeremiah 26:18 writes the name of this prophet as Micaiah, it would seem that Micah is an abbreviated form of the full name. He names Moresheth as his native village, distinguishing it clearly from Mareshah (1:14,15). This shows that he must not be identified with the prophet Micaiah, son of Imlah (1 Kings 22:8,9). From chapter 1:14 we learn that Moresheth was situated near the city of Gath, in the tribe of Judah, to the southwest of Jerusalem. Micah's close affiliation with Isaiah is evident from the fact that Isaiah 2:2-4 and Micah 4:1-4 read alike almost to the letter, so that it would be impossible to say to whom the revelation was granted originally if Isaiah had not claimed it for his own. Thus the united testimony of these two men became a powerful witness against the obstinate and rebellious people.

102. Book

Micah is another case in which the arrangement of the book betrays that it was written as a connected and summary review of the entire life's work of the prophet. It consists of three parts, each of which begins with the address "Hear" or "Listen" (1:2; 3:1; 6:1).

Micah directs his earnest admonitions to Judah and Israel, naming their capital cities. Rebuking the prevalent sins of idolatry, he foretells the destruction of both Samaria and Jerusalem and the exile of the people but also the deliverance of the true Israel. Since he denounces the idolatrous practices so severely and at the same time speaks of the destruction of Samaria as a future event (1:6,7), it is plain that he wrote the book before the reformation instituted by Hezekiah (2 Chronicles 30,31) and before the fall of the Northern Kingdom (between 728 and 722 B.C.).

Micah's prophecies have much in common with those of Isaiah, not only in the beauty of diction but especially in the clear vision of the messianic future. As a valuable supplement to Isaiah's announcement of the Son of the virgin, Micah foretold that the Savior was to be born in Bethlehem (5:2). We remember that this gospel message served to guide the wise men from the East to the manger of Christ.

Summary of contents

   I. A call to repentance, addressed to Judah and Israel, chapters 1,2.

  II. A rebuke of tyrants and deceivers of the people, together with a promise of the Messiah, chapters 3–5.

 III. Instruction concerning true godliness and the final blessedness of the righteous, chapters 6,7.

M. Nahum

103. Prophet

Of Nahum's personal history, we know no more than that he was a native of Elkosh, a small village of Galilee. There is no contemporaneous information concerning this place, but Jerome, who traveled through the Holy Land before he wrote his commentaries on the Bible (in the beginning of the fifth century after Christ), claims to have discovered a village called Helkesai. His suggestion that this might have been the ancient Elkosh has been generally adopted.

Nahum describes the Assyrian monarchy as a powerful sovereign over the nations, draws a lesson from the fate of Israel (2:2), and refers unmistakably to the defeat of Sennacherib (3:2,3). Accordingly, we date him immediately after Isaiah (between 660 and 650 B.C.).

That Nahum describes at length the greatness and magnificence of Nineveh does not warrant the assumption voiced by some commentators that he preached in that great city, because the knowledge on which he bases his description was common property throughout Western Asia at the time.

104. Book

Nahum's prophecy is called "an oracle concerning Nineveh" (1:1). He foretells the utter destruction of the proud Assyrian monarchy, which at that time was at the height of its power. His purpose is to comfort the people of Judah, who had not only witnessed the deplorable fate of the kingdom of Israel but had themselves suffered deep humiliation at the hands of the haughty victors.

Summary of contents

> I. The divine decree respecting the destruction of Nineveh, chapter 1.
>
> II. Resultant message to the people of God, chapter 2.
>
> III. Lamentation over the fall of Nineveh, chapter 3.

N. Habakkuk

105. Prophet

Habakkuk calls himself a prophet, but gives no other information to identify himself or his time. From the tenor of his discourse, however, we may conclude that he labored in the days of King Josiah, between 640 and 609 B.C., for in 1:5,6 he announces to the men of his own generation that they would live to see the invasion by the Babylonians

(Chaldeans), though the political situation at the time made such an occurrence seem unbelievable. Jeremiah points to the same time in 4:13 and 5:6, where he weaves certain words of Habakkuk into his discourse, according to his habit.

It is hardly possible, however, to prove from 3:19 that Habakkuk was a Levite or even a priest, although this idea must have found credence at an early date. The apocryphal tales of Bel and the Dragon at Babel, as we find them in the Greek version, still bear the title "From the prophecy of Habakkuk, son of Jesus, from the tribe of Levi." These tales show that the Jewish legend busied itself greatly with this prophet without feeling the need of basing its stories on fact.

106. Book

Habakkuk preaches of the judgment of God that was to be executed upon the Jewish people by the Babylonians. Then he proceeds to show that this heathen nation would also meet its fate on account of its sinfulness. He closes with a psalm of prayer, expressing the appropriate emotions of a believing heart.

It should be remembered that Paul quotes from Habakkuk the important statement that "the righteous will live by faith" (Romans 1:17), the very word of God that Luther pondered during his famous journey to Rome. It served to open his eyes to the worthlessness of his attempts at self-justification, even while he made the rounds of the sanctuaries at Rome.

Summary of contents

I. Prophecy of the Babylonian invasion, chapter 1.
II. A scathing denouncement of the haughty victors, chapter 2.

III. A psalm in praise of these proofs of the incorruptible justice of God, chapter 3.

O. *Zephaniah*

107. Prophet

During the reign of King Josiah, while Jeremiah and Huldah, the prophetess, labored among the people of Judah and Jerusalem (2 Kings 22:14), Zephaniah was likewise called into service, the last of the preexilic (before the Babylonian exile) prophets. He gives a detailed account of his descent, informing his readers that he was the son of Cushi, the son of Gedaliah, the son of Amariah, the son of Hezekiah. The unusual completeness of this genealogy surely means that its last member names a man of special importance. Since that name is identical with that of King Hezekiah, it would seem that Zephaniah was of royal blood, although we know only that Hezekiah had a son named Manasseh. It also appears that Zephaniah's work was done chiefly during the reformation instituted by King Josiah or immediately after it. He lays bare the wickedness of many prominent people, for example, who pretended in public to serve the true God while secretly they continued their idolatrous practices. We know that Josiah did not succeed in stamping out idolatry altogether. We learn from the historical books that the former abominations reappeared and flourished immediately after Josiah's death.

108. Book

Zephaniah obviously did not write all his discourses as they were delivered but compiled a condensed review of his prophetical messages. He writes in a fluent and vivid style. Alluding variously to the prophecies of former prophets, he shows that they had not been completely fulfilled by the tribulations already experienced but would be fully realized in the near future.

To show that the punitive righteousness of God is impartial, Zephaniah foretells the catastrophes that were to befall the neighboring heathen nations. Thus his theme is practically the same as that of Jeremiah.

At the same time, he does not forget to comfort God-fearing people with the promise of the restoring grace of God. He offers such rich consolation that Luther finds reason to say, "Though he is a minor prophet, yet he speaks more of Christ than many other and greater prophets, almost excelling even Jeremiah" (meaning, of course, in comparison to the extent of his writing). Luther refers to the gospel sense of Zephaniah's words, not to direct prophecies of Christ, for of these none were granted to this prophet.

Summary of contents

   I. Announcement of the destruction of the unbelieving people, chapter 1.

  II. The impending fall of neighboring nations, chapter 2.

 III. The promise that the small company of believers would be preserved in the midst of the catastrophe, chapter 3.

P. Haggai

109. Prophet

Haggai is the first of the postexilic prophets. The first company of returning Jews had reached Jerusalem in the first days of King Cyrus. In the following year, they laid the foundation of the new temple. But the intrigues of their heathen neighbors, whose offers of help and association had been rejected, served to delay the progress of the great work until the second year of King Darius. At last Haggai and Zechariah were inspired to urge the people to renewed efforts (Ezra 5:1).

The Scriptures tell us no more than this concerning Haggai. Some have misunderstood the Hebrew word for "messenger" in chapter 1:13 to signify that Haggai was an angel. He may have been one of the Jews who returned to their homeland under the leadership of Zerubbabel. Some commentators believe that the prophet claims to have been one of those who had seen the temple of Solomon before the people had been carried away by Nebuchadnezzar.

110. Circumstances

Haggai was granted four revelations within four months, which shows how earnestly God urged the people to continue building the temple after the long interruption. The tenor of Haggai's discourses also helps us to understand the task that was given to all the postexilic prophets. Because the people who had been brought back were greatly discouraged by the small beginnings of the restored kingdom, their prophets were to comfort them with the assurance that what they had lived to see was but a beginning and that the greater things promised in the older prophecies would be as surely fulfilled in glorious completeness as these beginnings that had been made. To Haggai was given the special work of promoting the erection of the temple, which was delayed by the indifference of the Jews as much as by the enmity of their northward neighbors.

111. Book

Laboring under these conditions, Haggai was compelled to rebuke the selfishness of his people, who gave all their thoughts to the building of comfortable houses for themselves and to the amassing of riches. But his chief mission was to strengthen the weak souls and to confirm their faith in the great promises. Hence he enriches the fund of messianic prophecies by adding the beautiful statement that the Messiah was to be the desire of all nations and that he was to glorify, by his personal presence, the temple that they were to build (2:6-9).

It is obvious that this prophet has recorded merely the themes of his discourses, for he surely did not confine himself to the brief statements that he has written. It was given to him to see satisfactory results of his preaching, as he himself (1:14,15) and Ezra (5:2; 6:14) testify.

Summary of contents

    I. The prophet rebukes the indifference of the people and urges them to renewed activity in restoring the temple, chapter 1.

    II. Haggai reveals the future glory of this new temple, 2:1-9.

    III. Haggai shows that certain afflictions had been sent in chastisement for the people's indifference, 2:10-19.

    IV. A promise of personal blessing for Zerubbabel, 2:20-23.

Q. Zechariah

112. Prophet

Zechariah began his prophetical labors two months later than Haggai, at Jerusalem. To distinguish his person from that of many other men bearing the same name, he informs us that he was a grandson of Iddo, the seer. His father, Berekiah, probably was a man of no special importance, since he is not even mentioned in Ezra 5:1. From Nehemiah 12:16 we learn that Zechariah and his family belonged to the tribe of Levi and that he came to Jerusalem with Zerubbabel. According to

2:4, he was quite young when first called as a prophet, but he attained old age. He was still living when all the priests and Levites were enrolled under Nehemiah, in the days of the high priest Joiakim (Nehemiah 12:12,16,26).

Many expositors believe that this prophet is identical with that Zechariah whom Jesus mentions in Matthew 23:35. Although the names agree, it is difficult to believe that the Jews would have dared to lay hands upon a priest and prophet so soon after their return from exile, nor is there any distinct record that the prophet Zechariah suffered death by violence.

113. Character

Though Zechariah's message was practically the same as that of Haggai, his manner of preaching was entirely different. Lacking the pleasing sweetness of diction that is characteristic of Isaiah and Haggai, his discourses abound in such daring thoughts, visions, and allegories that his book has ever been considered one of the most difficult to interpret.

This peculiarity troubled not only the Jewish commentators but also those Christian expositors who adopted the teachings of Christ as the true key of the Old Testament. There is not one commentator among those who are careful to follow the guidance of the Scriptures who may boast that his skill served to discover the meaning of all sayings of Zechariah beyond a justifiable doubt.

At the same time, it is a fact that Zechariah has many references to the Messiah and his kingdom, which describe the future with a remarkable wealth of detail, and that he is often quoted by the writers of the New Testament. Zechariah has given us the joyful message addressed to the daughter of Zion (9:9), which is quoted in Matthew 21:5.

The 30 pieces of silver and the potter's field (11:12,13) refer to well-known occurrences in the life of Christ (Matthew 26:15; 27:9,10). The statements in 12:10 and 13:7 are also mentioned in the New Testament as pointing to Christ and his work (John 19:37; Mark 14:27). Finally, the messianic import of the words in 6:12; 8:22; 13:1; and 14:9 is altogether beyond doubt.

114. Authenticity

Many critics have decided for themselves that for certain reasons the last six chapters of the book of Zechariah could not have been written by the prophet. Doubt first originated because in Matthew 27:9 certain statements of Zechariah (11:12,13) are quoted under the name of Jeremiah. Though this seems to indicate decisively that Zechariah did not write those words, all doubts are at once dispelled by comparing Jeremiah 32:6,7. It then becomes plain that Zechariah referred to those symbolical acts of the older prophet to explain their messianic character, and the Holy Spirit, speaking through Matthew, simply emphasized the unity of the two prophecies by naming the prophet to whom the revelation had first been made. Thus the only real difficulty as to the authorship of this book disappears.

The critics, indeed, have developed quite a number of other "proofs" for denying that the chapters in question are genuine, but as they have not been able to decide among themselves which of these "proofs" are really valid, we may confidently set them all aside. Soon after the death of Zechariah, when many were still living who had heard this prophet preach and had known him personally, the biblical books were assembled into the canon. It is simply unthinkable that under these circumstances such a large portion of the book should have been falsely ascribed to Zechariah either inadvertently or intentionally.

115. Contents

The prophet first records nine visions, which came to him in one night (1:8), and explains them, beginning with the state of the Jewish people in his day and proceeding to unfold their future up to the messianic period (chapters 1–6). The second part of the book (chapters 7,8) records an answer given by God in response to a question which the people had asked. Here serious admonition and merciful consolation appear side by side. The third part (chapters 9–14) contains two distinct discourses depicting the conflict between the kingdom of God and the great monarchies of the world, which ends with the victory of Christ's kingdom.

Summary of contents

    I. Nine visions exhibiting the struggle and the victory of God's kingdom, chapters 1–6.

    II. Admonition and consolation given in response to a question raised by the people, chapters 7,8.

    III. Two prophetic discourses concerning the advent of Christ's kingdom, chapters 9–14.

R. Malachi

116. Prophet

Malachi is the last link in the long chain of Old Testament prophets, and so his book very properly stands at the end of the Old Testament canon. We know nothing whatever of his person and history. But comparing Malachi 2:11-17 with Nehemiah 13:23-27 and noting the undeniable agreement of these two passages, we feel safe to say that Malachi preached at Jerusalem in the days of Nehemiah, supporting this leader of the people in his reformatory work.

Since the name Malachi may be translated "my angel" or "my messenger," it has been suggested that it's used here not as a personal name but as an official title used by the author, who may have been Nehemiah. This idea, however, must be rejected, not only because it is a mere guess but especially because the books of all the other prophets were put forth under the real names of their authors.

117. Book

Note the peculiar form of dialogue adopted by this prophet: the people call God to account, and God answers them. Malachi rebukes the religious indifference of the Jews, chiefly as it was revealed in their marriages with heathen women. He also has sharp words of criticism for the priests, who grossly neglected their duty of preaching the pure Word of God.

It should be noted too that in the discourses of Malachi, the promise of the Messiah was once more given to the people—this on the threshold of that four hundred–year period preceding the advent of Christ, during which there were no more prophets in Israel. Malachi calls Jesus the angel, or messenger, of the covenant, who was to cleanse the spiritual temple of God (3:1-4), and he also foretells the coming of Christ's herald, John the Baptist, whom he designates as the second Elijah (4:5,6).

Summary of contents

I. Malachi rebukes the sins of the people and of the priests, chapters 1,2.

II. Malachi prophesies Christ and his herald, John the Baptist, chapters 3,4.

Addendum to the Old Testament

A. Apocrypha

118. Meaning of the name

All Jewish writings handed down to us from the period after Nehemiah and Malachi have been named apocryphal books, or Apocrypha. Originally this term meant "hidden," in the sense that they were not considered canonical by the Jews. Afterward the term gradually came to be applied in the sense of "spurious." They were looked upon with suspicion, because the name of the author is given correctly for the book of Sirach alone.

119. Reception by the church

In the Jewish synagogues, these writings were kept in a separate locker and were never read in public meetings. The Roman Church, acting through the Council of Trent (1545–1563), has overridden all historical and theological doubts by decreeing that these books must be held of equal authority with the canonical books of the Bible and has thus adopted them as acknowledged sources of doctrine. The Roman Church even dared to corrupt the inspired text by inserting scraps of apocryphal writings into some of the canonical books, rendering it impossible for the reader of the Catholic Bible to distinguish the genuine from the spurious. By accepting certain apocryphal books, the Roman Church has decreed that some demonstrable errors and even false teachings must be acknowledged as words of God.

The Reformed churches have gone in the opposite direction by rejecting these writings altogether. As a consequence, very few editions of the English Bible contain translations of the Apocrypha. The English and American Bible societies are prohibited by their own laws from printing them in connection with the canonical books.

The Lutheran church, following the lead of Luther, has followed a sane middle course. Though we admit that these writings are not inspired and must not be held as equal in authority with the canonical books of the Bible, we say with Luther that most of them make interesting and useful reading. Selecting the best ones, Luther translated them and incorporated them into his version of the Bible.

120. Doubtful character

Except for the book of Sirach, we do not know definitely that any apocryphal book was originally written in Hebrew. All of them have at least been handed down to us in the Greek language. The book of Sirach doubtless is one of the oldest of the apocryphal writings and was once greatly valued by the Jews. In the introduction the grandson of Sirach relates how the book came to be written and declares that he translated it from the Hebrew. Some scholars have tried to show that the books of Judith, 1 Maccabees, and Tobit were also first written in Hebrew. Be that as it may, we have none of these books in the Bible language of the Old Testament. In their present form, they date from the period when prophecy had ceased and when the victorious campaign of Alexander the Great had made Greek the common language of Asia (333 B.C.).

There are many good reasons why the Apocrypha should be kept separate from the canonical books and must never be used as sources of religious doctrine. They are as follows:

(1) Some of the apocryphal books were issued under false names, and the true authors remain unknown. These books are the Wisdom of Solomon, the Book of Baruch,

and the Epistle of Jeremiah (Baruch, chapter 6). On the other hand, the books of the Maccabees, Judith, Tobit, and the additions to several canonical books are anonymous.

(2) None of these books was received into the canon of the Old Testament, not even the book of Sirach, who doubtless lived very shortly after the days of Nehemiah and was both a learned and a God-fearing man.

(3) They contain many statements that are legendary, erroneous, or even contrary to biblical doctrine. Thus the additions to the book of Daniel are easily recognized as fiction, of a very lurid and fantastic character. The first 11 verses of the book of Baruch contain many false statements contradicting the true record of Jeremiah. As examples of false doctrine, in the book of Tobit, an angel of God gives instructions for practicing witchcraft, and in 2 Maccabees 12:43-45 and 14:41-46, both the intercession for the dead and the act of suicide are spoken of with approval.

(4) These books are never quoted in the New Testament.

121. Classification

Luther considered some of the Jewish Apocrypha unworthy of the attention of the translator because they were no better than any heathen books. For this reason he did not translate the third and fourth books of Ezra and the third and fourth books of the Maccabees. Those that he put into German may be grouped as follows: (1) Spurious additions to the canonical books of the Old Testament (the prayer of King Manasseh, added to 2 Chronicles chapter 33; the Book of Baruch and the epistle of Jeremiah, added to the book of Jeremiah; the story of Susanna, the prayer of Azariah, the song of the three men in the fiery furnace, the stories of Bel and the Dragon, added to the book of Daniel; and additions to the book of Esther). (2) Legendary tales

(Tobit, Judith). (3) Jewish history of the period of the Syrian ascendancy in Palestine (Maccabees). (4) Books of wisdom (Sirach; Wisdom of Solomon).

122. Judith

The interesting book of Judith tells the story of Holofernes, commander-in-chief of Nebuchadnezzar's armies, who invaded the western countries and besieged the fortress of Bethulia. He was slain by Judith, a heroic Jewish woman, who thus became the savior of her people. The book itself offers the information that it was written after the return from Babylon (5:20). The writer, however, betrays his ignorance by many historical errors.

Luther believed that this book was not meant as history but was written "to be played as the Passion and other sacred stories are played among us," alluding to the "mysteries" of his day. This suggestion is based on the observation that the names of Judith, Holofernes, and Bethulia may well be understood in a symbolical sense. Judith stands for Judea, Holofernes means a heathen prince, and Bethulia, not otherwise known as the name of a city, signifies a virgin and may denote the people remaining true to God. Thus the composition becomes a great allegory, describing the victory of the Jewish people over heathendom.

123. Solomon

The title the Wisdom of Solomon names Solomon as the author, and he describes himself as king of Israel (9:7). In this way the real author sought to gain a hearing for his work, fearing that otherwise it would be without authority. It is supposed that he lived in Egypt not much more than a hundred years before Christ, at a time when the Jews had acquired full command of the Greek language and had also studied that Greek philosophy which the author shows to be the opposite of true wisdom.

Luther, who thought quite highly of this book, believes that it was meant as a solemn warning to cruel tyrants and vicious backbiters, while those who suffer persecution innocently are here comforted in their affliction. He also notes that there is hardly another book that has furnished so many suggestions for religious poetry as this one.

The author praises true wisdom, that is, the knowledge of the divine truth, and ascribes life-giving power to the Word of God (16:12). In the first part of his book (chapters 1–9), he sets forth the value of true wisdom and shows how it may be acquired. In the second part (chapters 10–19), he demonstrates the workings of God's wisdom as they appear in the history of all men, but especially in the history of the people of Israel. In this second part, we find some references to Jewish legends, which are treated as history, as in 12:9,17,22.

124. Tobit

The book of Tobit is a pleasant story relating certain experiences of one of the families that were carried to Nineveh as prisoners by Shalmanesar after he had destroyed the kingdom of the ten tribes. In simple and unaffected language, the writer describes the piety of the elder Tobit and his afflictions, the journey of the younger Tobit under the protection and guidance of an angel, and the desirable end of both the journey and the tribulations of the older man.

The date of the story is the century between 722 and 624 B.C. The elder Tobit was carried to Nineveh in 722, and the younger Tobit died in 624 at an age of 99 years. We have this book only in Greek, and nobody can show that it was first written in Hebrew, so the earliest date at which it can have been written is the year 300 B.C. The story may have been a part of Jewish folklore.

Luther, however, prefers to consider it as fiction of the same symbolical character as the book of Judith, depicting the tribulations of God-fearing families and the sure help of God. This assumption is sustained by the observation that the names of all persons mentioned by the writer may be taken as allegorical (Tobit means "the Righteous One"; Hannah, "the Delightful One"; Asmodeus, "the Destroyer"; Raphael, "God Heals"; Azariah, "Help of God"). The allegorical interpretation also explains the guardian angel who accompanies Tobit in visible human form.

The book betrays its human origin by introducing a piece of witchcraft. The angel instructs Tobit to use the liver of a certain fish as a talisman against the attack of evil spirits. This feature alone sufficed to deny the book a place in the canon.

125. Jesus Sirach

The book of Jesus Sirach is also called Ecclesiasticus (not to be confused with Ecclesiastes, the Preacher of Solomon, which belongs to the canon). It does not bear the name of the author but of his grandson, who translated and edited the book in Egypt about 130 years B.C. Jesus, a pious and learned Jew who lived after the exile, collected these wise sayings with great industry, in part from biblical, in part from other sources, and added some of his own observations. He bequeathed this Hebrew book to his son Sirach, and Sirach's son Jesus translated the treatise into the Greek world language for the use and benefit of his Jewish compatriots who lived in foreign lands.

While some of the chapters treat a definite theme, others consist of unconnected sayings. The most valuable part of the book is found in chapters 44 to 50, in which Sirach sets before his readers the faith and works of many God-fearing men of former years.

In the Greek Bible, the book is introduced by two prefaces, one by an unknown writer, the other from the pen of the translator, Jesus Sirach. Since they contain important information concerning the author, the contents, and the purpose of the book, we reproduce them here in free translation. The first preface says:

> This Jesus was the son of one Sirach and the grandson of a man named Jesus, like himself. He lived in a later period, after the captivity and the return, later than all the prophets. According to his own testimony, his grandfather was a studious and very intelligent man among the Hebrews, who collected not only the sayings of wise men who lived before his days but also his own dicta, which were full of understanding and wisdom.

> When that first Jesus fell asleep, he left the book fairly complete to his son Sirach, who took it and again bequeathed it to his son Jesus. This man put it together into a well-arranged whole and called it his own, his father's, and his grandfather's wisdom, hoping to stimulate the reader so much the more to give careful consideration to the book because of the name of wisdom.

> It contains wise sayings, apothegms, allegories, fragments of sacred history, references to men who had been well pleasing to God, together with a prayer and a hymn, and also a demonstration as to how God blessed his people with good gifts and punished their enemies. In this

manner this Jesus became a successor to Solomon, being held in no less esteem by reason of his wisdom and learning, since he was not only a scholar but was also called one.

The preface by Jesus Sirach reads as follows:

Since the Law, the Prophets, and the Writings joined with them have transmitted to us the knowledge of so many and so great things, by reason of which Israel should be duly praised for wisdom and piety, and since it is needful that not only the readers themselves should obtain true understanding but that the lovers of wisdom should become useful to those who are without, by reading and writing, my grandfather, having diligently read the Law, the Prophets, and the other Writings of the fathers and having thereby acquired sound knowledge, was urged in his mind to write something himself that might serve to promote wisdom and understanding. Those who are eager to learn, being attracted thereby, might also be induced to lead a life according to the Law.

You are therefore requested to read this book with kind and pious attention and with forbearance, if those who know the language should find that I have failed to render some words correctly. For in translating from the Hebrew into another language, you do not always find a word of exactly the same meaning. Not only this, but the Law and the Prophets and the other Writings exhibit a great diversity of diction. For when I came to Egypt in the 38th year of King Euergetes and remained there for a length of time, I discovered quite a great difference in

117

doctrine. Hence I considered it highly necessary to apply myself with some diligence and labor to the translation of this book. In the course of time, I have spent much study and care in order to lay this book into the hands of those who are eager to learn, though living abroad, so that they might order their ways according to the Law.

126. Baruch and Jeremiah

The book of Baruch and the epistle of Jeremiah, though quite distinct, were joined together by Luther and put under one title in his translation. They contain admonitions that are alleged to have been addressed to the Jews in Babylon and Jerusalem after the destruction of the latter city.

That these documents are spurious can be demonstrated from the very first chapter, which abounds in historical misstatements. We may safely assume that Baruch, the close companion of Jeremiah, did not forsake the prophet when he went from Jerusalem to Egypt, but it is claimed in this book that Baruch read it before the ears of the captives in Babylon. We know that the temple had been laid in ruins, that all Mosaic forms of public worship had ceased to be observed, and that the vessels of the temple were not returned until the days of Cyrus. This book, however, declares that the vessels were returned five years after the destruction of Jerusalem and that Baruch admonished the Jews to bring sacrifices to the temple and to observe the holy days.

As far as we know, this book never existed in a Hebrew form. Luther was greatly tempted to set it aside altogether; he writes:

> This book is very poor, whoever this good Baruch may have been. It is unbelievable that

Saint Jeremiah's servant, who was also called Baruch and to whom this epistle is ascribed, should not have been gifted with higher intellectuality than this Baruch. Thus I very nearly discarded him together with the third and fourth books of Ezra. We admit Baruch into this company because he writes so strenuously against idolatry and declares the Law of Moses.

127. Maccabees

The books of the Maccabees were written long after the days of Malachi. Since the history of the first book carries us down to the year 135 B.C., it hardly could have been issued more than 125 years before the coming of the Lord. Its author repeatedly mentions with regret that there were no prophets in Israel at the time (4:46; 9:27; 14:41). He does not himself, therefore, claim to possess the prophetic spirit, nor does he demand canonical honors for his history.

Both books aim to tell the story of the Jewish people under the Seleucidian rulers, who controlled the Syrian kingdom as successors of Alexander the Great and were named after Seleucus Nicator (312–280 B.C.). In consequence of the persecution that the Jews suffered for their faith, especially under Antiochus Epiphanes, surnamed the Illustrious, five sons of the priest Mattathias at length placed themselves at the head of a small force. After a hard struggle of nearly 40 years (175–135 B.C.), they succeeded in establishing religious freedom and suppressing idolatry.

The oldest son of Mattathias, Judas, was surnamed Makkab, that is, the "Hammer," probably on account of his vigorous leadership. This surname passed from him not only to his brothers but to all those who exhibited their courageous faith in those troublous times.

The family of the Maccabees is also known as the house of the Hasmoneans, after one of its ancestors. The Hasmoneans were men of influence until the days of Christ. Their power was finally broken by that Herod under whose reign Jesus was born, but even Herod found it advisable to marry Mariamne, a Hasmonean woman.

The two books of the Maccabees are not connected with one another, except by name. Though they cover nearly the same ground, they were written by different authors and differ greatly in historical value.

The first book of Maccabees deserves great confidence as a source of historical information and always has been esteemed accordingly. It is a tale, simply told, of the chief occurrences of the Maccabean time and thus furnishes a supplement to the history of the Jewish people. On comparing its statements with those of heathen historians of the same period, the investigator finds the author to be a very reliable witness. The Christian reader, moreover, discovers here a tangible proof of the truth of prophetic vision, for from this book we learn how the prophecy contained in the 11th chapter of Daniel was fulfilled.

Luther declares that this book is very similar to the other biblical books in style and diction and that it would not have been unworthy of a place among them.

The second book of Maccabees is greatly inferior to the first in almost every respect. History and legend are mingled so confusingly that the author cannot be regarded as a safe informant. His aim, rather, seems to have been to produce an edifying narrative without strict regard to truthfulness. He admits, moreover, that his tale is not the result of careful study on his part. He says, "These and other things besides, which Jacon (of Cyrene in Africa) has recorded in five books, we propose to condense into the briefest compass" (2:14). This remark also shows that the whole composition originated in northern Africa, where the Jews long had become accustomed to the use of the Greek language.

The story of the book does not go beyond Judas Maccabeus and covers no more ground than the first seven chapters of the first book of Maccabees. The statements concerning intercession for the dead (12:43-45) and the defense of suicide (14:41-46) prove that both the religious and the moral judgment of the author was grievously warped. Accordingly Luther says:

> We permit it to pass because of the beautiful story of the seven Maccabean martyrs and their mother and other portions besides. But it looks as though it were not the work of a master but had been patched together from many books. Moreover, it has a hard knot in the 14th chapter, which tells of the suicide of Rhazis, which also troubled Augustine and the old fathers. Briefly, just as it would have been proper to number the first book among the sacred writings, so this second book was properly thrown out, though it contains some good things.

Among the Greek Apocrypha, a third and a fourth book of Maccabees have been preserved, but they are such wretched and bungling efforts that they were not even received into the Latin version.

128. Additions to Esther and Daniel

The additions to the books of Esther and of Daniel were written in Greek and are therefore spurious. Luther found them incorporated into the text of the canonical books in the Latin version used in the Roman Church. He eliminated them and assigned them to their proper place among the Apocrypha.

These fragments show, however, that the Jews studied the books of Esther and Daniel with great interest and used their fancy freely to elaborate certain brief statements of the canonical text. As far as these additions profess to relate occurrences, they are fiction, pure and simple. But the prayers are conceived in a spirit of piety and are based entirely upon passages of the Bible. Luther says:

> Here follow some few pieces which we did not wish to translate in the Prophet Daniel and in Esther. We have plucked out such cornflowers, because they are not found in the Hebrew Daniel and Esther, but in order that they might not be destroyed, we have planted them in separate gardens, or beds, because, nevertheless, many good things, and especially the song of praise *Benedicite,* are found in them.

The *Benedicite* that Luther refers to is the song of praise of the three men in the furnace of fire.

129. Prayer of Manasseh

The prayer of Manasseh is a supplement to 2 Chronicles 33:12,13. King Manasseh, who had been carried away to Assyria as a captive, repented there of his sins and was reinstated into his kingdom. According to the Jewish legend, he spoke these words while confined in the belly of an iron ox heated to redness, whereupon the image burst to pieces and Manasseh was carried to Jerusalem by an angel.

B. A brief review of Jewish history

The main features and many details of Jewish history should become familiar to children in our Christian elementary schools through the study of what we call Bible history. Such knowledge is presupposed in the following review, which passes over many epochs very swiftly in order to gain space for more detailed discussion of those periods that are rarely or never studied in the elementary school nor enlarged upon in the pulpit.

130. Primeval period, from the creation to the flood (I), 4004–2348 B.C., or 1–1657 after creation

After creation and the fall of the first parents, mankind multiplied very rapidly. But from the outset, men separated into two distinct classes. The God-fearing descendants of Adam, being of one mind with him, put their trust in the gospel promise, while the descendants of Cain (the Cainites) forsook God and were enslaved in idolatry and other heinous sins. Under the guidance and instruction of their great leaders, the children of God at first kept strictly to themselves, avoiding all familiar association with the Cainites. But in the course of time, many of them became indifferent to God's truth and began to intermarry with their ungodly neighbors.

The result was corruption and an increase of wickedness, which rose to such a height that God at length threatened to destroy the whole world by the flood. This message was proclaimed by Noah, the preacher of righteousness (2 Peter 2:5). But men had become so callous that nobody gave heed to the portentous announcement. When the catastrophe came, only Noah and his family were saved, his sons, Shem, Ham, and Japheth, becoming the progenitors of a new human race (Shemites, Hamites, Japhetites).

During this period many men, especially those prominent among the children of God, attained a remarkably high age. This was so apparently because the weakening influence of

123

sin upon the physical constitution of man developed gradually, so that primeval man was better able to resist the inroads of disease. At the same time, God made proper use of this circumstance for his plan of salvation. The longevity of those who were the teachers of God's church ensured the faithful and energetic transmission of the divine revelation. Note that Adam lived together with Methuselah for nearly 250 years and that Noah enjoyed the instruction and example of Methuselah for six hundred years.

We also note in passing that according to the witness of the Scriptures, the arts and sciences were cultivated first by the Cainites.

131. Period of the patriarchs, from the flood to the migration of Jacob into Egypt (II), 2348–1526 B.C., or 1658–2478 after creation

For about one century after the flood, the new human race dwelt together. But though Noah continued to preach faithfully, men once more began to turn away from God and finally became so arrogant and overbearing that the Lord scattered them abroad by confusing their languages. From the midst of an idolatrous people, God then chose Abram, son of Terah, born about 2166 B.C., called him from Ur of the Chaldees about 2091 B.C., and guided him to the promised land of Canaan. Except for a brief sojourn in Egypt, Abram continued to dwell in Canaan as a stranger and looked forward to the fulfillment of the promise concerning the blessed Seed.

Fourteen years after Ishmael, Isaac, the son of promise, was born. From him the promise passed on to Jacob, Isaac's younger son, who was forced to flee to Mesopotamia because Esau, his brother, sought his life in violent jealousy and hatred. Blessed with abundant wealth, Jacob returned to

Canaan some 20 years later, accompanied by his 2 wives and 12 sons. Under the providence of God, Joseph, Jacob's son, became the savior of his father and his brothers in Egypt and secured for them a desirable place to live, not only during the years of famine, but for many centuries thereafter.

132. Period of Moses, Joshua, and the Judges (III), 1526–1050 B.C., or 2478–2954 after creation

After the people of Israel had increased greatly in Egypt under the protection of the Lord, the time at last arrived when they were to take possession of the Promised Land. In order to make them dissatisfied with the country where they had found refuge, God permitted them to be sorely oppressed by the Egyptian rulers until they cried aloud for deliverance.

By divine appointment, Moses assumed the leadership of Israel. After many miraculous demonstrations of divine power, the people were guided through the Red Sea and into the desert of Sinai, where the Lord intended to renew his covenant with them and to confirm it by a glorious revelation.

From Mount Sinai the people heard the voice of their Lord, who then employed Moses as a mediator, through whom they received the commandments, statutes, and judgments of God. Thus God established the theocracy in Israel, enthroning himself as their sole ruler, who intended to regulate even their social and civil life without the intervention of human governors.

The road to Canaan lay open before the chosen people, and they would have entered it without serious mishap if they had not sinned grievously against their Lord. To chastise them for their stubborn thanklessness, he condemned them to wander in the wilderness for 40 years, in order that the generation which had come out of Egypt should perish without seeing the Promised Land. Joshua and Caleb alone survived, for even Moses was permitted only a distant view of Canaan from the summit of Mount Nebo, where he died.

Under the leadership of Joshua, the successor of Moses, Israel at length crossed the river Jordan, conquered the land with many wonderful exhibitions of divine assistance, and distributed it among the 12 tribes according to the instructions given by God. Because they failed to exterminate the heathen inhabitants of Canaan, as they had been instructed to do, but left them in possession of certain sections of the country, they suffered the just consequence of their disobedience. Seduced by their heathen neighbors, they adopted various idolatrous practices and thus provoked the wrath of God, who chastised them severely by giving them into the hands of the heathen to be oppressed.

But as often as the people returned to the Lord with contrite hearts, he raised up judges, valiant leaders, who delivered them from their oppressors. These judges were not merely zealous patriots, who sought the welfare of their people. In every instance they obeyed a special call of God, which was often conveyed to them by direct revelation. They never ruled over the people as lords but were recognized as deliverers and saviors (Nehemiah 9:27). During the period of the judges, Ruth, a Moabitess, was received into the fellowship of Israel and became an ancestress of David.

133. Period of the kings to the Babylonian exile (IV), 1050–586 B.C., or 2954–3416 after creation

Though Israel experienced many unmistakable proofs that God himself helped them through the judges, the wayward people at length became dissatisfied with the existing order of things. Even the beneficent and successful leadership of Samuel, the last of the judges, failed to quell their desires. With barefaced and shameless ingratitude, they demanded that a king be given to them who might be their official and visible ruler and so increase the political honor and prestige of Israel. They would not recognize that they thus rejected the kind guidance of their gracious God.

Their request was granted. God gave Saul, the son of Kish, to be their first king. When Saul entered upon his new duties, he was a God-fearing man and proved to be both an excellent general and a wise ruler. But only two years later, he fell into wicked ways, and from that time onward, it became ever more apparent that his heart had fallen away from God. In persecuting David, an upright and innocent man, Saul showed that he was indeed a king like the kings of the heathen (1 Samuel 8:5). He perished miserably after he had given further proof of his wickedness by seeking comfort and advice in the house of a sorceress. He ruled over Israel 40 years (1050–1010 B.C.).

Saul's successor was David, son of Jesse, from the tribe of Judah. After Saul had been rejected by the Lord, David, then a youth of 18 years, had been anointed by Samuel to be the next king of Israel. He gave evidence of the God-fearing spirit that dwelt in him by waiting quietly and modestly for the day of his elevation to the throne. Not once did he sin against Saul, his king, in word or deed. Being a skilled musician, he was called to the royal court to entertain the king but returned to his shepherd's work when the war against the Philistines began.

David was sent to the camp by his father to carry provisions to his brothers. His trust in God prompted him to undertake the unequal combat with Goliath. His unexpected victory earned him great renown but also the jealous hatred of Saul. During the persecution in which Saul openly sought the life of his fancied rival, David bore his sufferings with patient hope, until God ended Saul's career 12 years after David's first anointment.

After an election by the people, David was publicly anointed at Hebron as king over the house of Judah. But Abner, who had been captain of Saul's host, rebelled against David on behalf of Saul's son and began a civil war. This uprising, however, was unsuccessful and lasted but a short time. The unrest was soon quieted, and all the tribes of Israel swore allegiance to King David.

By mighty deeds of valor, David overwhelmed the enemies of Israel one by one and secured peace for his people. He captured the city of Jerusalem, which had until then been in possession of the Jebusites, and made it the seat of government for his kingdom. Under the guiding hand of God, David extended his power until even Syria was compelled to pay tribute and a Jewish garrison controlled the mighty city of Damascus. The immense riches that David brought home from his campaigns were used to beautify Jerusalem.

When David planned to build a temple, the Lord refused his permission. He promised, however, not only that David's son should be king after him but also that the Messiah should spring from the posterity of David. David began to gather treasures of many kinds and all materials for the future temple and appointed the service of the sanctuary by distributing the priests into various classes, to each of which was assigned certain work pertaining to public worship.

Being a gifted poet and inspired by God, David also composed many psalms for the use of the congregation of Israel. The severe chastisements that followed upon his dreadful fall, the shocking occurrences that happened in his own family (Amnon, Absalom), the rebellion of Sheba, the punishment called forth by David's sin of numbering the people—all served to keep David truly humble in the midst of his astounding successes.

After a reign of 40 years (1010–970 B.C.), being then 70 years old, David placed his scepter into the hands of Solomon, his son, and was gathered to his fathers soon thereafter. As he was not only a great political ruler but also one of the forefathers of the Savior, an enlightened prophet, and a person typifying the future Messiah, David stands forth as one of the most noteworthy persons of Old Testament history.

Under the scepter of Solomon, the kingdom of Judah and Jerusalem attained their greatest glory. Though his wars were few and none of them of special importance, the renown of his power caused many rulers of adjacent kingdoms to seek his friendship. By developing extensive trade routes, along which his fame was carried to many distant lands, he amassed such wealth as never before had been known by his people.

Solomon's supreme achievement, however, had its root in his zealous love for the worship of his God. He built the great temple, which in beautiful grandeur and richness of ornamentation surpassed all similar structures in the world. For seven years many thousand workers toiled to erect this extraordinary edifice, and when it was dedicated in the presence of a rejoicing people, the Lord himself took possession of it and sanctified it to be an abiding place of his grace.

The Holy City was further beautified by other magnificent buildings (the king's palace!), and its defenses were carefully strengthened, so that it became a capital upon which a great people might look with just pride. The fame of Solomon extended far beyond the boundaries of his land, not only for his power and wealth but also for his surpassing wisdom, which drew the queen of Sheba to Jerusalem.

Toward the end of his life, however, Solomon, following the practice of heathen rulers, took unto himself a great number of wives, many of them from idolatrous nations, and through their influence he contaminated himself with idolatry. To make him understand the heinousness of his sin, God told him that his kingdom would be divided after his death. But there is good reason to believe that Solomon died truly repentant, for at a great age he wrote the book called Ecclesiastes, which is plainly meant as a confession of his wrongdoing. His reign, like that of Saul and David, endured for 40 years (970–930 B.C.), so that the first three kings of Israel guided the fortunes of the people for 120 years.

Solomon had barely closed his eyes in death when the calamitous division of the kingdom took place as a result of the wickedness of Rehoboam, his son and successor. When the ten northern tribes sent messengers to petition Rehoboam for a mild government, Rehoboam dismissed them with a domineering, tyrannical refusal, which estranged the hearts of those tribes so much that they seceded and set up a separate kingdom.

Only the two tribes of Judah and Benjamin remained true to the house of David, and as Benjamin had gradually dwindled into insignificance, the Southern Kingdom was thereafter known as the kingdom of Judah. With its mere 3,400 square miles of territory, as against the 9,400 square miles controlled by the kings of Israel, it was a sorry remnant of the powerful kingdom over which Solomon had ruled. Its northern boundary never was far from Jerusalem, though it shifted repeatedly according to the varying power of the northern kings. The capital of the Northern Kingdom was first located at Shechem, then at Tirzah, and finally at Samaria.

The Northern Kingdom, Israel, continued for 250 years after the separation. During this period, Israel had 19 kings from nine different families. Not one of them kept himself free from idolatry.

The Southern Kingdom, Judah, which continued for 380 years, had 20 kings, all from the house of David, as God had promised, and six of these (Asa, Jehoshaphat, Uzziah, Jotham, Hezekiah, and Josiah) are described as having walked in the ways of the Lord.

134. Northern Kingdom

While Solomon yet lived, Jeroboam, son of Nebat, an Ephratite from Zereda, was designated as the future king of the ten tribes by Ahijah the prophet and fled to Egypt because Solomon sought to take his life. When the kingdom was divided, the northern tribes chose him as their ruler, and he made Shechem his capital. Because he feared that his people, being without a sanctuary, would continue to make pilgrimages to Jerusalem and thus might be persuaded to return to the house of David, Jeroboam set up two golden calves as objects of worship, one at Dan, the northernmost, the other at Bethel, the southernmost city of his kingdom. Thus he seduced his people to gross idolatrous practices. This is the sin of Jeroboam by which he made Israel sin, the underlying cause for the final destruction of the Northern Kingdom and of the house of Jeroboam.

Nadab, Jeroboam's son and successor, reigned but two years when Baasha rose up against him, killed him and every soul belonging to Jeroboam's family, and became king in his stead. Baasha held the throne while he lived, but Elah, his son and successor, was slain after two years by Zimri, who also destroyed all the offspring of Baasha and proclaimed himself king. Zimri's triumph was shortlived.

After seven days while Zimri sat at the new capital, Tirzah, the people made Omri, captain of the host, king over Israel.

When Omri succeeded in entering Tirzah at the head of an army, Zimri withdrew into the royal palace, set fire to it, and died there. Omri chose Mount Samaria as the site for a new capital, which he called Samaria after the name of the mountain. From that time this city remained the seat of government in the Northern Kingdom. Omri did worse in the eyes of the Lord than all his predecessors, so that Ahab, his son, found idolatry firmly established in the kingdom when he ascended the throne six years later.

Ahab, however, was not content with the heathenish practices bequeathed to him by his father. When he married Jezebel, daughter of a Sidonian king, he introduced all the abominations of the Phoenician religion. In vain did Elijah thunder his powerful protests against the horrible practices of the priests of Baal. Elijah's only reward was the violent and bloodthirsty hatred of both Ahab and Jezebel. When Ahab filled the measure of his sins by murdering Naboth, the vengeance of God was visited upon him and his house. He was mortally wounded in a fight against the Syrians.

Two years later Ahaziah, Ahab's son and successor, died from injuries received in a fall and was followed on the throne by his brother, Jehoram. In the 12th year of his reign, Jehoram was returning wounded from a campaign against Syria when he was met by Jehu, the chosen avenger of the wickedness of Ahab's house, who slew the king and destroyed Jezebel, together with all that remained of Ahab's descendants.

Jehu reigned over Israel for 28 years. Though he did away with the worship of Baal, he preserved the golden calves of Jeroboam and thus became guilty of Jeroboam's sin. Then the Lord began to cut Israel short (2 Kings 10:32), and the Northern Kingdom drifted toward its inevitable doom. Jehu was followed by four kings of his own blood. The first two, Jehoahaz and Joash, reigned 33 years in all. They retained the worship of the calves and even gave room to the abominations of Baal. To chasten them, the Lord gave the Syrians power to defeat Israel and to oppress the people most grievously. Nevertheless, they recovered sufficiently under Joash to repel a wanton attack of Amaziah, king of Judah. They even took Jerusalem by storm and pillaged the wealthy city.

The power of Israel was once more raised to a great height under Jeroboam II. He held Judah in subjection and extended his rule to the Euphrates on the east, to Damascus on the north, and beyond the Dead Sea on the south, so that his domain covered practically the same territory as that of David. His renown is recorded by two prophets, Hosea and Amos, who preached in Israel in his days, together with Jonah.

When the second Jeroboam died, Zachariah, the last of Jehu's posterity, was to succeed him. But he reached the throne only after a long period of disorder and held it for but six months. Shallum, who murdered Zachariah, was slain by Menahem after one month.

During Menahem's reign the Assyrians for the first time became a factor in the history of the Jewish people. King Phul (Tiglath-pileser of Nineveh) threatened to destroy Israel, and only by paying a heavy tribute could Menahem retain his title for ten years. He was followed by Pekahiah, his son, who was murdered two years later by Pekah. In order to strengthen himself against Assyria, Pekah planned to subdue Judah with the assistance of Rezin of Syria. Tiglath-pileser, however, to whom King Ahaz of Judah had submitted, invaded Israel the second time and punished

Pekah by leading into captivity the inhabitants of the country east of Jordan.

By murdering Pekah, Hoshea acquired the crown of Israel. As he made no effort whatever to curb idolatry among his people, the measure of their wickedness was filled during his reign. A third Assyrian invasion had made him tributary, but turning traitor, he sought aid against Assyria from So, king of Egypt. Then Shalmaneser brought up an army and besieged the city of Samaria. Hoshea succeeded in defending himself for two years, and Shalmaneser died during the siege. Sargon, his son, finally broke into the city and led away all its inhabitants, together with all the people of the Northern Kingdom, into the Assyrian captivity (722 B.C.). The captives were colonized in various places, and these colonies were the scene of the history of Tobit.

After that time the ten tribes disappeared from history. They seem to have been absorbed by the peoples of Asia without leaving a trace. That the country of Samaria might not lie waste, however, Esarhaddon, king of Assyria, repopulated it with strangers from Babylonia. These new settlers intermarried with the few remaining Israelites, and thus there came into existence a hybrid people, called the Samaritans, who were addicted to idolatry, though they were not without some knowledge of the God of Israel. Between them and the Jews, a state of hostility developed, which became unpleasantly apparent when the Jews returned from the Babylonian exile and was still evident in the days of Christ.

135. Southern Kingdom

We now turn back to the year when Solomon's kingdom was torn asunder in order to review the history of Judah, the Southern Kingdom. Rehoboam, Solomon's successor, would have tried to whip the northern tribes into subjection by force of arms, but at the word of Shemaiah the prophet, the army, which had been gathered in haste, disbanded. Between Rehoboam and Jeroboam, however, bitter enmity existed as long as they both lived.

In the days of Rehoboam, Jerusalem was captured for the first time by a foreign enemy. Shishak, king of Egypt, entered it by force and despoiled both the royal palace and the temple. Idolatry in the most varied forms began to prevail and resulted in much dissolute, licentious living. Rehoboam was followed by Abijah, his son, who walked in the footsteps of his father in everything, except that he fought with Jeroboam and gained a signal victory.

Abijah was succeeded by Asa, a God-fearing man, who put his trust in the Lord and hated idolatry. After defeating Zerah the Ethiopian, Asa inaugurated a religious reform throughout his kingdom, in the course of which even the idol worshiped by his mother was destroyed. Toward the end of his reign of 41 years, when Baasha of Israel threatened to invade Judah, Asa made a covenant with the king of Syria against the will of God and even laid hands on Hanani, the seer who reproved him for his unbelief. In his last sickness, he also failed to put his trust in the Lord but relied on the skill of his physicians.

Jehoshaphat, Asa's son, walked in the ways of David altogether. Not only did he suppress idolatry, but he caused priests and Levites to travel throughout the land and teach the Law of God to the people. He also took pains to improve the administration of justice, admonishing the judges to be mindful of their responsibility to God. For these reasons the Lord was with him. The neighboring peoples did not dare to molest Judah but, rather, sought Jehoshaphat's favor with rich presents.

Jehoshaphat committed one grave error when he made common cause with wicked King Ahab of Israel for an attack upon Syria, in utter disregard of the warning sent him by the mouth of Micaiah the prophet. In this campaign Ahab was slain, while Jehoshaphat escaped unhurt. But instead of learning a lesson from his deliverance, he continued in his friendly relations with the house of Ahab. After a remarkable victory over the Ammonites and Moabites, he not only joined the wicked King Ahaziah in extensive commercial enterprises but also married Jehoram, his son, to a daughter of Ahab. The trade plans miscarried because the Lord destroyed the ships by a storm, and Jehoram's marriage resulted in deplorable misfortune for the entire kingdom.

When Jehoram ascended the throne of his father, he proved to be a cruel and godless ruler. To secure his throne, he murdered his brothers and exhibited great zeal in establishing various idolatries. As a fitting reward, he lost large portions of the rule he had inherited and finally died from a horrible disease, as Elijah the prophet had foretold.

Jehoram's son, Ahaziah, was a willing tool in the hands of Athaliah, his mother, who taught him to walk in the sins of the house of Ahab. He was slain by Jehu, the avenger of God over Ahab and all his kin. When Athaliah heard this, she caused all royal offspring to be murdered, and only the infant Joash (also called Jehoash) escaped through the bravery of his father's sister and of his nurse. Athaliah then wielded the scepter for six years. At length Jehoiada, the high priest, found courage to incite the people against that tyrannous woman.

They removed her and all priests of the idolaters and raised the rightful heir, Joash, to the throne. Since he was only seven years old, he remained under the tutelage of Jehoiadah for some time and followed his guidance willingly.

Idols were destroyed wherever found. The true worship of God was restored, and the temple was furnished according to the means supplied by the people. But when Jehoiadah died, Joash followed the unholy counsels of the princes of Judah to permit idolatry, and when Zechariah, son of Jehoiadah, dared to lift up his voice against this wickedness, he was stoned to death by order of the king. As a judgment the Lord brought about an invasion of the Syrians, who departed with rich spoils and left the king behind them, sorely wounded. Finally, Joash was slain by conspirators.

Amaziah, Joash's son, did that which was right in the sight of the Lord but not with a perfect heart. After defeating the Edomites, he carried their idols back with him to Jerusalem and worshiped them. When a certain prophet rebuked him, he rejected the reproof with great scorn. His wanton spirit prompted him to send a challenge of war to Jehoash of Israel, and he refused to keep the peace, though Jehoash earnestly desired it. After a disastrous defeat, Amaziah was taken to Samaria as a captive. Several years later, when he was permitted to return to Jerusalem, he too lost his life at the hands of conspirators.

For a hundred years after his demise, the kingdom of Judah enjoyed an era of comparative quiet and prosperity. The powerful testimony of Isaiah and other prophets served for a time as a check to the spread of corruption, and of the four kings who reigned during this period, only one was notorious for shameless wickedness.

Uzziah, son of Amaziah (called Azariah in 2 Kings 14), enjoyed a long and blessed reign. He was greatly successful in his wars and rebuilt the fortifications of Jerusalem, which had been dismantled during his father's reign. Toward the end of his life, however, he insolently presumed to usurp the priestly office and burned incense upon the altar of the

Lord. Thereupon he was struck with leprosy and was thus compelled to resign the government into the hands of Jotham, his son.

In the year when Uzziah died, Isaiah was called as a prophet. The biblical record passes over the 16 years of Jotham's reign very briefly, stating that he feared the Lord and departed not from his ways all his life. Thus he and his people enjoyed prosperity for a time.

A sudden change for the worse set in when Ahaz ascended the throne. Not a trace of the piety that had been so characteristic of his father graced the new king. In fact, he fairly wallowed in all the wickedness of heathen idolatry and even burned his own sons in sacrifice to Baal.

For these reasons his reign brought a succession of misfortunes upon Judah. King Pekah of Israel invaded the country and carried with him to Samaria many thousand captives and great spoils. The Edomites on the east and the Philistines on the west encroached upon the territory of Judah. For a short season, Ahaz secured the support of the king of Assyria. But afterward, Tiglath-pileser made war against him, and then Ahaz introduced even the gods of Syria into Jerusalem, because they, as he thought, had helped the Syrians against Assur. Dishonor pursued him even in death, for he was not buried in the sepulcher of the kings.

Hezekiah, Ahaz' son, was a God-fearing man, whose supreme desire was to restore the worship of the Lord God of Israel. He destroyed all images and accessories that might be used for idolatrous practices, including even the bronze serpent of Moses, to which some of the people had burned incense. His messengers went throughout the land, from Dan to Beersheba, inviting all the people of Israel of all the tribes to join in a general celebration of the Passover. All the people of Judah and a few Israelites assembled at Jerusalem and kept the feast for 14 days with great rejoicing. They were also found willing to contribute freely to the support of the sanctuary.

Their faith in the Lord was put to a supreme test when Sennacherib of Assyria besieged Jerusalem with a powerful army and haughtily demanded immediate surrender. Sustained by the strong words of comforting promise spoken by Isaiah, Hezekiah suppressed the fear that had begun to shake him and was rewarded by witnessing the utter destruction of Sennacherib's army through the intervention of God. His faith was further confirmed some time thereafter, when he was delivered from a deathly sickness.

Rejoicing over his escape, Hezekiah failed to preserve true humility toward the Lord and was properly rebuked with the announcement that the destruction of the kingdom was at hand. He was promised, however, that the catastrophe would not take place while he lived. Just what this threat meant was readily understood by Hezekiah, who witnessed the final downfall of the Northern Kingdom.

After the death of Hezekiah, the kingdom of Judah descended to its doom with rapid strides. Manasseh, son of Hezekiah, surpassed even Ahaz in wickedness. All abominations of heathenism were not only tolerated but fostered, until the people were more corrupt than the heathen tribes that God had expelled before them. A severe visitation of God finally brought Manasseh to his senses. He was carried to Babylon as a captive and remained there for several years. In this affliction he repented and was permitted to return to Jerusalem.

Then Manasseh earnestly endeavored to undo the evil that he had caused, but it soon became apparent that the people were too utterly depraved. Moreover, when Amon succeeded his father, he proved to be a wicked man and confirmed the people in their defection from the Lord. After two years Amon was murdered, and Josiah ascended the throne.

Josiah's administration was the last God-pleasing period in the history of Judah. He zealously tried to purge Jerusalem and Judah of all heathenish abominations, and when the high priest Hilkiah discovered a copy of the book of the Law while the temple was being repaired, the king redoubled his efforts to restore the true worship of the Lord. In this most praiseworthy undertaking, he was probably assisted by the prophet Jeremiah. After a reign of 31 years, Josiah foolishly opposed Pharaoh Neco, king of Egypt, who had set out to invade Babylonia. In the battle Josiah received a fatal wound and died at Jerusalem soon thereafter. Jeremiah wrote a lamentation to be sung by the people in Josiah's memory.

From that day Judah became a pawn in the war between Egypt and Babylon, who were struggling for worldwide dominion. The people made Jehoahaz king, but Pharaoh Neco deposed him after three months, carried him to Egypt as prisoner, made Eliakim king (after changing his name to Jehoiakim), and exacted a heavy war contribution. Neco, however, lost the battle of the Euphrates, and then Nebuchadnezzar of Babylon forced Jehoiakim into subjection.

In the year 605 B.C., Jehoiakim revolted against Nebuchadnezzar and hoped to offer effective resistance by combining with Egypt, Syria, and Tyre. Nebuchadnezzar at once came up to Jerusalem, defeated Jehoiakim, and carried off much treasure and a multitude of the people to Babylon. This was the beginning of the Babylonian captivity, the first deportation, in which Daniel and his companions were taken to Babylon. Still relying upon his allies, Jehoiakim continued to refuse payment of tribute to the Babylonian monarch, but he died before enduring the punishment intended for him.

After a brief reign, Jehoiachin, Johoiakim's son, was carried off to Babylon, together with many spoils. Nebuchadnezzar also deported a large part of the populace, with the most influential men, among whom was Ezekiel, later called to be a prophet. The throne was given to Mattaniah, an uncle of Jehoiachin. Nebuchadnezzar changed Mattaniah's name to Zedekiah.

Zedekiah was wicked, like his two predecessors, fostering the abominations of heathenism among his people. He refused to heed the faithful warnings of Jeremiah but, rather, encouraged the people to scoff and persecute this prophet and his fellow workers. Jeremiah had especially advised against defection from Nebuchadnezzar, but Zedekiah, in the ninth year of his reign, revolted openly against his overlord. Immediately the host of Babylon moved against Jerusalem and surrounded the city. The siege lasted two years and caused a dreadful famine. Finally the besiegers forced an entrance. The king fled but was overtaken near Jericho. Wreaking vengeance, Nebuchadnezzar caused Zedekiah's sons to be slain before him and then had his eyes put out.

Thus the last king of Judah was carried to Babylon in chains, a pitiable captive. With him, his people were carried away. Jerusalem was razed to the ground, and a meager remnant who were left behind, the prophet Jeremiah among them, dwelt among doleful ruins. Seven months later Gedaliah, whom Nebuchadnezzar had set as ruler over the land, was assassinated, and the remnants of the people, fearing the vengeance of the Babylonians, fled to Egypt.

136. Period of the four monarchies from the Babylonian captivity to the birth of Christ (V), 586–4 B.C., or 3416–4004 after creation

The four world monarchies under which the people of Israel lived in the four centuries just preceding the advent of Christ were the Babylonian, the Medo-Persian, the Greek, and the Roman empires. The Babylonian (more properly, *Neo*-Babylonian) kingdom was established by Nabopolassar when he overthrew the last Assyrian king, in 606 B.C., and destroyed the city of Nineveh. He was the father of Nebuchadnezzar, who destroyed Jerusalem while still crown prince, though he had been admitted to joint rulership with his father and bore the title of king.

The glory of the Babylonian empire was short-lived. After 70 years, when Nabonid was king and had elevated Belshazzar, his son, to joint regency, Cyrus succeeded in overthrowing the power of Babylon and founded the Medo-Persian monarchy, which continued until 330 B.C.

Then the West sent forth that meteoric conqueror Alexander the Great, who under God's providence became an important factor in preparing the world for the rapid spread of the gospel in the days of the New Testament by implanting the speech and culture of Greece in western Asia and Egypt. He lived to extend his dominion to the river Indus in the East. In Egypt he founded the city of Alexandria, which afterward grew to be an influential center of commercial and literary activity.

The early death of Alexander was the signal for the disruption of his empire. In Egypt, Ptolemaeus Lagi founded the dynasty of the Ptolemies; in Syria, the Seleucidian kingdom was established by Seleucus Nicator. These and all other Greek states were unable to resist the gradual advance of the Romans, and so the Roman monarchy was at the height of its power when Christ was born.

The Babylonian exile of the Jews lasted 70 years (606–536 B.C.). After the destruction of Jerusalem, the Jews began to understand that it was vain to hope for a return before the time foretold by the prophets and settled down quietly in the land of their captivity, as Ezekiel the prophet had advised them to do. That they did not forget Jerusalem is evident from several psalms that date from that period. Their faith and hope were nursed and upheld by Ezekiel and Daniel, and they surely also sought comfort and strength in the study of the older prophecies, especially those of Isaiah.

At last their longings for deliverance were fulfilled. Cyrus had defeated the Babylonians in 538 B.C., but he made Cyaxares ruler over Babylonia. Daniel, who once more rose to a position of high honor under this king, calls him Darius the Median. But when this Darius died, in 536 B.C., Cyrus enthroned himself at Babylon and was moved by God to permit the return of the Jews to their country not, indeed, as an independent nation but in full enjoyment of religious liberty.

Under the leadership of Zerubbabel, a descendant of David, and Joshua, the high priest, the people journeyed back to the Promised Land. Their first attempts at restoration were so feeble that the older people, who had seen the glory of the first temple, burst into tears when the foundations for the new house of worship were laid. They also suffered greatly from the hostility of the Samaritans, who had been refused admission to the fellowship of the Jews. The Samaritans successful intrigues blocked the way to a rapid completion of the temple. In those dark days, Haggai comforted the people with the promise that this very temple was to see the revelation of the glory of God in the fullness of time. Finally, in 516 B.C., exactly 70 years after the destruction of Solomon's magnificent temple, the Jews were enabled to dedicate their new house of worship under Darius Hystaspes.

During the subsequent 60 years, most probably during the reign of King Xerxes, the Jews who had remained at Babylon experienced the oppression and merciful deliverance recorded in the book of Esther. In the year 458 B.C., God raised up Ezra, a priest and a scribe, to be a new leader for the exiled people. With the permission of King Artaxerxes Longimanus, who also granted considerable gifts of silver and gold, Ezra took the second great company of exiles back to Jerusalem. He found to his dismay that various intolerable abuses had become common practice among those who had returned before, but he succeeded in remedying them by energetic measures of reform. Yet his efforts to secure the welfare of the people appear to have failed of lasting success. After 13 years the report was carried to Babylon that the remnant of Israel was in great affliction and reproach.

Nehemiah, cupbearer to King Artaxerxes, was moved by this distressing news to resign from his high position in order to hasten to the assistance of his people. Acting under a commission from the king, he offered successful resistance to the enemies of the Jews round about, fortified the city, and established law and order. Cooperating with Ezra, he then restored the true worship of the Lord and eradicated the abuses that once more had become sadly prevalent.

When Nehemiah returned to the Persian court, other governors succeeded him. Almost immediately transgressions of the Law and other disorders began to spread again. Sanballat, a Moabite leader of the Samaritans who had long endeavored to destroy the independence of the Jews, even managed to marry his daughter to a man of the family of the high priest. Nehemiah regarded it as his duty to return once more to Jerusalem in order to frustrate the sinister designs of Sanballat. This energetic action convinced the Samaritans that they must not hope for an alliance with the Jews on the basis of an unholy disregard for religious differences. Sanballat built a temple on Mount Gerizim and appointed his son-in-law high priest of the new sanctuary (John 4:20).

It is beyond reasonable doubt that about this time the biblical books of the Old Testament were assembled and arranged in the canon as we now have it. The book of the prophecies of Malachi was the last one to be incorporated into the sacred collection. From that time inspired prophecy ceased in the land of the Jews. It was the beginning of the last period of expectation, which finally ended with the advent of the Messiah. From the captivity up to within a hundred years before the birth of Christ, the Jewish people had no royal rulers of their own. The high priests were in full control and became highly influential.

137. The Jews under Alexander, the Ptolemies, and the Seleucids

Even before Alexander the Great overturned the power of the Persian kings, the Jews had acknowledged him as their overlord. After he had taken Tyre, the Phoenician metropolis, he proceeded upon his way to Egypt, passing through Judea.

Great consternation prevailed in Jerusalem, but Jadduah, the high priest, conceived a daring plan to gain favor with the Greek king. Attired in his robes of office and accompanied by the priests in their distinctive raiment, he set forth from the city at the head of the entire populace to meet the conqueror. Alexander immediately made obeisance to Jadduah, explaining that he had once, in a dream, seen a man so attired who had promised him dominion over Asia. The king was conducted into the city and visited the temple, where he was even permitted to offer a sacrifice under the eye of the high priest.

The story goes that he was also shown the prophecies of Daniel, which gave him great pleasure, because of their obvious reference to his success, and thus served to strengthen his friendship for the Jews. He distributed gifts, remitted taxes because it was a Sabbath year, and decreed complete religious liberty for the Jews. But the blazing star of Alexander set only ten years later, when he died because of his excesses. As he left no son to inherit his immense empire, it was split into several kingdoms by his generals.

After a long struggle, Ptolemaeus Lagi acquired possession of Egypt and Judea, and the Ptolemies continued in power for more than a century. Both the founder of their dynasty and his immediate successor, Ptolemaeus Philadelphus, were men of culture who fostered science and literature and made use of the Jews in this direction. Many thousand Jews were transferred from their old homes to Egypt, not always with their consent but never without the granting of great privileges. Most of them settled in Alexandria and in the course of time became quite thoroughly versed in Greek learning. Ptolemaeus Philadelphus established a great library at Alexandria, and it is reported that he caused the Hebrew Bible to be translated into Greek in order that it might be added to his remarkable collection as a part of the world's literature (the Septuagint, see section 142).

About the year 247 B.C., when Ptolemaeus Euergetes reigned, the old feud with the Seleucidian dynasty of Syria broke out anew, and the struggle lasted for nearly

50 years. Judea was frequently the battleground. Its inhabitants suffered greatly not only from the warring parties but also from their hostile neighbors, the Samaritans, who seized the opportunity of the upheaval to harass the Jews in many ways.

When Antiochus III, called the Great, had definitely defeated the Ptolemeans, it seemed as though an era of peace and quiet had settled upon Judea. Antiochus aided the Jews in repairing their temple, assisted them with gifts of animals for sacrifice, and remained their true friend as long as he lived. At his suggestion many Jews settled in the cities of Asia Minor. Others lived as colonists in Babylonia and Mesopotamia. These scattered Jewish communities were afterward called the Diaspora, that is, the dispersion (see 1 Peter 1:1).

The second successor of Antiochus III, called Antiochus Epiphanes, surnamed the Illustrious, exhibited quite another character. He saw his opportunity to interfere in Jewish affairs when Jerusalem was agitated by a stubborn struggle among several persons, all of whom claimed the office of high priest. In the course of this disruption, a Jew named Jason who was imbued with Greek ideas seized the office and at once introduced Greek games, built a Greek gymnasium, and even began to establish Greek forms of worship in the Holy City. This Jason was a favorite of Antiochus, and when the Jews expelled him, the king took a forceful hand in the matter. He placed a garrison in Jerusalem, despoiled the city, massacred many thousands, and sold other thousands into slavery. Later he tore down the walls of the city and finally declared that the Jewish religion was abolished. Then he decreed that all the peoples of his domain should have but one religion, adding the special order that the Jews must adopt the idolatry of the heathens.

138. The Maccabees and Herod

In this persecution many Jews denied their faith. Others, however, remained steadfast, though they faced martyrdom in its cruelest forms. At last an old man, Mattathias, became the energetic leader of those who would remain true to the faith of their fathers. With great scorn he rejected the temptation to deny his religion for a money bribe and as a price for the king's favor. Fired by zealotism, he killed a Jewish apostate and also a lieutenant of the king and then escaped to the mountains with many followers. From his retreat he raided the country in all directions, defeated the armed forces of the heathens, destroyed the altars of the idolaters, and strengthened the faithful.

When Mattathias finally died at the age of 146 years, three of his sons assumed the leadership in succession. Judas, after whose surname Makkabi (from *makab,* "hammer") the whole family came to be named the Maccabees, proved to be a successful champion, defeating the Syrians in several battles. He took possession of Jerusalem and reestablished the true worship of God. In memory of this noteworthy occurrence, the Jews thereafter celebrated the Feast of the Dedication (John 10:22). Antiochus descended upon Judea with a great army, but he was suddenly seized with a terrible disease and died. Under his son, a lad of nine years, peace was restored to the Jews, and the decree abolishing their religion was annulled.

Though later the struggle against the Syrians had to be renewed, the Maccabees succeeded in increasing their advantages. In the course of a family feud, waged for the possession of the throne, Jonathan, brother of Judas, sided with Alexander, who thus gained the ascendancy and designated Jonathan as high priest. Simon, the third brother, secured for himself a hereditary claim to the throne and bequeathed it to his son, Johannes Hyrcanus. This ruler became very powerful, both as prince and as high priest. He defeated the Samaritans and destroyed their temple on Mount Gerizim. He also subdued the Idumeans, compelling them to adopt the Jewish religion, and extended his domain until the Jewish kingdom was nearly as large as at any time before.

Finally, in the year 106 B.C., Aristobulus, son of Hyrcanus, assumed the royal title and thus restored this last evidence of political independence. After him, his brother Alexander Jannaeus extended the boundaries of the kingdom both eastward beyond Jordan and westward to the sea, until it equaled the kingdom of David. He spent almost the entire period of his administration (103–76 B.C.) in warlike enterprises. As he united in his person the office of high priest with that of king, he found opposition in a party of strict observers of the Law, who abhorred the lowering of the high priest's prestige implied in the king's acts. These were the Pharisees, who for many years stood opposed to the Sadducees. They upheld the requirements of divine Law against the unwarranted claims of the Hasmoneans (Maccabees) upon the office of the high priest, while the Sadducees defended this departure from the divine ordinance.

One day, on the Feast of Tabernacles, the assembled multitude, incited by the Pharisees while Alexander Jannaeus was offering a sacrifice, pelted him with fruits from the boughs of trees that they had brought to the temple. Though the king took bloody revenge upon the Pharisees for the outrage, he could not alter the sentiment of the party. After his death Salome, his widow, ascended the throne, while Hyrcanus, his son, became high priest. This seemed unbearable to the Pharisees. Arranging for a revolt, they entrusted the leadership to Aristobulus II, the younger son of Alexander, and drew up before Jerusalem with an armed force.

In the further course of this civil war, Pompey, a Roman general who was just then conducting a campaign in Syria, saw his opportunity to interfere. As the fighting parties refused to arbitrate their differences, Pompey finally took the city of Jerusalem on a Sabbath Day of the year 63 B.C. The Sadducees desperately defended the heights of the temple but were at length overwhelmed by the Romans. On this occasion the Roman general even entered the Holy of Holies, but he spared the temple and did not interfere with the worship of the Jews. In this manner the Jews became vassals of the fourth world power and remained politically dependent until Jerusalem was destroyed.

Pompey carried Aristobulus and his children to Rome, where they were compelled to adorn the triumphal procession of the victor. Hyrcanus II was made ruler and high priest, but he proved so inefficient that Caesar appointed Antipater, an Idumean prince, to be an associate ruler. In reality, Hyrcanus actually remained high priest only. He was captured while engaged in a campaign. Then Antipater had himself appointed Roman governor.

In this way the last vestige of political autonomy was wrested from the Jews and particularly from the Sanhedrin. They tried, indeed, to recover their lost glory by repeated revolts, but always encountered the iron hand of the Romans, who finally made it possible for Herod to be appointed king after the death of his father, Antipater. This development showed that the party of the Hasmoneans, or Maccabees, had been definitely shorn of all influence.

Herod took a fearful toll of his opponents. Not only did the heads of all prominent Sadducees fall, but death was the fate of every person of Hasmonean extraction. Even Mariamne, Herod's queen, and also his mother-in-law and finally his own sons born of Mariamne had to die because the blood of the Maccabees coursed in their veins. The cruel Idumean spilled the noblest blood so freely that the massacre of the babes of Bethlehem, which also was his work, is not even mentioned by profane historians of that day. It was too insignificant an event to be chronicled.

Herod soon changed the appearance of the city by building theaters and setting apart areas for athletic games. In order to curry popular favor, possibly also with the intention of minimizing his atrocities, he beautified the temple and remodeled it at great expense. His character remained unchanged to the end. When he was about to die from a loathsome and incurable disease, which had come upon him as a judgment of God, he gave orders to execute one of his sons by his second wife. When he felt the weakness of death stealing upon him, he had six thousand prominent Jewish men imprisoned in the Hippodrome at Jericho, instructing the guards to slaughter the unfortunate men as soon as the message of the king's death was received, in order that there might be some real mourners at the king's demise. Fortunately, this fiendish scheme of the dying tyrant was not carried out, and so it came to pass that Herod actually died unmourned. This was in the year 4 B.C., the 751st year after the founding of Rome.

139. The religious climate

In this long period of unceasing strife and political unrest that followed the exile, the Jewish people gradually developed those religious characteristics with which we are familiar from the gospel stories of the New Testament. As God no longer gave them prophets, they were to cherish the wealth of promises that had been given them, looking forward hopefully toward the light of salvation that was to arise in Christ. And, surely, there always were some faithful souls who waited quietly and steadfastly for the coming of the Promised One.

But in the stress and disorders of those turbulent days, the leaders of the people and their followers lost sight of the true messianic hope. It should be noted that the Messiah is not even mentioned in the apocryphal books of the Maccabees. The great heroes of the Hasmonean house were completely engrossed with their own schemes for attaining political power and independence. When the conquest of the Romans deferred this goal to the distant future, the promise of the Messiah was remembered, indeed, but the misguided people looked forward to him as to a valiant hero who would restore the political power and glory of Israel.

Having lost their political importance, the sects of the Pharisees and Sadducees thereafter spent their time in endless squabbles over questions of faith. From the New Testament, we know the Pharisees as great sticklers for the law, preaching the righteousness of works as the true way of salvation. They required literal fulfillment of the law, to which they had added numberless restrictions and demands (the "tradition of the elders," Matthew 15:2), so that whoever accepted their leadership lived in miserable spiritual bondage. The Sadducees, on the other hand, were frankly rationalistic, rejecting all tenets that seemed unreasonable to them. Thus they denied the doctrines of immortality, eternity, the existence of spirits, and resurrection and advocated a life of carnal self-indulgence.

There was a third sect, called the Essenes, much less popular and influential, that at first was scattered among the people but later found a haven of refuge in the desert places lying westward of the Dead Sea. There they lived in close communion, rejected marriage, and made the service of the needy the chief rule of their lives. We know very little about their religious views, but it seems that they were greatly given to philosophical speculation and for that reason were often classed with the heathen mystics.

140. The Herodians

After the death of Herod, Palestine was divided among his three sons. Archelaus, who had been educated at Rome, was made ruler of Idumea, Judea, and Samaria under the title of ethnarch (Matthew 2:22). Since his appointment had been violently opposed, he began to persecute his enemies most cruelly as soon as he was enthroned. The Jews, however, carried their complaints to Rome, and the emperor deposed the tyrant, banishing him to Gaul. For a time his province was ruled by governors, among whom was Pontius Pilate. They were under the supervision of the Roman legate for Syria and dwelt at Caesarea, visiting Jerusalem only occasionally.

Another son of Herod, Philip, a mild and just man, was appointed tetrarch of the district east of the Jordan. He reigned peacefully and prosperously for 37 years.

Herod Antipas, third son of Herod the Great, was tetrarch of Galilee and Perea. He is the Herod whom John the Baptist rebuked for marrying his brother's wife, who also first imprisoned and then beheaded the fearless preacher. He likewise took part in torturing Jesus after his capture. Being a crafty schemer (a "fox," Luke 13:32), he contrived to retain the favor of the Roman emperors, until Herodias, his ambitious wife, persuaded him to visit Rome in hopes of securing the title of king. Certain charges brought against him by his nephew, Herod Agrippa I, proved his undoing. He was deposed from his office and was sent to Gaul with his wife, a pair of sadder and wiser exiles.

During the administration of Herod Agrippa I, a grandson of Herod the Great, all Palestine was gradually reunited by a series of imperial decrees and became an independent province, separate from Syria. This Herod caused James the apostle to be executed and Peter to be imprisoned, to please the Jews (Acts 12:1-4). Soon after these vicious acts, when he permitted the populace to acclaim him as a god, he was struck with a loathsome disease, worms eating his body alive.

Agrippa II, Herod's son, began ruling when only 17 years old and was granted the title of king as a ruler of the several parts of Palestine. Before this ruler Paul spoke in his own defense (Acts 25,26). After Agrippa II had reigned 26 years, Jerusalem was destroyed (70 A.D.), and he was unable to ward off the catastrophe.

During the preceding 70 years, a new party had arisen, the Zealots, who strove to realize the kingdom of God on earth as they dreamed it. They were a fanatical element, spurning peace under Roman dominion and always ready for armed rebellion. Their repeated uprisings finally exhausted the patience of the Romans, who became the executors of the divine judgment: The Jewish people ceased to be a nation.

C. The first translations of the Old Testament

141. Targum and Talmud

During the Babylonian captivity and the period immediately subsequent to it, the Jews not only learned the language of their overlords but also began to use it more and more among themselves. Gradually the Hebrew tongue, in which the books of the Old Testament are written, disappeared from common use altogether and was supplanted by the Aramaic, or Chaldee, language. Hence it soon became apparent that the assembled people no longer understood the Scripture lessons when they were read in the synagogue on the Sabbath Day, and it was found necessary to supplement the reading with an interpretation in the new dialect.

In Aramaic a translation is called targum, and this general term is now used as a proper name for the Aramaic paraphrases of the Old Testament that have been handed down to us. At first the scribes undoubtedly produced a translation *ex tempore* as the lesson was read, and even afterward the interpreter was not permitted to use written notes in the synagogue. For this reason it is improbable that we have any written remains of the oldest Targums.

It is certain, however, that the Targums still extant date from a very early period. There is the Targum of Onkelos on the books of Moses, but scholars to this day are not agreed on who wrote it. The Jerusalem Targum on the Pentateuch and the Targum Jonathan on the prophets are also worth special mention, but there exist Targums on almost all the books of the Old Testament. These versions rarely reproduce the literal meaning of the Hebrew text but are mostly paraphrases, which are sometimes expanded into veritable commentaries on the text.

The Targums must not be confused with the Talmud, which the Jews esteem so highly that they place its authority above that of their Bible in practice, though they acknowledge in theory the superior sacredness of the canon.

The Talmud consists of two distinct parts, the Mishnah and the Gemarah. The former is a collection of ancient precepts developed from the Mosaic Law, while the latter is a voluminous exposition of the Mishnah. The whole is written in Aramaic. Certain portions of the Mishnah were assembled before the days of Christ, and it is probable that our Lord refers to them as the "traditions of the elders," which he condemned. In its present form, this part of the Talmud dates from about the end of the second century after Christ. The beginnings of the Gemarah are of a later date, and the work was added to periodically until the end of the sixth century.

The two great versions of the Talmud, that of Jerusalem and that of Babylon, differ only in the Gemarah. Each exhibits the rabbinical opinions of many hundred Jewish scholars; the Talmud Yerushalmi contains the Gemarah of rabbis who lived chiefly in Galilee, while the Talmud Babli displays the wisdom of Jewish teachers who lived in the Diaspora at Babylon. The bulk of the Talmud, which has been printed in 12 large folio volumes, is a witness to the amazing diligence of the contributors and collectors.

142. The Septuagint

When the Greek language had become universally used in Palestine and the adjoining countries as a result of the conquests of Alexander the Great, it became apparent that the Old Testament ought to be translated into the new world language. This would not only benefit those Jews who adopted the Greek language entirely but also the Gentiles who desired to become acquainted with the literature and religion of the Jewish people.

Egypt with its large Jewish population, whose scholars had developed a decided leaning to Greek science and literature, naturally became the birthplace of that important Greek version of the Old Testament which is known as the Septuagint. This name, which means "Seventy," is a perpetual reminder of the legendary origin of this translation. The story goes that when Ptolemaeus Philadelphus was collecting books for the great library at Alexandria, his librarian, Demetrius Phalereus, suggested that the king should seek the aid of the high priest Eleazar at Jerusalem in order to obtain a translation of the books of Moses. Eleazar dispatched 72 learned men, six from each tribe of Israel, who carried a beautiful copy of the Law with them to Egypt. These men were placed on the island of Pharos, each in a separate cell, and they completed their work in 72 days. Developing this story, later legends have it that those diligent scholars translated the entire Old Testament and that, miracle of miracles, all of the 72 versions agreed to a letter. From this legend, substituting a round number, the version was called the Septuagint, and it is frequently represented by the Latin numerals LXX. It is certain that this translation was made in Egypt, most probably at Alexandria, the center of culture and learning. As the grandson of Jesus Sirach already knew and used it, it must have been commonly known before the year 132 B.C. Since the version is not equally reliable and exact throughout, it is also quite certain that it is the work of several translators. It is not a literal translation but often assumes the form of a paraphrase. In this great work, the books of Samuel, Kings, and Chronicles, which consist of one volume each in the Hebrew, were each split into two parts, and all later versions follow this example.

At the time of Christ, the Septuagint was very widely known and was esteemed so highly by the Jews that they readily accepted the legends referred to above. The holy writers of the New Testament usually quote Old Testament passages according to the Septuagint version. Sometimes we notice that the quotation does not agree literally with the Hebrew text. But in such cases we recognize that by quoting the words of the Greek version, the Holy Spirit endorses them as a true exposition of the Hebrew original, often bringing out shades of thought that might otherwise be overlooked. To the student of the Old Testament, the Septuagint lends valuable assistance in determining the significance of many difficult words and phrases.

D. The geography of Palestine

143. General outline

When God informed Abraham about the country that his descendants were to occupy in due time, God named the Euphrates as the extreme eastern and the river of Egypt as the extreme western boundaries (Genesis 15:18). Further details are recorded in Exodus 23:31, where God says, "I will establish your borders from the Red Sea to the Sea of the Philistines, and from the desert to the River." There the eastern and western boundaries are defined.

Adding to this the most explicit description given in Numbers 34:2-12, we find that according to the promises of God, the inheritance of the people of Israel was to extend on the east to the edge of the desert that stretches from the southern end of the Dead Sea to the Euphrates, on the south from the northern point of the Red Sea to the Dead Sea, on the west to the river of Egypt and the Mediterranean Sea, and on the north from the Mediterranean to the Euphrates.

Because the people of Israel failed to execute the judgment of God upon the heathen peoples of this territory, they did not obtain full control of it until the days of David, and even then their possession was only temporary. The various events recorded in sacred history mostly transpired in Palestine proper, which is bounded by the mountains of Lebanon and Anti-Lebanon on the north, by the river Jordan on the east, by the Mediterranean on the west, and by the Arabian Desert on the south. To this must be added the country east of Jordan, which was given as a heritage to the tribes of Reuben, Gad, and half of Manasseh.

The river of Egypt, which is mentioned as part of the western boundary, is apparently not the Nile but a small brook that flows into the Mediterranean due north of Mount Sinai. It dries up in summer and is so insignificant in itself that most of our maps do not even indicate its position.

The name Palestine is a Greek corruption of the word Philistaea, originally the name for the southwestern part of the country, which even the Jews eventually applied to the whole land. It was called Canaan after the fourth son of Ham, some of whose descendants, the Canaanites, had settled there. It was the Promised Land because it had been promised to Abraham and his descendants. We justly call it the Holy Land not only because it was the scene of the great works that God did on behalf of his people but particularly because the Savior of the world spent his holy life there and has thus given the many places that he visited a significance which no other places in the wide world can have for a Christian.

Palestine proper, together with the land east of Jordan, has an area of about 12,000 square miles, which is about the size of the state of Maryland. Its natural boundaries, such as mountains, deserts, and the Mediterranean Sea, were barriers of isolation and made it a suitable home for that people whom God had destined to hold an exclusive position among all nations. There the Israelites might have lived quietly and peacefully, looking forward to the fullness of time, if they had not frustrated the purposes of God by their disobedience.

Though small in area, Palestine exhibits all possible variations of surface. It may be divided into four distinct strips, which run side by side in a general north and south direction, namely, (1) the coastal plain, (2) the mountain region, (3) the Jordan valley, and (4) the high plateaus east of Jordan.

144. The coastal plain

The coastal plan extends along the Mediterranean Sea in an unbroken sweep, except where it is cut in two by the western end of Mount Carmel. North of Carmel lies the narrow edge of seashore once inhabited by the Phoenicians, who were never disturbed in their occupancy by the Israelites. East of Mount Carmel extends the beautiful plain of Esdraelon, which though actually lying within the mountain region, is nevertheless a physical part of the coastal plain. South of Mount Carmel lie the plains of Sharon, and south of these, the land of the Philistines, who were bitter enemies of Israel for centuries. There the plain broadens until it reaches a width of nearly 20 miles, at the point where it touches the desert. This part was known as the Shefelah, that is, "low hills," the foothills of the mountain region. The soil of the entire coast strip is rather sandy but extremely productive, and its undulating surface lies between one and two hundred feet above the level of the sea.

All the greater cities of this strip were built on the seashore. The narrow territory of Phoenicia offered no inducements to the farmer and herdsman, but the rich and powerful cities of Tyre and Sidon controlled the sea lanes in their day, sending their traders beyond the Straits of Gibraltar and even to the British Isles. The Phoenician colonies along the northern coast of Africa proved a serious impediment to Rome when it was about to develop into the mistress of the world.

On the shores of Sharon lay the cities of Joppa and Caesarea. Joppa, one of the most ancient cities of the world still existing today, always was, and is now, the one good harbor of Palestine. Whoever travels to Palestine by water leaves the ship at Joppa. Caesarea is often called Caesarea Palaestina (the Philistine Caesarea), to distinguish it from other cities of the same name. It was a place of considerable importance.

Of the cities belonging to the Philistines, Ashkelon in particular gave much trouble to the Jews and also showed bitter enmity against the Christians in later years. When the Crusades began, it was used as a landing place by the European invaders, who also destroyed it in 1192. To the south of Ashkelon, also on the seashore, lay the city of Gaza. Because it stood at the edge of the southern desert, it was a desirable stopping place for caravans coming up out of Egypt. On the caravan road leading from Jerusalem to Gaza, Philip baptized the eunuch. Along the foothills, the Philistines had the towns of Ashdod, Ekron, and Gath, well known in the history of the kings of Israel. Today, Ashdod alone exists—as an insignificant village.

The short rivers of the coastal plain flow only in the rainy season. The most southern one is the river of Egypt, which forms the boundary of Palestine. The only watercourse of any importance is the Kishon, which drains the Plain of Esdraelon. It is familiar from the story of Sisera and Elijah the prophet.

145. *The mountain region*

The mountain region of Palestine extends from Mount Lebanon southward to the Dead Sea. There most of the important events of Jewish history took place. Except for narrow plains along the River Jordan, Galilee, Samaria, and Judea (the three chief parts of the land) exhibit all the aspects of a mountain country with its alternate high hills and pleasant valleys.

Abutting on the northern boundary of Palestine proper lie the notable mountain ranges of the Lebanon and the Anti-Lebanon. *Lebanon* means "White Mountains," called so either because the highest summits of the range (9,000 feet) are usually covered with snow throughout the year or because of the color of the chalk formations. Even to this day, a great part of this mountain region is tilled with great care and usually brings good crops on account of the many springs of cool water. Not far below the highest ridge, the modern traveler sees the last remnants of those magnificent forests of cedar trees that furnished much of the building material for Solomon's temple. Many of the inhabitants of Lebanon are Christians, called Maronites.

Separated from Lebanon by the broad valley of Coelesyria, Anti-Lebanon raises its peaks to the same height. The most famous is called Mount Hermon (also known as Sirion, or Senir), which forms the southern end of the range and consists of a group of considerable peaks, the highest of which rises to an altitude of 10,000 feet above sea level. Snow usually lies on its summit throughout the year. In ancient days this snow was harvested and carried to Tyre to be used for cooling drinks. On Mount Hermon rise the unfailing springs of Jordan, and its dew waters adjacent valleys.

From Lebanon and Anti-Lebanon, waters flow to the four points of the compass. From their heights the traveler's eye carries eastward to Damascus, northward to Antioch, westward to Tyre and Sidon, and southward into the reaches of the Holy Land.

146. Galilee

From the southern foothills of Lebanon, the country of Galilee extends southward to the range of Mount Carmel. In the distribution Galilee became the home of the tribes of Asher, Naphtali, Zebulun, and Issachar.

Upper Galilee includes the mountains of Naphtali, with Jebel Jermuck as the highest peak (4,000 feet). As one travels toward the south, he sees the mountains decrease in altitude until they reach an average height of 1,800 feet in the southern part. Between them lies the Plain of Zebulun, where many of the cities were located that are so familiar from the story of Jesus. The great Plain of Jezreel (Esdraelon), which was shared by Issachar and Zebulun, lies still farther to the south, along the foot of Mount Carmel.

In Lower Galilee the traveler of today is shown the Mountain of the Beatitudes, where Jesus is supposed to have preached the Sermon on the Mount, and Mount Tabor, which was formerly believed to have been the scene of Christ's transfiguration.

The general aspect of Galilee is that of a high plateau, which descends to the coastal plain on the west, to the Plain of Jezreel on the south, and to the Jordan and Lake Gennesaret on the east.

This district, which is now largely a deserted waste, sustained an almost incredible population in Old Testament days. According to Josephus, a Jewish historian whose reliability, however, is not above suspicion, Galilee had 204 cities, each of at least 15,000 inhabitants (a total of 3,060,000 souls).

There is no doubt that Galilee was the most productive district of Palestine. At its northern edge lay the very ancient city of Dan, the northernmost city of the Holy Land (as Beersheba was the southernmost city of the country, the expression "from Dan to Beersheba" meant the same as "throughout the land"), close to the headwaters of the Jordan. Dan existed when Abram came from Chaldea but was known as Laish until captured by the Danites. Cana, where Jesus performed his first miracle, was situated in the Plain of Zebulun. Along the Sea of Galilee, going from north to south, lay the cities of Korazin, Bethsaida, and Capernaum, which, though populous at the time of Christ, have disappeared so completely that even their sites are in dispute. Tiberias, however, built by Herod the Great and named after Emperor Tiberius, is today a village of four thousand inhabitants. Nazareth, which may be reached from Cana on foot in two hours, is situated against the southern slope of the plateau, facing the Plain of Jezreel, in a bowl-shaped valley between white hills of chalk. Its present inhabitants still show the house of Joseph, the well of Mary, and other alleged points of interest connected in some way with the life of Jesus. Within the Plain of Jezreel, we find the village of Nain, which, though very small today, must have been a city of considerable size in the time of Christ.

147. Samaria

Mount Carmel, the Little Hermon, and the hills of Gilboa together form a distinct natural boundary between Galilee and Samaria. It was not physical features, however, that separated Samaria from Judea on the south. There the political boundary underwent many and various changes as the centuries rolled by.

Samaria was greatest in the days of Jeroboam I, who held the city of Bethel and made it a place of idolatrous worship. The district that became Samaria was settled by half the tribe of Manasseh and by the powerful tribe of Ephraim, from which the kingdom of the ten tribes derived one of its names. The name Samaria originated during the period of the kings, when Omri built his new capital city and called it by that name (1 Kings 16:23,24). After the ten tribes had been deported, the king of Assyria populated the district with alien colonists, and by intermarriage of these with the few remnants of Israel, there came into existence the hybrid people called Samaritans, who were bitter enemies of the Jews.

In Samaria there are no great plains whatever. Its mountain summits (the Mountains of Ephraim) rise to an average height of 2,500 feet above sea level. The valleys are hardly inferior in fertility to those of Galilee. When Canaan was conquered by the people of Israel, at least 50,000 families settled in Samaria. The range of Carmel, which reaches a height of about 1,700 feet, received its name ("God's vineyard") from the productiveness of its slopes, which were carefully tilled in the old days. The range of the Little Hermon belonged in part to Issachar and in part to Manasseh. On Mount Gilboa in the northeastern corner of Samaria, King Saul suffered his final defeat and died.

Two other noteworthy heights are Gerizim and Ebal, between which lay the city of Shechem. The former was called the Mount of the Blessings, the other, the Mount of Cursings, according to Deuteronomy chapter 27 and Joshua 8:33,34. Mount Gerizim was afterward held sacred as a place of worship by the Samaritans (John 4:20).

Shechem was the oldest city of Samaria. Abraham visited it in the course of his wanderings, and Jacob lived there for a time. Situated between Gerizim and Ebal, it became the residence of the king immediately after the establishment of the northern kingdom. After Tirzah, the second capital, which lay northeast from Shechem, had been burned by Zimri, Omri turned to the northwest and built the city of Samaria. This capital was destroyed by the Maccabean leader Johannes Hyrcanus, but Herod the Great rebuilt it and called it Sebaste (the Greek equivalent for Augusta) in honor of Emperor Augustus. To the south of Shechem was Shiloh, where the ark of the covenant rested in the days of Eli and where Samuel was educated. Bethel, formerly called Luz, belonged to Samaria most of the time, though it lay within the heritage assigned to the tribe of Benjamin.

148. Judea

There is no change in the character of the landscape as the traveler passes from Samaria into Judea. The mountains of Judah also reach an average height of 2,500 feet, and numerous fertile valleys lie between them. On the west this district descends into a section of very productive foothills, which gradually merge into the Philistine Plain of Shefelah.

At Hebron begins a great valley, with many branches on both sides, which divides the mountainous country into two sections and extends toward the seacoast in the west. On the south Judea touches the Arabian Desert. There lies the Desert of Judah, a wild and uninviting district, in which David passed many years of his life as an outcast, undergoing many hardships.

The Mount of Olives (Olivet) near Jerusalem is the most noteworthy elevation of the Judean heights. At the point where the mountains descend toward Jericho, the traveler is shown the steep peak of Quarantania, where, it's conjectured, Jesus fasted 40 days and was thereafter tempted by Satan.

Among the cities of Palestine, Jerusalem is unique, not only because it became the center of the true worship of the Lord after the temple had been built but chiefly because the wonderful divine work of redemption was ultimately accomplished in and near this city. Hence it is not romance but intense religious interest that has prompted Christian scholars to devote much study to the history and topography of Jerusalem in order to seek solutions for many problems that the biblical record raises.

In point of age, Jerusalem is one of the most venerable cities on earth. It flourished in the days of Abraham, who was blessed by Melchizedek, king of Salem, which is Jerusalem. Afterward it was the chief city of the Jebusites and was called Jebus. In vain did Joshua attempt to wrest it from the hands of the Canaanites, nor were the Benjamites more successful after him. David finally captured it, made it his capital, and called it Jerusalem. During the days of the kings, it was frequently captured and pillaged by hostile armies, but it remained for Nebuchadnezzar to destroy it utterly in 586 B.C.

The returning exiles began to rebuild it in 536 B.C., and it quickly grew to its former size after Nehemiah had restored its walls in 444 B.C. Though often sorely harassed, Jerusalem then stood for more than five centuries, until Titus, a Roman general, once more leveled it to the ground, in 70 A.D.

Fifty years later the Emperor Hadrian built a new city on the ruins, calling it Aelia Capitolina, and this name persisted until Constantine the Great restored the ancient name of Jerusalem. Not only Jews and Christians but also the Muhammadans hold this city sacred; the latter call it El-kudsh, "the Holy One."

Jerusalem lies 32 miles from the Mediterranean, 18 miles from the Dead Sea, 19 miles from the Jordan, and 36 miles from Samaria, at an elevation of about 2,500 feet above sea level.

Three valleys and four hills, which lie within its precincts, determine the general appearance of the city. The four hills are spurs of the Judean mountains and have the following names: Bezetha, lying to the north and east; Moriah, on the southeast; Akra, on the northwest; Zion, on the southwest. The eastern slopes of Bezetha and Moriah descend into the valley of the brook Kedron (Valley of Jehoshaphat). The Tyropoean Valley (Valley of the Cheese-makers!) separates Zion and Moriah at its southern end, while its two northern branches cut in between Akra and Bezetha, as well as between Akra and Zion. Bezetha and

Moriah are separated by a slighter depression. On the west the city touches the Valley of Hinnom, which unites with the Tyropoean and the Kedron valleys south of Jerusalem. Thus the great city was protected on three sides by deep valleys, and only the northern wall offered a convenient point of attack to besiegers. Hence many successful assaults, as that of Titus, were launched against it from that side.

On Mount Zion the Jebusites had their castle, and there David built his palace. As a result, that part of the city was known as the City of David. Later it was called the Upper City. There also stood the palace of Herod the Great. Opposite to Zion and to the eastward, on Mount Moriah of ancient memory, Solomon erected the first temple. In the northwestern corner of the great space stood the Castle of Antonia, which was the scene of a fierce and bloody struggle when the Romans stormed the city. On the place where the temple had stood, Caliph Omar in 637 built the mosque called Kubet es-Sakhra, which is one of the most cherished sanctuaries of the Mohammedan world to this day.

Mount Akra, the Lower City, and the height of Bezetha, the New City, are later additions to Jerusalem. The former was first enclosed with a wall in the days of the Maccabees, while the walls of the latter were not built until after the ascension of Christ. Thus the various sections of the triple wall of Jerusalem were erected at different periods. David and Solomon built the first wall around Zion and Moriah. The second wall protected the height of Akra; no one has as yet been able to show where it met the first wall on Moriah. The third wall, enclosing Bezetha, begun by Herod the Great, was completed shortly before the Roman siege.

The Mount of Olives faces Jerusalem from the east, across the valley of the Kedron, and consists of several distinct knolls. The southernmost of these is called the Mountain of Offense, because Solomon there built an idol sanctuary. Next to it rises the Mount of the Prophets, so called because several prophets are said to have been buried there. The knoll in the middle is known as the Mount of the Ascension, but it is assumed with good reason that the ascension of Christ took place on the eastern slope, rather than on the summit and in sight of the city. Next to this comes the Mount of the Galileans; there the angels are said to have appeared to the apostles after Christ's ascension. The knoll farthest north is called Scopus, that is, the outlook, for from this point Titus is said to have obtained his first view of the Holy City.

Near the place where the three valleys meet below Jerusalem, the Pool of Siloam was located. On the slope opposite to it, the natives still point out Aceldama, the field of blood.

Bethlehem, where Christ was born, lies five miles south of Jerusalem. It was called Bethlehem Ephratah, to distinguish it from a village of the same name in Galilee. The present inhabitants, who are Christians, till the productive soil successfully. In Bethlehem the modern traveler is shown the alleged Grotto of the Nativity and also the Church of Mary, which was built by the Empress Helena. Near Bethlehem the caravan route passes the Tomb of Rachel.

Eighteen miles to the south of Jerusalem still lies the ancient city of Hebron, which flourished in the days of Abraham and became the burial place of the three patriarchs. After the conquest it was assigned to Caleb as a heritage. It was designated as one of the cities of refuge and as one of the Levitic cities, where the descendants of Aaron were to have their permanent residence. After David became king, he resided at Hebron for nearly eight years.

Beersheba, a border city, is 45 miles from Jerusalem to the southwest.

Going eastward from Jerusalem along the southern slopes of Mount Olivet, the traveler in Christ's day first reached Bethphage, then Bethany, both situated on the road to Jericho. Bethphage has disappeared without a trace. Bethany is now a small Arab village.

After traveling from Jerusalem through a lonely desert for about 13 miles, the visitor reaches Jericho, called the City of Palms on account of its fertile, semitropic environment. After suffering many conquests, it has degenerated into a dirty Arab settlement.

Gilgal, where the people of Israel had their first camp west of Jordan, was situated close to the river, not far from Jericho.

The small village of Emmaus lies almost due west of Jerusalem.

149. Valley of the Jordan

The Valley of the Jordan, which the Arabs simply call the Ghor, that is, the Valley, extends from the foot of Mount Hermon straight south to the Dead Sea. In itself rather an insignificant stream as rivers go, the Jordan is still a most remarkable watercourse. Not only is it entirely landlocked, but it also sinks far below sea level as it approaches its terminus. While its sources lie high up on the mountain slopes, at an altitude of 1,000 feet, it discharges its waters into the Dead Sea at a level of 1,300 feet below that of the ocean. Within a distance of 134 miles by air, its waters thus fall 2,300 feet. Because its course is winding, its actual length is 200 miles.

Three strong springs combine to form the headwaters of the Jordan. The northernmost one is found at Hasbeya, on the slopes of Mount Hermon. Near the location of Dan, the spring called Tel-el-Kady adds its contribution. To the east of this, near Caesarea Philippi, is the spring of Banias, which the Jews believed to be the real headwaters of Jordan, declaring that it draws its waters, through an underground connection, from a small lake lying toward the northeast, called Phiala.

The upper part of the river, from Hasbeya to Lake Merom, is 40 miles long. In a space of 12 miles, the river drops 1,000 feet and thus reaches sea level. There it enters Lake Merom, called El-Hule by the Arabs, which is shaped somewhat like a triangle, with the apex pointing to the south. The northern edge measures about 3 miles, and the distance between the point of entrance and the exit of the river is 4 miles. This lake is surrounded by lowlands overgrown with reeds, and it is so shallow that it often almost disappears in the hot summer months; hence it looks much more like a marsh than a lake. Nevertheless, it abounds in fish and therefore sustains great flocks of waterfowl.

In its middle course, between Lake Merom and the Sea of Galilee, the river traverses barely 11 miles of actual distance, but it descends 682 feet. While its current is sluggish as it enters Lake Merom, its bed soon narrows toward the south, and 2 miles beyond the exit, the stream rushes headlong between forbidding walls of rock. At this place it is spanned by Jacob's Bridge, built of great blocks of basalt, over which Jacob is said to have crossed when he returned from Mesopotamia (an error in tradition, see Genesis 32:22). From times immemorial this bridge has been used by caravans plodding their slow way from Damascus to the port of Akka (north of Mount Carmel).

The Sea of Galilee is also called Lake Gennesaret and Lake Tiberias, after a district and a city lying on its shores. In

the Old Testament, its name is Chinnereth. It is shaped somewhat like a pear, its greatest width being 7 miles, its length
nearly 13 miles. In depth it varies between 100 and 160 feet.
Its surface lies 682 feet below the level of the ocean.

Snuggling between the barren cliffs on the Sea of
Galilee's western shore lie a number of fertile valleys, where
great cities and villages once flourished (Korazin, Bethsaida,
Capernaum, Tiberias, Magdala). Today, however, this district
is almost desolate.

The eastern shore rises steeply, its frowning cliffs presenting an aspect of forbidding dreariness. In the days of
Christ, very few towns or villages could be found there. This
explains the deep anxiety of the disciples when Christ suggested that they should feed the multitudes that had assembled near the shore to hear him.

As a rule, the surface of the lake is smooth and quiet,
but at times fierce storms rush down upon it quite unexpectedly and threaten ships with disaster. Because the lake
is below sea level, the climate along its shores is almost
tropical, so that all fruits of the torrid zone may be grown.
The northern part of the lake abounds in fish to this day;
hence the name Bethsaida, "fish town." Along both shores
of the lake, hot water rises to the surface from springs, the
most important being found at Tiberias, where the tempera-
ture reaches 137 degrees Fahrenheit.

Having deposited the silt brought down from the mountains in the broad bowl of the Galilean Sea, the Jordan
begins its lower course with a rush of clear water, which it
then carries over a distance of 66 miles into the Dead Sea.
On this part of its journey, it descends 600 feet more, forming some 30 distinct falls and many rapids. After plunging
through a narrow gorge, it emerges into the fertile Plain of
the Jordan at Bethshean, where the fields of Jericho and of

Moab lie on opposite sides of the stream. This plain expands to a width of 14 miles. Even this delightful district, however, is mostly desolate today.

Every year on the Monday after Easter, many thousand pilgrims wend their way from Jerusalem through Jericho to the place where, as the local tradition declares, Jesus was baptized by John. There they bathe in the rushing stream and hope to obtain forgiveness of sins through this ceremony.

The Jordan is fed by numerous tributaries along its entire course and especially in its lower reaches. Most of these, however, carry no water except in the rainy season. Only two larger rivers, both coming from the east, flow into the Jordan steadily, the Hieromax (called Yarmuk in Arabic but not mentioned in the Bible) and the Jabbok. All these additions hardly suffice to offset the losses that the river suffers through evaporation. Saline springs, moreover, pour their waters into the Jordan along its entire lower course, so that the river finally carries a great amount of salt into the Dead Sea.

The Dead Sea is called Salt Sea by Moses, the East Sea by Ezekiel and Joel. Josephus names it the Asphalt Sea; the Talmud, Sea of Sodom; the Arabs, Sea of Lot (Bahr Lut). The name Dead Sea was introduced into Christian literature by Jerome.

This body of water measures 46 miles in length and has a width of 5 to 9 miles. Its surface lies 1,300 feet below sea level. Since it is completely surrounded by high cliffs, the great beat of the sun is held as in a deep basin, causing tremendous evaporation. While this explains why this land-locked sea should be salty, it must be added that rivulets of strong saline water coming from salt deposits flow into the Dead Sea from the southeast. In this manner the water has become so saturated with salt that its density prevents the swimmer from sinking.

The surroundings are barren and hideously desolate. There is no vegetation except in a few spots, where springs of sweet water flow. Rarely does a bird venture to wing its way across the waste of water, and no living thing has ever been found in it, not even the smallest mussel. Indeed, all fish that happen to be swept into the Dead Sea by the Jordan die in the briny waters. When the spring floods fill the bed of the Jordan to overflowing, the level of the Dead Sea also rises a few feet. As this surplus of water evaporates rapidly, a heavy crust of salt is deposited along the shore.

At both the northern and the southern ends of the sea, marshes are found, which exhale pestilential vapors, causing much sickness among the natives, even as far north as Jericho. Europeans almost invariably succumb to their effects if exposed.

Several explorers who dared to sail upon the Dead Sea paid for their venture with their lives.

Along the shores are large deposits of sulphur and asphaltic lime. Frequently, especially after an earthquake, the waves throw pieces of asphalt upon the shore. This is a reminder that a part of the Dead Sea covers the former Vale of Siddim, that delightful and promising district which Lot chose for his home, where in the days of Abraham, asphalt was taken from pits (Genesis 14:10; NIV, "tar pits"; KJV, "slime-pits").

Sodom and Gomorrah flourished in this garden of God until the Lord overturned them and destroyed them with fire and brimstone from heaven. On the eastern shore of the Dead Sea, somewhat below the center, a peninsula projects into its waters, and it is supposed that Sodom and Gomorrah lay to the south of this point, where the water, hardly more than a lagoon, nowhere reaches a depth of more than

15 feet. In the northern part of the sea, the depth frequently reaches 1,300 feet.

Besides the Jordan the Dead Sea has few tributaries of any size. Among them is the Kedron, which rises near Jerusalem, and the Cherith, beside which Elijah dwelt when he was being fed by the ravens.

150. The land east of the Jordan

The land east of the Jordan, extending from the foot of Mount Hermon to the brook Arnon, which empties into the Dead Sea, was chosen as a heritage by the tribes of Reuben and Gad, together with half the tribe of Manasseh. Manasseh dwelt in the north, Reuben in the south, and Gad between the two, the three districts roughly corresponding to the three divisions west of the Jordan, Galilee, Samaria, and Judea. South of Reuben dwelt the Moabites. Later, all this country was called Perea, that is, the land beyond, from the point of view of those who lived west of the Jordan, but this name is often used for the southern portion of the district alone.

From the north almost to the Dead Sea, the banks of the Jordan rise up steeply in rugged cliffs. In the north there are several great plateaus, which are displaced by hill forma-tions in the southernmost part. Geographically, the district is divided into three parts, Bashan (the Hauran), Gilead, and the mountain country of Abarim.

The Bashan of the Bible, now known as the Hauran, is bounded by Mount Hermon on the north, by the desert on the east, by the Jordan and the Sea of Galilee on the west, and on the south by the river Hieromax (or Yarmuk). Rising steeply from the Valley of the Jordan, the hills of Bashan merge into an immense plateau, which extends far to the east and is there enclosed by the great Hauran mountains. As the underlying rock, which frequently crops out from the

175

surface, consists of black basalt, the general appearance of the country is somewhat dreary. But the numerous deposits of lava, which have crumbled in the course of time, offer many opportunities for successful farming.

At the time of Christ, Bashan was divided into five districts, the names of which are partly used by the Arabs today. Gaulanitis (in Arabic, Golan) was situated along the upper and middle courses of the Jordan. To the northeast of it lay the province of Iturea. The northeastern part of Bashan formed the province of Trachonitis, probably identical with the biblical Argob and known to the Arabs as El-Lejah. There King Og was defeated at the city of Edrei. South of Trachonitis lay Batanea. The remaining section, enclosed by the other four and bounded by the Hieromax on the south, was called Auranitis (from Hauran).

In the New Testament, a large part of Perea was called Decapolis, the Ten Cities. We are unable to define the precise limits of this section because the list of the ten cities varies in the records, and most of them were afterward destroyed by the Jews. The greater number of them undoubtedly lay in Bashan, but Damascus also belonged to the group. These were heathen cities, established in the midst of a Jewish population, and were protected in their independence by the Roman government.

The Mountains of Gilead rise south of the Hieromax. This district is divided into almost equal parts by the river Jabbok. Its southern boundary is formed by the brook of Heshbon, which flows into the Jordan near the mouth of that river. (Note that the name Gilead is used in a wider sense in Deuteronomy 34:1.) While basaltic rock prevails in Bashan, where the people must fashion their building material most laboriously, Gilead has much white limestone, which is so easily worked that the inhabitants often prefer to live in caves cut into the living rock (troglodytes).

Between the brook of Heshbon and the rivulet of Arnon, we find Mount Abarim, formerly the dwelling place of the tribe of Reuben. This is a fertile but treeless plateau, marked to this day with the ruins of ancient cities. In the eastern part of the plateau stands Mount Nebo, a peak of the range of Pisgah, from the summit of which Moses was permitted to look across the Jordan into the Promised Land before he died.

151. Climate and products

Since it is situated within 32 degrees of the equator, Palestine, generally speaking, enjoys a warm climate. Winter is hardly more than a rainy season. Though snow sometimes falls even around Jerusalem, it never stays on the ground.

The Bible often mentions the two rainy periods that are of vital importance for Palestinian agriculture. The early rain, which comes in autumn and is so called because the Jewish year begins about that time, is needed for the winter grains, such as wheat and barley. The latter rain is expected in spring, shortly before the summer harvest, and moistens the soil for the summer crops, such as durra, beans, tobacco, and cotton.

Because the various cities stood on different levels, harvesttime varied considerably. As a rule, the people around Jericho threshed their wheat when this crop was still green in the fields near Hebron and on Mount Carmel.

The remarkable promises that God had made through Moses concerning the fertility of the Promised Land and the future prosperity of the Jewish people (Deuteronomy 8:7-10; 11:10,11) were fulfilled to the letter. When David ordered the people to be numbered, Joab discovered that Israel could assemble 800,000 valiant men and Judah 500,000. These figures signify that a total population of 6,500,000 souls was supported by the small country. In later days even more people dwelt there.

In the old days, the soil of Palestine produced heavy crops of various grains, such as wheat (durra), spelt, millet, and lentils. Flax and cotton supplied material for garments, which, however, were too costly for the common people. The gardens were luxurious, with many varieties of vegetables for the tables. The vine, the fig tree, the date palm, and the olive tree bore their fruit in season. Valuable gums were procured from such shrubs as the balsam and the myrrh. The Plain of Sharon was noted for its great wealth of flowers, but other parts of the country were not less resplendent with bloom at certain seasons. Special mention could be made of the rose of Jericho, also called the resurrection plant. The trees that furnished most building materials were the cedar, the cypress, the terebinth, and the oak.

From the catalog of clean and unclean beasts (Deuteronomy 14; Leviticus 11), it appears that the country abounded in animal life. The desert places were infested by such carnivorous animals as lions, bears, panthers, foxes, jackals, and hyenas. Of domestic animals the Bible mentions sheep, goats, cattle (the bulls of Bashan, Psalm 22:12), asses (besides the wild ass), and horses (these latter, however, were usually imported from Egypt).

The south wind frequently carried swarms of locusts up from the Arabian Desert, which fell as a plague upon the fields. Deliverance came by the east wind, which would brush the pests into the sea. Bees found an abundance of food on the flowering fields, so that honey truly flowed in the valleys and glens (1 Samuel 14:25,26).

152. Sinai Peninsula

We turn for a moment to the Sinai Peninsula, where the people of Israel spent the 40 years of their sojourn in the desert. It lies to the southwest of Palestine and projects into the Red Sea like a broad wedge, forming the gulfs of Suez and Akabah (the ancients called them the Gulf of Hierapolis and the Aelanitic Gulf). In days of old, the peninsula was called Arabia Petraea, after the city of Petra, which lay near its northeastern edge.

The people of Israel entered this peninsula after crossing the upper end of the Red Sea and journeyed southward along its western coast, until they reached the mountainous country of the southern point. There loom the naked, forbidding peaks of Horeb, among them Mount Sinai, noted for being the place where God proclaimed the Law. Explorers have not been able to identify this peak with certainty. Some decide in favor of the height called Jebel Musa by the Arabs; others prefer to ascribe the honor to Jebel Serbal or to the peak called Ras-es-Sufsafeh.

From Sinai the people turned to the northeast, journeying along the edge of the Desert of Paran, which occupies the middle portion of the peninsula and is called El-Tih, that is, the Wandering, by the Arabs. Then the Israelites finally reached the Desert of Zin, the Arabah, a narrow strip extending from the Dead Sea to the Gulf of Akaba.

The last 38 years of desert life for the people of Israel were probably spent in this northeastern portion of the peninsula, but it is impossible to identify their various stopping places. No one can determine the routes along which they wandered. To the east from the Desert of Zin, in the land of Seir, or Moab, lies Mount Hor, where Aaron died and was buried.

The peninsula contains about 11,200 square miles. It is now inhabited primarily by several thousand Bedouins, whose herds of sheep and goats find fair pasture and a large number of springs on the plateau, to which they are driven in summer. The valleys between the mountains facing the coast are also clothed in green. In some places even gardens and groves of date palms are found. Feiran, the largest oasis, lies in the northwestern part; it seems quite probable that this was the Elim of the Bible (Exodus 16:1).

E. Weights and measures of the Bible

153. General character

In many cases it is not possible to express the value of the biblical weights and measures in the units with which we are familiar. Exactness of measurement as we know it was and is foreign to the Oriental mind. Thus, of the eight "ells" described in the buildings of ancient Egypt, no two are exactly alike. Moreover, none of the ancient Hebrew standards of measure, a few coins excepted, have survived the ravages of time. We also know that the same measure had entirely different values at different times, because the Jews, adopting the measures of the nations among which they lived, applied to them the names of those Jewish measures which most closely approached them in value. Hence the statements given below must always be taken as tentative only, and they will not always be found to agree with information given in other books.

154. Measures of time

It is uncertain whether the Jews in Old Testament days always divided the day exactly into a certain number of hours. The sundial of Ahaz, however, seems to indicate that this way of dividing the day was known (Isaiah 38:8). From

Genesis 1:5 and Leviticus 23:32, it appears that the day was reckoned from one sunset to the next one. When periods are indicated, parts of days must be counted as full days (1 Samuel 30:12,13; Matthew 27:63,64) and parts of years as full years (Jeremiah 25:1). The night seems to have been divided into three watches: the first watch (Lamentations 2:19), the middle watch, and the morning watch (Exodus 14:24).

Under the Roman dominion, the Jews adopted the Roman division of time. The day, divided into 12 hours, was reckoned from sunrise to sunset, without regard to the season of the year. Hence the hours were slightly longer in summer than in winter. The night had four watches, each of approximately 4 hours.

The Jewish year began in the month of Ethanim (or Tisri), its first days coinciding with the last days of our September or the first days of our October. Each month began with the new moon, and thus the year was actually a lunar year, shorter by several days than the solar year. Hence an extra month was added about every three years. This manner of computation renders it almost impossible to make Jewish dates agree exactly with our calendar.

Just as each week had a day of rest, the seventh, so every seventh year was counted as a year of rest, the Sabbath Year, in which the fields were not to be cultivated (Leviticus 25:2-7,20-22). After each cycle of seven "weeks" of years (49 years), the 50th year brought the Great Jubilee, for which special ordinances governing social and civil life had been given (Leviticus 25:8-16).

155. Linear measure

Small units of linear measure were taken from certain parts of the human body, such as finger's breadth (Jeremiah 52:21); handbreadth (1 Kings 7:26); span (Isaiah 40:12, KJV); and ell, or cubit. The first two of these terms require no explanation. A span is the distance between the point of the thumb and the points of the fingers extended opposite to the thumb. An ell, or cubit, was measured from the tip of the middle finger to the elbow; hence its length varied between 18 and 22 inches among different people.

The following larger units of measurement are mentioned in the Bible: rod (Ezekiel 40:5), stadium (Luke 24:13; KJV, "furlong"; NIV footnote), mile (Matthew 5:41), day's travel (Luke 2:44), Sabbath Day's walk (Acts 1:12), orguia (Acts 27:28; KJV, "fathom"; NIV footnote). A reed was six cubits long. The Greek term *stadium* represented a measure of 607 feet, according to Roman notation. The mile of the Bible is undoubtedly the Roman mile, 1,000 double paces, about 5,000 feet. A day's travel naturally varied in length and probably never exceeded 30 miles. A Sabbath Day's walk was defined in the traditions of the elders as a distance of not more than 2,000 paces beyond the walls of Jerusalem. An orguia, a nautical measure, was almost identical with the fathom used by modern seafarers; it was about 6 feet long.

Table of Linear Measures				
1 finger	= $^7/_8$ inch			
1 hand	= 4 fingers	= 3$^1/_2$ inches		
1 span	= 3 hands	= 12 fingers	= 10$^7/_8$ inches	
1 cubit, or ell	= 2 spans	= 6 hands	= 24 fingers	= 21 inches
1 reed	= 6 cubits	= 144 fingers	= 126 inches	
1 stadium (KJV "furlong")	= 607 feet			
1 mile	= 5,000 feet			
1 day's travel	= 20 to 30 miles			
1 Sabbath Day's walk	= 2,000 paces			
1 orguia (KJV "fathom")	= 6 feet			

156. Dry measure

The smallest unit of dry measure was the cab (2 Kings 6:25), which amounted to a little more than a quart. A seah (KJV, "measure," Genesis 18:6; 1 Samuel 25:18; 2 Kings 7:1,16,18; 1 Kings 18:32) was about equal to our peck. Three seahs made 1 ephah, which therefore contained about 3 pecks. The ephah also was part of a decimal system, for it held 10 omers (Exodus 16:36), and 10 ephahs made 1 homer (Leviticus 27:16). A cor (also "measure," KJV, 1 Kings 4:22; Luke 16:7) contained as much as a homer, that is, between 7 and 8 bushels. In the New Testament, the Roman term *modius* occurs (KJV, "bushel"; NIV, "bowl," as in Matthew 5:15; Mark 4:21; Luke 11:33); this was about 1 pint less than 1 peck.

Table of Dry Measures				
1 cab	= 1⅓ quarts			
1 seah	= 6 cabs	= 1 peck		
1 omer	= 2⅖ quarts			
1 ephah	= 3 seahs	= 18 cabs	= 10 omers	= 3 pecks
1 homer, or cor	= 10 ephahs	= 100 omers	= 7½ bushels	

157. Liquid measure

The largest unit of liquid measure was called a bath (1 Kings 7:26); in cubic contents it was about equal to 1 ephah and held between 7 and 8 gallons (Luke 16:6 footnote). The 6th part of a bath was called a hin (Exodus 29:40), and the 12th part of a hin was a log (Leviticus 14:10).

Table of Liquid Measures		
1 log = ²⁄₃ pints		
1 hin = 12 logs	= 8 pints	
1 bath = 6 hins	= 72 logs	= 6 gallons

158. Weights

The greatest measure of weight was called a kikkar (translated "talent," as in Exodus 25:39), which was probably not always a definite quantity. According to 2 Kings 5:23, it was a sufficient burden for one bearer. From Exodus 38:25,26 it seems to appear that a kikkar contained 3,000 shekels. Moreover, the kikkar was always divided into 60 minas (KJV, "pound," as in 1 Kings 10:17), making 1 mina the equivalent of 50 shekels.

There were three kinds of kikkar, varying in value. The kikkar of silver weighed about 117 pounds troy. Its shekels were the shekels of the sanctuary (Exodus 38:25), having a value of about 50 cents each. The kikkar of gold (Exodus 25:39) weighed about 131 pounds troy. Its shekels were worth about 10 dollars each. The kikkar of the king (2 Samuel 14:26) weighed about 158 pounds troy, making its shekel worth about 75 cents. Actual monetary values today might vary considerably.

Luke 19:13-25 also uses minas (KJV, "pounds"). In John 12:3 the term translated "pint" (KJV, "pound") comes from the Greek term *litra,* which was about equivalent to our pound (John 19:39).

The word *talent* (Matthew 18:24; 25:14-30), of Greek derivation, also denotes a certain weight, though it is uncertain whether the writers of the New Testament followed the Greek or the Syrian usage of the term. According to the

Greek valuation, a talent of silver was worth several thousand dollars, whereas the Syrian talent of silver amounted to about one-fifth as much.

To understand why the units of weight are described chiefly in terms of monetary values, remember that the use of weights as applied to commodities other than valuable metals was a secondary development. This also explains the fact that such minute weights as the gerah (that is, "bean," about ¹/₂ dram avoirdupois; the 20th part of a shekel, Exodus 30:13) and the bekah (¹/₂ shekel, weighing about a quarter of an ounce, Genesis 24:22) were definitely adopted at a very early date. Even the ancient Orientals felt the need of exact measurement when giving or receiving precious metals.

159. Money and coins

The use of coined money seems to have been unknown among the Jews until their return from the Babylonian captivity. Until then it had been customary to weigh the precious metals when buying or selling. This, however, does not imply that the ancient nations had no medium of exchange similar to our money. It would seem that pieces of gold and silver of definite weight were freely circulated. Such money certainly was used by Abraham when he bought the cave of Machpelah from Ephron. And the wedge of gold that tempted Achan (Joshua 7:21), as also the piece of silver that Saul offered the prophet (1 Samuel 9:8), were almost certainly recognized as pieces of money.

In earlier days the precious metals seem to have been worked into rings of certain weight, which were then used as money (compare the gifts that Eliezer gave to Rebekah, Genesis 24:22, and the "money pouches" belonging to Joseph's brothers, Genesis 42:35). The Egyptian monuments furnish ample evidence that such forms of money were made and circulated in the land of the Nile.

The first coins (darics) are mentioned in 1 Chronicles 29:7 as a part of the treasures that David gathered for the purpose of building the temple. The same coins are referred to as drachmas in Ezra 2:69. These were gold pieces of Persian origin, and it may well be assumed that Persian silver coins came into circulation at the same time. Simon Maccabaeus was authorized in the year 139 B.C. to stamp coins bearing his own image (1 Maccabees 15:6). Soon after this, copper coins, representing fractional parts of the shekel, began to be circulated.

In the days of Christ, the Jews used coins of gold, silver, copper, and bronze, some bearing a Jewish stamp, but most of them of Greek or Roman origin. The smallest coin was called a lepton (KJV, "mite," Mark 12:42; Luke 12:59; 21:2), worth a fraction of a cent, coined by the Jews because only Jewish money was accepted in the temple. Two lepta made 1 quadrans, the fourth part of the Roman *as* ("farthing," Matthew 5:26; Mark 12:42). The as, or *assarion* (NIV, "penny"; KJV, "farthing" in Matthew 10:29; Luke 12:6), was worth about 14 leptas.

The lepton, quadrans, and as were made of copper or bronze. Ten *asses* made 1 *denarius* (KJV, "penny," Matthew 18:28; 22:19). The denarius was a Roman silver coin, bearing the image of the emperor and known as the tribute money. Together with the Greek *stater*, it formed the bulk of the money that circulated in Palestine. The stater ("four-drachma coin," Matthew 17:27) was a Greek silver coin of about the same value as 1 Jewish shekel. But in Matthew 17:27 the Greek name is probably given to a Jewish coin, called didrachma in verse 24 and valued at $^1/_2$ shekel, because the Lord is speaking of the contribution to the temple treasury, which amounted to $\frac{1}{2}$ shekel for every Jew. In Luke 15:8 the "silver coin" is 1 Greek *drachma,* which was of the same value as 1 Roman denarius. The same translation is used for *argyrion* in Matthew 26:15 and Acts 19:19. In the first case, argyrion probably denotes the Jewish shekel; in the second, the Roman denarius.

Table of Money		
1 lepton (KJV, "mite")	= a fraction of a cent	
1 quadrans (KJV, "farthing")	= 2 lepta	
1 as (assarion, "penny")	= 4 quadrans	
1 denarius	= 16 asses	= a laborer's daily wage

PART TWO

The New Testament

Chapter 1
The New Testament in General

A. *Origin of the books of the New Testament*

160. The transition period

Our Lord Jesus based his whole message upon the Word as written in the Old Testament and was always eager to explain its significance, publicly or privately. When the messengers of John the Baptist asked him, "Are you the one who was to come?" he called their attention to a prophetic word, the fulfillment of which was taking place before their eyes (Matthew 11:2-6). At Nazareth Jesus preached from a text taken from Isaiah (Luke 4:16-21). On several occasions he expounded to his disciples all the Scriptures in Moses and the Prophets concerning himself (Luke 24:27,44-47). He reminded Nicodemus of the bronze serpent and rebuked him because he, a learned scribe, failed to understand the teachings of Jesus despite his knowledge of the Old Testament (John 3:10,14). In fact, as we have pointed out repeatedly, the witness of Christ is an irrefutable proof of the divine origin of the Old Testament.

The apostles, having been eyewitnesses of the things that they were to proclaim and having been schooled in the understanding of the Old Testament by the Lord himself, needed no new writings on which to base their discourses. If it became necessary to prove to the Jews that the old prophetical promises had been fulfilled in Christ and his kingdom, they quoted the words of the prophets and expounded them in the light of the fulfillment (Acts 2:16-21, 25-31; Christ's exhortation of the twelve apostles, 3:22; 17:2,3; and so on). When called upon to bear witness to Jesus' life, suffering, and death, the apostles spoke confidently, as those who had heard and seen, and through the power of the divine Spirit, their testimony was effective as truth infallible.

161. The period of writing

While Jesus lived among men and preached the gospel in its new development, there was no need of written records. For this reason we possess no written testimony from the hand of Jesus. A certain epistle that he is said to have written to Abgarus, governor of Edessa in Syria, is the work of a forger of the third century.

Again, as long as the apostles could carry on their work without any restraint and labored in the small circuit of the first churches, which they were able to visit personally at short intervals, no one felt the immediate need of new writings.

But this state of things could not last. Within 30 years after the ascension of Christ, in the first years of the sixth decade of the first century, such a change had come over the outward circumstances under which the apostles labored that the personal visits of the great teachers necessarily became more infrequent, and it even was apparent that they might cease altogether very soon. Churches had been founded far from Jerusalem and scattered abroad over large portions of three continents. Many of them could only be reached by letter. Christians everywhere in the Roman Empire were filled with forebodings of the approaching cruel persecutions, and it could be foreseen that the leaders of the Christian church would probably be among the first victims.

Under these circumstances the Holy Spirit prompted the apostles to write down what was to serve the church to the end of the world as her great treasure of divine truth, as a source of saving knowledge, and as a guide for faith and life. Knowing that they were writing the truth of God, the apostles expected the churches to accept their teachings as given by divine revelation, in which even single words were not brought forth by human wisdom but by the inspiration of the Holy Spirit. Read 1 Corinthians chapter 2, for example, where Paul is speaking of all apostles!

B. Classification of apostolic writings

162. General character

Though the gospel is the one great message of the New Testament, it is never preached alone in the New Testament. As the gospel cannot be understood or appreciated by man unless the law has brought him to a true knowledge of sin, Christ and his apostles always preached the law of God without modification when it was needed. On the other hand, there is no book in the New Testament that contains only law. Everywhere the gospel shines forth in its saving glory (compare section 3).

163. Differences

Divine truth is presented in various forms also in the New Testament. Therefore we categorize the apostolic writings in three great classes. There are 5 historical books, 21 doctrinal books, and 1 prophetical book.

191

Setting these books side by side with those of the Old Testament, we find that the doctrinal books of the New Testament correspond roughly with the poetical books of the Old. Although it is quite reasonable to conclude from Colossians 3:16 and Ephesians 5:19 that New Testament songs and hymns soon made their appearance in the churches and were sung in public worship, there is no indication whatever that the apostles, following the example of the old prophets, composed such songs under the inspiration of the Holy Spirit.

The doctrinal books were written as the needs of the churches or of single people seemed to demand that the apostles should set forth the Christian doctrine in the form of epistles, or letters.

The historical books of the New Testament tell the story of the life and work of Jesus Christ from his birth to his ascension and then describe how the Christian church was spread among Jews and Gentiles until near the time of Jerusalem's destruction.

Prophecy concerning the earthly destinies of the church is quite a secondary feature in the New Testament, because the visible form of the church is now no longer defined by divine law. Nevertheless, God has given us one book in which the future of the church unto the end of days is set forth at length, though altogether in symbols and visions.

Summary of classification

I. Historical books: The gospels according to Saint Matthew, Saint Mark, Saint Luke, and Saint John; the Acts of the Apostles.

II. Doctrinal books: Epistles of Paul to the Romans, Corinthians (2), Galatians, Ephesians, Philippians, Colossians, Thessalonians (2), Timothy (2), Titus, and Philemon; of Peter (2); and of John (3); plus the epis-

tle to the Hebrews; the epistle of James; and the epistle of Jude.

III. Prophetical book: The Revelation of Saint John.

C. *Writers of the New Testament*

164. Persons of the writers

With the exception of Paul and probably Luke, the writers of the New Testament were not learned men, but they came from the common people. They were called to their exalted office by Christ himself or were subsequently moved by the Holy Spirit to record the divine truth revealed to them, as his penmen.

Matthew, the apostle and evangelist, was called from a tax collector's booth by Jesus. Peter, John, James, and Jude were natives of despised Galilee, and we know definitely that John and Peter were fishermen before they were called by the Lord. Of Mark and Luke we know very little. They most likely did not belong to the upper class, though we know that Luke had been trained as a physician. (Read and apply 1 Corinthians 1:26-29.) Paul alone was a highly educated man and therefore surpasses all his fellow workers in intellectual achievement.

In the writings of the evangelists and apostles, the practiced eye will notice many evidences of the great differences in the men's characters and training. There, as in the case of the prophets of the Old Testament, such personal peculiarities could well exist without casting any doubt as to the divine inspiration of any of these writers.

165. Agreement in doctrine

Because we accept as divine truth what Paul says of himself and his apostolic colaborers in 1 Corinthians 2:7-13, we know that they all stood equally under the inspiration of

193

the Holy Spirit. Therefore neither their historical nor their doctrinal statements can possibly contain evidences of disagreement. Every careful student of the New Testament will admit that there are certain statements difficult to harmonize, especially in the gospels. We feel sure, however, that we fail to see the agreement only because we do not quite understand the statements themselves or because we are not sufficiently informed concerning all the circumstances involved. In fact, the information brought to light by historical research has tended to corroborate the accounts given in the New Testament in the most remarkable manner.

Much less will any Christian be disturbed by the fanciful theory of rationalistic critics, who maintain that the church passed through a long period of doctrinal dissension in which Paul and Peter antagonized one another. Such critics suggest that Paulinism was liberal, while Petrinism was narrow-minded and Judaistic; that the epistles of the two apostles were written as campaign literature; and that the struggle was brought to an end at last by various compromises. No one who believes the New Testament was given by divine revelation will be able to discover any traces of such ungodly and unholy strife in the beautiful epistles of these two great men. Criticism of the kind just described merely reveals the hostile unbelief of its authors and fails in its attempts to discredit the Scriptures.

166. The date

All the sacred writers of the New Testament finished their labors before the end of the first century after the birth of Christ. The leaders of negative criticism have not only attempted to show from alleged internal evidence (that is, peculiarities of style and diction and so-called contradictions) that the books of the New Testament are not genuine, but they also have tried to demonstrate that these writings were issued much later than the apostolic era. It would be unprofitable to discuss their so-called arguments in this connection. That they disagree among themselves stamps them as false witnesses, who speak lies knowingly.

We have ample historical proof that the books of the New Testament were in existence before the year 100. The following are some witnesses:

(1) The writings of the apostolic fathers, pupils of the apostles, were issued between the years 107 and 175 of the Christian era. They contain many allusions to, and actual quotations from, almost all the books of the New Testament. To this interesting literature belong certain epistles of Ignatius, bishop of Antioch, and of Polycarp, bishop of Smyrna, both pupils of the apostle John. The former died in the year 109, the latter in 155, both as martyrs of their faith. While such men lived, no deceiver could have successfully published forgeries under the name of the apostles.

(2) Other fathers of the church, who were contemporaries of the apostolic fathers and some of whom were their pupils, quote the New Testament in corroboration of their doctrines. We mention Justin Martyr (died at Rome in 166); Irenaeus, who was bishop of Lyons in Gaul and a pupil of Polycarp (died a martyr in 202); and Tertullian, a presbyter of Carthage in northern Africa who later joined the heretical sect of the Montanists and died in 220.

(3) Before the year 177, Tatianus, a pupil of Ignatius, compiled the first harmony of the gospels, that is, a book in which the four gospels are woven together into one continuous narrative. The importance of this witness is that the gospel according to Saint John, probably one of the last books of the Bible to be written, must have been common

property of the church for many years before Tatianus began his task.

(4) Even some heretics of the second century must here serve unwittingly as witnesses of the truth. Thus Marcion, who was active about the year 150, accepted the gospel according to Saint Luke and ten Pauline epistles as sources of Christian truth and rejected the remaining books of the New Testament. He had not found them to be spurious, but he believed that their authors had fallen back into Judaism, even though they were apostles. He, therefore, considered the writing genuine but disagreed with the doctrine contained in the books. Wouldn't he have denied that the apostles had written such things if the least doubt had existed in his day concerning the apostolic authorship?

(5) The flood of apocryphal books written in the second century furnishes a similar, indirect proof. In them the narrative of the genuine gospels was expanded by copious fantastic additions. How could we explain that the writers of these worthless stories expected them to be received as supplements to the apostolic narratives if the latter had not been known and received as genuine long before?

In short, it can be shown that no book of any heathen writer can boast of so many witnesses to its authenticity as the books of the New Testament.

D. The canon of the New Testament

167. Distribution

The circumstances under which the single books of the New Testament were written make it plain that not only the letters of the apostles but also the gospels and the book of Acts at first found only a small circle of readers. But even then the apostles began to urge a wider distribution of their writings. It is reasonable to conclude from Colossians 4:16, for example, that Paul would encourage all his churches to get copies of his epistles. The success of this effort is attested by Peter (2 Peter 3:15,16), who appears to take it for granted that all the Pauline epistles and the "other Scriptures" were known to his readers.

The distribution of the apostolic writings was promoted by the close communion established among the various churches through the visits both of the apostles and of other members. We may well assume that Christians generally were eager to acquire all obtainable sources of inspired information. A stranger could hardly offer a more welcome and valuable gift to his Christian host than a copy of one of the gospels or of an epistle, brought from his home church. Furthermore, skillful copyists, who made it their business to reproduce literary works, were at that time to be found in every larger city of the Roman Empire.

168. Collections

We have indisputable evidence that collections containing all or most of the books of the New Testament were actually in use near the middle of the second century. In 1750 a most valuable document was discovered in the Ambrosian Library at Milan by Ludovico Antonio Muratori, after whom it is called the Muratorian Canon. This manuscript, written in very poor Latin, and somewhat mutilated at that, contains a list of those New Testament books which were acknowledged as genuine and canonical in the church at Rome. As far as the record is undamaged and decipherable, it mentions four gospels, the Acts, 16 epistles, and Revelation. According to all indications, the list was written at Rome about the year 160, demonstrating that Rome possessed an almost complete collection of the apostolic writings in the middle of the second century.

The Itala, a Latin version of the Bible, carries us still further back, probably before the middle of the second century. Tertullian, who died in 220, quotes from it more freely than from other versions that he possessed, because it was the best known. Since the various writings of Tertullian exhibit quotations from nearly every book of the New Testament according to the Itala, the collection of the books must have been completed very much earlier.

The third document of importance in this connection is the ancient Syriac version called Peshito. There was an early need for this collection because Syria soon could boast large congregations of Christians. Some scholars maintain that the Peshito was completed before the year 150. It contains all the books of the New Testament except 2 and 3 John, 2 Peter, Jude, and Revelation.

169. Degrees of canonicity

Almost from the very first, some circles of the Christian church wavered in their acceptance of certain apostolic epistles and of Revelation. Eusebius, bishop of Caesarea (born 260, died 340), addressed this issue. While traveling through the countries along the eastern shore of the Mediterranean, he collected the material for his great work that earned him the honorary title "Father of Church History." In his book he declares that according to his observations, the books of the New Testament as we now have them are of two kinds. One kind he calls homologumena, that is to say, those which were universally accepted; the others are antilegomena, that is to say, they were spoken against in some churches because of certain doubts concerning their apostolic origin. He found the following books were homologumena: the four gospels, Acts, the Pauline epistles, the epistle to the Hebrews, 1 Peter, 1 John, and Revelation. Second Peter, 2 and 3 John, Jude, and James were antilegomena.

Though the canon of the New Testament was thereafter defined by some church councils (for instance, at Hippo, in Africa, in 393), it is obvious that the historical fact reported by Eusebius cannot be discarded by an ecclesiastical decree. Consequently we preserve the distinction between the homologumena and the antilegomena (or protocanonical [first] and deuterocanonical [second] books) as a matter of record. Nevertheless, we receive the latter, though of "the second degree of canonicity," as inspired apostolic writings because it appears that the doubts concerning their origin were not sufficiently substantiated.

E. The language of the New Testament

170. Native language of the Jews

When the Jewish people returned from the Babylonian captivity, the generation that had been born in the years of the exile had fully learned the language of the conquerors and used it in their daily life. We read of this transition from one language to another in Nehemiah 8:8, where we are told that when the Law was read to the people in Hebrew, the priests gave an interpretation, so that the hearers might understand. In this way the Hebrew language of the Old Testament fell into complete disuse in the course of time, giving way to the Aramaic, or Syro-Chaldean, dialect.

Aramaic, then, was the language of the Jewish people in the time of Christ. Though we cannot show that our Lord used it exclusively when he spoke, we feel safe in saying that he used it extensively. This explains why the writers of the gospels quote some sayings of the Lord in Aramaic, sometimes adding a translation for the benefit of their Greek readers, as in Mark 5:41; 7:34. From Acts 21:40 and 22:2, we learn that the apostles also used Aramaic when addressing Jewish gatherings.

171. Use of the Greek language

The most important and lasting result of the victorious campaign that brought all Asia under the scepter of Alexander the Great was the introduction of the Greek language among the conquered nations. In the time of Christ, Greek was spoken in all parts of the great Roman Empire, and in Palestine even the uneducated people understood it well. This appears from Acts 22:2, where we are told that the assembled Jews were favorably impressed when Paul addressed them in Hebrew, that is, in their Aramaic mother tongue, instead of using Greek.

It is certain that many Greeks lived in Palestine. The Decapolis, the "Ten Cities," were probably inhabited by Greeks exclusively. Thus Jesus must have had frequent opportunity to use that language. He certainly did so during his trial before Pilate. Among the apostles there surely was not a single one who was unfamiliar with Greek, though they naturally spoke it with a Jewish accent.

172. Sacred language of the New Testament

A book written in those days, even if designed for Jewish readers exclusively, fulfilled its purpose perfectly if the author used the Greek language. This is evident from the Greek Apocrypha of the Old Testament, which found interested readers among the Jews for whom they were written. Consequently there was no urgent reason for any book of the New Testament to be written in Hebrew or Aramaic. Moreover, as the New Testament was to be the source of true religious knowledge for all mankind and not for the Jews alone, the divine plan of salvation required that all its books should be written in the language universally spoken at that time. Therefore we find that all the inspired writers of the New Testament employed the Greek language when they began to write under the inspiration of the Holy Spirit, so that their books became immediately available for practically all the world.

Chapter 2
The Historical Books of the New Testament

A. General remarks concerning the gospels and Acts

173. Titles and order

Though it is hardly probable that the titles of the gospels and Acts were given by their inspired authors, the origin of the titles dates back to the earliest days. The four narratives of the life of Jesus Christ were called gospels because they proclaim, in historical form, the blessed news of the incarnation of the Son of God and of the completion of his redemptive work. We call them the gospels according to Saint Matthew, according to Saint Mark, and so on but not in the sense that these books were written by someone else according to the tradition of the persons named. The title means that the one gospel of the advent and the work of Jesus Christ was written by Matthew, Mark, Luke, and John, according to the manner in which they were inspired by the Holy Spirit.

Acts, which was recorded by Saint Luke as a continuation of his gospel story (Acts 1:1), tells us how the Christian church was established and spread by the activity of the apostles, especially Peter and Paul.

The order in which the gospels are placed in our Bibles is also based on ancient tradition, which was old even in the days of Irenaeus (who died in 202). He says that Matthew wrote first, then Mark, then Luke, and finally John. It is true that other writers of that period give the order as follows: Matthew, John, Mark, Luke. This, however, is not meant to indicate the historical succession of the books.

This arrangement places side by side the two evangelists who were apostles and the other two who were apostolic men, that is, disciples of the apostles.

174. Independence of the holy writers

Though it is certain that the later evangelists knew the writings of their predecessors, it is just as certain that none of them was dependent upon any other person but that each one wrote according to a definite plan and for a definite circle of readers. Since all four evangelists wrote under the same guidance and inspiration of the Holy Spirit, it goes without saying that not one of them had need to use the work of his predecessor or set out to remodel and improve it. In our subsequent discussion of the single gospels, we shall learn that each evangelist had in mind a definite audience and molded his presentation according to its needs.

We find, accordingly, that the gospels, though similar in a general way, each have their own distinct character, a fact that was always recognized by the church. Matthew preaches Jesus as the Messiah in whom all promises of the Old Testament were fulfilled. Mark exhibits him as the Savior from all evil, who demonstrated his almighty power in his miracles. Luke emphasizes that Jesus is the Savior of all mankind. John sets out to identify him as the Son of God, mighty in words and deeds. The understanding of these distinctive features has always been so definite that from the very earliest days, pious men declared that the fourfold gospel was a realization of a wonderful vision recorded by Ezekiel (1:3-21). To Matthew they assigned the figure of a man or an angel; to Mark, that of a lion; to Luke, that of an ox; and to John, that of an eagle.

Besides these general characteristics, each evangelist has his own minor peculiarities and mannerisms of diction and style, which show that he wrote quite independently of any other author.

In the first three gospels, there is an obvious similarity of arrangement and of expression, which has caused them to be grouped together under the name of the synoptic gospels, that is, gospels that treat the story of Christ from the same, or a similar, point of view. This similarity, however, may be explained quite naturally. Among Oriental peoples it was and still is customary for pupils to commit to memory the statements of their teachers word for word, the teacher assisting in this process by frequent repetitions of his sayings. The disciples of Jesus undoubtedly acquired much of their knowledge of his teachings precisely in this manner. Afterward, when they told and retold the wonderful story of his life, not only in the Christian churches but also to those whom they tried to win over to the faith, naturally their narratives assumed not only a definite but a similar form, to which they also adhered when, moved by God's Spirit, they made their written record.

175. True authors

All efforts of modern negative criticism to discredit the genuineness of the gospels have failed most decidedly. With great effort rationalistic scholars have built up an artful tissue of lies with which to dispose of forever the glory of the divine revelation. Their testimony, however, fails to agree, so they suffer the fate common to all false witnesses. One will say that the first three evangelists were dependent upon some written document that they call the Urevangelium, that is, the original gospel, of which, however, nobody has ever been able to produce even a trace. Another one will say that Matthew furnished copy for Mark and Luke. A third maintains that Matthew and Luke were mere followers of Mark.

A fourth one will argue most learnedly that Luke was the one who wrote first and furnished a pattern for Matthew and Mark to follow. Their views obviously clash because they are based largely upon imagination.

But such scholars agree, in the fundamental principle of rationalism, that the evangelists recorded not the revelation of God but their own ideas of what this revelation ought to have been. The only statement of Scripture that seems to favor their general proposition, the preface of Saint Luke's gospel (1:1-4), does indeed show that many written records of the life of Jesus were actually in existence at the time, but it surely does not imply that the evangelists had need of such sources when they began to write under the inspiration of the Holy Spirit.

176. General contents

The story of the life of Jesus is told with practically the same arrangement of the material in all the four gospels. Each of them may be divided into three large sections: (1) the historical introduction; (2) the story of the prophetical work of Christ; (3) the narrative of Jesus' suffering, death, and resurrection.

To the historical introduction belong all passages telling of the birth and the work of John, the herald of Christ, together with the information given concerning the birth and childhood of Jesus. This section is well elaborated by Matthew and Luke, while Mark and John pass over it briefly.

The narrative of the prophetical work of Christ begins with the story of his baptism by John and of the 40 days in the desert. To this section belong all sermons addressed to the people or to his disciples, his discussions with individual people, and his miracles, through which he proved the divine origin of his teaching and his person.

With the story of Christ's sufferings and death and his glorious resurrection, the gospel narrative comes to an end. Only Mark and Luke mention the ascension, and that in very few words.

B. The gospel according to Matthew

177. Evangelist

Practically all that we know of Matthew is recorded by himself (9:9-12), by Mark (2:13-17), and by Luke (5:27-32). Matthew was called by Jesus from his place of business, a tax collector's booth, to become one of the apostles of our Savior. His father was one Alphaeus, a man otherwise unknown to history. The father of James, a man with the same name, was doubtless a different person (Matthew 10:3; Acts 1:13).

While he was a tax collector, Matthew was known by the name of Levi. Since this name occurs in none of the lists of the apostles, it would seem that Matthew discarded it altogether after he joined the circle of Christ's disciples. We have no means of determining whether he really bore both names before he was called or whether he took a new name for the old one in order to put aside everything, as it were, which might serve as a reminder of his former dubious calling. The tollbooth under his supervision was on the shore of the Sea of Galilee, probably not far from Capernaum.

During the three years of Christ's activity, Matthew never was prominent among the disciples in any special degree. As to his life after the first Pentecost, we have but meager and unreliable information. It is said that Matthew preached at Jerusalem for 15 years after Christ's ascension and that he then set out to proclaim the gospel among other people, such as the Ethiopians, the Macedonians, the Syrians, the Persians, and the Medes. In the catalog of martyrs, the day of his death is given as September 21, but many ancient documents fail to mention that he died a martyr's death.

178. Gospel

The New Testament nowhere mentions that Matthew wrote the Gospel that bears his name. The superscription is not part of the inspired Word, having been added later to distinguish this gospel from the others. But we have numerous witnesses that in the middle of the second century, it was a matter of common knowledge in the Christian church that Matthew wrote this book.

This agreement, which was not marred by the slightest doubt at the time, would be inexplicable if it had not corresponded with known facts. Matthew did not enjoy such special renown compared with the other apostles, so that everybody would have picked him at random as the author of so important a document. Besides, at the date indicated, many persons were living who were qualified to investigate the truth of such a tradition and were honest enough to contradict it if they had found it to be fictitious.

In fact, the only people to call the matter into question are the unbelieving critics, and their arguments are so plainly the result of prejudice that they fall to pieces when soberly tested. There, as always, negative criticism rests upon the hypothesis that miracles are impossible and that all stories of miracles are untrue. Therefore, critics of this class maintain that the first gospel cannot have been written by an apostle, since it fairly teems with miracle stories. Generally speaking, it is the habit of rationalistic critics to determine in their own minds what an apostle might, could, and should have written. When the biblical books do not measure up to that manufactured standard, they are declared to be spurious—a procedure that is utterly unscientific and stems from unbelief.

179. Purpose, place, and date

Matthew makes it plain that he intended his gospel primarily for Jewish readers. He prefaces his narrative with a genealogy that establishes the claim that Jesus is truly the Son of David, a fact of vital interest for Jewish converts. Furthermore, Matthew clearly makes it his special task to show most convincingly that the prophecies of the Old Testament were fulfilled in Jesus, so there can be no doubt as to the messiahship of the Lord. To this must be added that he never explains Jewish customs and practices nor introduces any information about the geography of the Holy Land. Obviously, his intended readers must have been well informed on these matters. It should also be noted that Matthew records more instances of the clashes between Jesus and the Jewish sects than the other evangelists.

The fact that Matthew wrote for Jewish Christians would seem to indicate that he wrote the gospel while he was in Palestine. It is quite improbable that he would have found time for such a great undertaking while traveling from place to place as a missionary.

For the date of Matthew's writing, we do not depend altogether upon guesswork, for he seems to indicate it quite plainly. In 27:8 we read, "That is why it has been called the Field of Blood *to this day"* and in 28:15: "And this story has been widely circulated among the Jews *to this very day."* These remarks would have been superfluous if Matthew had written immediately after the occurrences to which he refers. Because he considers it noteworthy that such sayings should have been preserved to the date of his writing, considerable time must have elapsed since the resurrection of Christ.

On the other hand, these remarks indicate that Matthew wrote before the year 66. In that year the great war began, which soon ended all local traditions in Palestine. This assumption is strengthened by the contents of chapter 24, where the evangelist records a sermon of Christ in which the Lord paints one great picture of the future judgments of God, combining the destruction of Jerusalem and the end of the world in one description. Matthew would surely have remarked that part of this prophecy had been fulfilled if he had written after the fall of Jerusalem. These and other similar considerations make it fairly certain that Matthew wrote the first gospel about the year 60.

180. Original language

It is certain that Matthew wrote his gospel, as we now have it, in the Greek language, the sacred tongue of the New Testament. This we maintain despite the confident assertion of modern critics that our first gospel is merely the translation of a book that Matthew originally wrote in Hebrew. Like many other alleged results of the prowess of modern science, this assertion is not based on provable facts but upon theories that appeal to the spirit of unbelief. If the Greek Testament contains only a translated Matthew and not the original book, our claim that the first gospel as we possess it is the inspired Word of God is suspect—all of which is highly desirable from the viewpoint of rationalism, because of the many miracles contained in this gospel! So here again the wish is father of the thought.

The idea of a Hebrew Matthew was suggested by certain remarks found in the books of ancient writers, which have been misunderstood and misinterpreted. The story originated as follows. Papias, bishop of Hierapolis in Asia Minor, a pupil of John the apostle, writes, "Matthew made a collection of these words *(logia)* in the Hebrew language, and everybody translated them as well as he could." Pantaenus (died 202) is reported to have found this Hebrew book among the peoples of India, and Jerome (died in 420) claims to have seen a copy of it among the Nazarenes of Syria. Other writers of the church also speak of this book, but without claiming to have laid eyes upon it. Nobody has a word to say as to when and by whom this Hebrew text was put into Greek.

Against these vague and doubtful records, which furnish modern critics their only arguments, we list the following facts:

(1) Since the most ancient Christian writers quote from our Greek Matthew, this Greek book must have been received as a work of the apostle in the beginning of Christian history.

(2) Far from exhibiting traces of a translator's labors, the gospel itself contains unanswerable proof that it was written in Greek by the author. A translator, when handling the quotations from the Old Testament, would surely have pursued one of two systems: he would either have translated every such text from the Hebrew, or he would have transcribed the quotation from the Septuagint. Matthew did not, however, feel bound by any such method but made his quotations in whatever way best suited his purpose. We may also mention a play upon words found in the Greek text of 6:16, which could not have been translated from the Hebrew, even as it disappears in our modern translations.

(3) The ancient Syriac version of the New Testament, the Peshito, which was made in the second century, produced Matthew's book from the Greek that we possess and not from some unknown Hebrew original.

These facts may serve to throw some light upon those statements of the ancient writers mentioned above. It is not at all impossible that Matthew made some sort of record in Hebrew at a very early date, but it is altogether certain that he wrote our first gospel in Greek, as we have it now. It is also quite possible that those writers are speaking of a translation of this gospel, made by certain sects for their own purposes and then published as the original work of Matthew.

Summary of contents

    I. Historical introduction, chapters 1,2.

    II. The prophetical work of Christ, chapters 3–25.

    III. Christ's sufferings, death, and resurrection, chapters 26–28.

C. *The gospel according to Mark*

181. Evangelist

The name of Mark occurs frequently, both in Acts and in the epistles. We learn that Mark was also called John, having a Hebrew as well as a Greek name (Acts 12:12,25; 15:37; in 13:5,13 he is simply named John). His mother, Mary, had a house in Jerusalem, where the first church was accustomed to assemble. The legend says that he was one of the 70 disciples whom Christ sent out to preach on a certain occasion. But this does not agree with 1 Peter 5:13, where the apostle calls Mark his son, for this statement always has been taken to mean that Peter converted Mark.

Being the cousin of Barnabas (Colossians 4:10), Mark was chosen to accompany Paul and Barnabas as their attendant on their first missionary journey. But he deserted the travelers midway and returned home (Acts 13:13). This act of Mark caused a sharp contention between Paul and Barnabas when they were about to prepare for a second journey (Acts 15:37-39), because Paul refused to accept Mark again as an attendant. Barnabas, however, would not yield. He preferred to separate from the apostle and took Mark with him to the island of Cyprus. Subsequently Mark must have adjusted his differences with Paul, for the apostle mentions him as his fellow prisoner and fellow laborer in the epistles that he wrote during his two captivities in Rome (Colossians 4:10; Philemon 24; 2 Timothy 4:11).

According to a very old report, Mark is said to have evangelized the great city of Alexandria in Egypt, founding the church at that place. A legend invented at a much later date declares that his body was carried to Venice and buried there (the Church and Piazza di San Marco at Venice).

182. Authority

Mark was not himself an apostle, but he was a disciple not only of Paul but also of Peter, for the latter declares that Mark was with him in Babylonia (1 Peter 5:13). The ancient tradition of the church adds the information that this "pupil and interpreter of Peter" wrote down his gospel according to the discourses of the apostle. It is true that the sources do not quite agree. Some say that Peter caused Mark to write the gospel; others, that he spoke neither for nor against the undertaking; and still others, that he endorsed the gospel after it was written.

The manner in which Mark discusses certain occurrences in the life of Peter is strong internal evidence that the apostle must have been personally interested in the work of his disciple. On the one hand, Mark 8:29 omits the praise that the Lord bestowed upon Peter according to Matthew 16:17. On the other hand, he not only mentions the sharp rebuke that Matthew also records (Mark 8:33; Matthew 16:23), but in the story of Peter's denial, he mentions some aggravating circumstances that the other evangelists passed over in silence (14:54,68). We would expect that Peter, acting under the impulse of his genuine repentance, was in the habit of calling attention to his weakness and sin in unsparing words, while the other apostles did not dwell upon the shameful details of the denial.

If the second gospel was actually written by Mark under the eyes of Peter, this would also serve to show why his gospel immediately came to be accepted by the church as canonical, though its writer was not himself an apostle. At the same time, however, we maintain that Mark wrote under the inspiration of the Holy Spirit and not merely as a mouthpiece of Peter.

183. Authenticity

No valid arguments have ever been presented by any critic to show that the second gospel was not really written by Mark. Only the most unblushing opponents of divine truth, such as the notorious Tuebingen school of critics, have dared to question the genuineness of this gospel. Their alleged proofs are not worth serious discussion. It is obvious that Mark was entirely independent of the other evangelists for his material. His book shows such definite and consistent purpose that some scholars, going to the other extreme, have designated it as the source from which Matthew and Luke drew their information. It should be mentioned, however, that some reasonable doubt exists as to the genuineness of the closing section (16:9-20), which is missing in several of the oldest manuscripts that we possess. This evidence is not at all conclusive, however, for there may have been other reasons why the copyists who made those manuscripts failed to add that section. In the Greek text, the story would end with unusual and unbearable abruptness if the last verses were omitted.

184. Purpose and distinctive features

Mark makes a practice of explaining Jewish customs and of locating the places in Palestine that he mentions. Thus he describes the custom of handwashing (7:3,4), explains the Hebrew word *Corban* (7:11), describes the doctrine of the Sadducees (12:18), the location of the Mount of Olives (13:3), the custom of the first day of the Passover (14:12), an Easter custom of the governor (15:6), and the meaning of the day of preparation (15:42). This makes it obvious that his book was intended primarily for readers who were unfamiliar with the life and the country of the Jews.

A notable feature of Mark's style is evident when we compare his narrative with those of Matthew and Luke. Though this gospel contains only a few short sections that cannot be duplicated from the first and third gospels, Mark has a habit of adding certain details that serve to make his brief narrative very picturesque. For particulars compare Mark 2:1-4 with Matthew 9:1,2; Mark 3:5 with Matthew 12:3 and Luke 6:8; Mark 5:2-5,13 with Matthew 8:28,32 and Luke 8:27,33; Mark 5:25-34 with Matthew 9:20-22 and Luke 8:43-48; Mark 6:35-44 with Matthew 14:15-21 and Luke 9:12-17. Mark omits the longer addresses and sermons of Jesus and thus produces a narrative that is remarkable for its quickness of action.

185. Place and date of writing

We have no certain information regarding the place where Mark wrote his gospel. There is an ancient tradition that Mark wrote at Rome. Since Peter declares that Mark was his companion at the metropolis, which he calls Babylon (1 Peter 5:13), that tradition may be true and would help to explain why Mark wrote for people other than Jewish Christians. It would also be a good reason for the use of certain

Latin words that Mark introduces into his Greek narrative. Thus in 12:42, he remarks that the two mites (NIV, "small copper coins") of the widow amount to one quadrans (NIV, "fraction of a penny"), which was a Roman coin. In the story of the crucifixion of Christ, the captain of the soldiers is always called a centurion (15:39), whereas the other evangelists use the corresponding Greek title.

These few Latinisms, however, do not warrant the assumption definitely voiced by scholars of the Roman Catholic Church that Mark originally wrote his gospel in Latin. An alleged manuscript of this Latin Mark, found in the great library at Venice, was easily shown to be the copy of a Latin translation. Moreover, the ancient church declares without a single dissenting voice that Mark wrote in Greek.

As to the date of writing, we have none but the most vague indications. If it is true that Mark wrote when he was at Rome with Peter, who did not visit the metropolis until shortly before his death, during the persecution of Nero, it would seem that the date of the gospel must be set for the year 66 or thereabouts.

Summary of contents
    I. Historical introduction, 1:1-8.
    II. The prophetical work of Christ, 1:9–14:31.
    III. Sufferings, death, and resurrection of Christ, 14:32–16.

D. The gospel according to Luke

186. Evangelist

According to the most ancient and dependable tradition of the church, the third gospel, together with its continuation in Acts, was given to the world by Luke, a pupil and companion of Paul. Without a dissenting voice, all ancient writers of the church agree that the author of this gospel is the same person whom Paul mentions as his companion in Colossians 4:14; 2 Timothy 4:11; and Philemon 24.

Luke joined the great apostle at an early date, for he speaks of the events of the second missionary journey of Paul as an eyewitness (Acts 16:10). After that he probably remained with Paul almost continually, for we hear that he was at the apostle's side both in the first and in the second captivity (Acts 27:27; Philemon 24; 2 Timothy 4:11).

A later tradition would have us believe that Luke was one of the 70 disciples who were sent out to preach by Christ (Luke 10:1), but Luke seems to set himself apart from those "who from the first were eyewitnesses" (1:2). Besides, Paul distinctly fails to class him with those who were of Jewish descent (Colossians 4:11-14). We must conclude, therefore, that Luke was converted from heathenism, a fact borne out by the observation that his language is much more free of Hebraisms than that of the other evangelists. An unsupported tradition has it that he was born and converted at Antioch. We know that he was a man of some education, because Paul tells us that he was a physician.

187. Authenticity

Very few critics have undertaken the hopeless task of showing that the third gospel is not from the pen of Luke, and their best efforts have failed to shake the universal testimony of the ancient church. The very fact that the book of Acts begins with a reference to this gospel is sufficient to prove that the gospel was written in the apostolic era.

According to his own statement, Luke had "carefully investigated everything from the beginning" (1:3) before he began to write this gospel under the inspiration of the Holy Spirit. His words do not disclose where he made his inquiries. We do not know whether his sources were oral or, in part, written. It may well be, for instance, that Zacharias, the priest, had made a written record of the remarkable circumstances surrounding the birth of John the Baptist and that Luke had read the document. On the other hand, Luke may have derived all his knowledge concerning the life of Jesus from Paul, whose companion he was for so many years. Paul undoubtedly had gathered all information obtainable on that subject of vital interest. At any rate, there is good evidence that Luke profited by the oral instruction of Paul (compare Luke 22:17-20 with 1 Corinthians 11:23-26; Luke 24:34 with 1 Corinthians 15:5). It is impossible to decide, however, whether Luke as a writer stood in the same relation to Paul as Mark did to Peter.

188. Purpose

We learn from the introduction that Luke wrote this gospel for the instruction of a certain Theophilus, of whom we know nothing beyond what is indicated by Luke (1:1-4). The evangelist addresses this man as the "most excellent" Theophilus (1:3), employing a title that he otherwise uses only for men of high official station (Acts 23:26; 24:3; 26:25). It has been taken for granted, therefore, that Theophilus was a very prominent man.

Luke also tells us that Theophilus was a new convert to Christianity and stood in need of the instruction concerning the life of Jesus that Luke was about to give him in this gospel. Again, it seems sure that Theophilus was unacquainted with Palestine and the eastern part of the Roman Empire generally. While Luke gives information concerning certain places in Palestine (1:26; 4:31; 24:13; Acts 1:12) and even concerning some places lying more westward (Acts 16:12; 27:8,12), he refers to some very insignificant villages of Italy merely by name, without adding a word of explanation (Acts 28:12,13,15). This makes it seem certain that Theophilus was a Roman and lived in Italy.

Luke most assuredly did not design his two books for the use of one man alone but recognized him as a representative of that part of the church which had been converted from heathenism. Therefore he makes it his special business to show that Jesus is the Savior of all men and lays particular stress upon those sermons and parables of the Lord in which the universality of salvation is most clearly expressed. With this purpose in mind, Luke carries the genealogy of Christ back not only to Abraham, as Matthew does, but to Adam (3:38), in order to set forth Christ as the second Adam (1 Corinthians 15:45), given to all mankind as the source of life and salvation.

189. Date and place of writing

It seems most reasonable, considering the known facts, to assume that Luke wrote this gospel at Rome. He had ample time for this great undertaking during the two years that he spent at Rome as a companion of Paul during the apostle's imprisonment (Acts 28:30). The date of writing seems to be fixed by the fact that the story of Acts is not carried to the death of Paul but only to the end of those two years of imprisonment. Since Acts was written after the gospel, the latter must be dated about the year 63 or 64.

Summary of contents

    I. Historical introduction, chapters 1–3.

    II. The prophetical work of Christ, 4:1–22:39.

    III. Sufferings, death, and resurrection of Christ, 22:40–24:53.

E. The gospel according to John

190. Evangelist

The author of the fourth gospel makes so many definite allusions to his person that we scarcely need the unanimous testimony of the ancient church to recognize him as John the apostle, whom we know as the disciple specially beloved by our Lord.

John was a native of Galilee, a son of Zebedee and Salome, and a brother of James the Elder. In company with his brother, like Peter and Andrew, John earned his bread by fishing in the Sea of Galilee, near the port of Bethsaida. When John the Baptist began to preach, John, the future apostle, became his disciple. He also was one of the two whom the Baptist directed to Jesus (John 1:37-40). Soon thereafter Jesus called John and others to be his apostles. Together with Peter and James, he was privileged to witness some significant acts and experiences of the Lord, such as the transfiguration, the resurrection of the daughter of Jairus, and the great agony in Gethsemane.

His personal relation to Christ was much more intimate than that of any other disciple (see John 13:23, for example). For this reason, most probably, Jesus entrusted his mother to the tender, filial care of John before he died on the cross, and John gladly took her into his own home (19:27). Tradition has it that John provided for her until she died in the year 48.

In the church of Jerusalem, John ranked as one of the pillars (Galatians 2:9), and it seems that he labored only there at first. Later, probably after the close of Paul's activity but before the destruction of Jerusalem, John went to Asia Minor, choosing the city of Ephesus as his home. Soon after this change, perhaps during the Neronian persecution, in which Paul and Peter died as martyrs, John was banished to the island of Patmos and there received the revelation (Revelation 1:9). From there, however, he returned to Ephesus and labored for many years yet in his capacity as apostle. According to legend he died near the close of the first century, the only one of the apostles who, to our certain knowledge, did not suffer a martyr's death.

John had an intense and fiery nature (one of the "Sons of Thunder," Mark 3:17) and devoted himself to the Lord with burning love. None of the other apostles excelled him in the zealous study of Christ's sayings and teachings, and none was granted a deeper contemplation of the divine mysteries. Hence the church, applying the great vision of Ezekiel, gave to John the symbol of the soaring eagle, and an old Latin poem says of him:

> The eagle flies to boundless height;
> No prophet in his vision's flight
> Did e'er beyond him soar;
> Fulfillment attained, fulfillment to be—
> Did saintly men e'er clearer see
> So much mysterious lore?

The love and reverence in which John was held shines forth in the numerous legends that became popular after his departure. The imagination of a later generation found an attractive suggestion in the words of Christ (John 21:22) and evolved the fanciful tale that John had not really died but that he slept in his grave, awaiting the second advent of Christ. In proof of this, it was said, the mound covering his body moved gently with the rhythm of his breathing.

191. Authenticity

While John nowhere calls himself the author of the fourth gospel, he comes as near doing so as possible. While he never mentions his own name, to which the other evangelists refer so often, he always speaks pointedly of the disciple whom Jesus loved. To this must be added the testimony of 19:35, for we know with certainty that John stood under the cross. Consequently the early church never wavered as to the certainty of John's authorship. In fact, the earliest writers of the church refer to this gospel as written by John the apostle.

In the face of this testimony, all doubts raised by unbelievers become ridiculous. The very magnificence of this gospel has only spurred on the rationalistic critics in their vain efforts to disprove John's authorship. But all their alleged arguments merely go to show that their real intention is to demolish its authority.

Of all their alleged "proofs," only one is worth mentioning, namely, that John seems to contradict the other evangelists especially in his account of the death and resurrection of Christ. This very disharmony, however, should be looked upon as proof of the authorship of John. Any forger would certainly have been extremely careful to avoid the least shadow of a contradiction with the other evangelists, in order not to betray himself. Besides, though we may not always be able to solve the difficulties in question to the satisfaction of everybody, we should remember that many other and more important matters mentioned in the Bible remain inexplicable to us simply because we don't know all the facts, and yet the Bible does not cease to be God's own truth on that account.

192. Purpose

The evangelist has given us full information as to the purpose of his gospel. It was written so that its readers might "believe that Jesus is the Christ, the Son of God, and that by believing [they] may have life in his name"

(20:31). This, then, is the purpose of this gospel for all time, since the apostles were to be teachers of the world to the end of days.

Knowing this great purpose, we have no problem grasping the special reason why John wrote this gospel, though he was familiar with the three first gospels, which had been in the church for quite a long time. We note that John passes by most of the stories that the other evangelists had recorded, except in the narrative of the sufferings and death of Christ. His gospel consists mostly of information that the other evangelists had not given. For this reason it has been supposed that John wrote his gospel as a supplement to the preceding gospels, and this may indeed have been his intention in part.

On the other hand, the fourth gospel is so unlike the other gospels and so unique in its character that the attentive reader involuntarily will seek for some special reason why this book should have been written. We find it in this, that during the latter years of John's life, the church was confronted by a dangerous heresy, which made it necessary to describe the life of Christ precisely from the point of view that John chose.

It seems that a certain Jewish agitator by the name of Cerinthus began to deny the essential and true divinity of Jesus Christ, rejecting the truth that the Son of God suffered death for us. That must have been the beginning of the heresy which later became known as Gnosticism, which attempted to weld together the Word of God and heathen philosophy and, consequently, fell into blasphemous error. It is very likely that John, recognizing the danger in its beginnings, wrote his gospel against the errors of Cerinthus, since he consistently makes it a point to demonstrate the divinity of Christ.

193. Readers, place, and date

Because he lived in Ephesus, John naturally took into consideration that most of his immediate readers would be of Greek extraction. Therefore, he considered it necessary to translate the Hebrew words he quoted and to explain the Jewish customs he mentioned (1:38,41; 4:9; 5:2; 6:4; 7:3; 11:18). The earliest sources of information agree not only that John wrote this book in the city of Ephesus but also that he wrote it near the end of the first century, when he was a very old man.

194. Distinguishing features

John knew that his readers were familiar with the first three gospels, so he recorded very few miracles of Christ and said little about the Lord's prophetical work in Galilee. The outstanding feature of his mode of presentation, however, is the lengthy discourses of Christ that he records. They are so important for his purpose that the historical statements often merely serve to set the scene for Christ's words. Thus the miraculous feeding of the multitude (chapter 6) led to the wonderful discourse on the Bread of Life. The story of the healing of the blind man (chapter 9), though highly instructive in itself, is told because it prompted the comforting discourse concerning the Good Shepherd and his sheep (chapter 10).

Many of these discourses also exhibit a custom of Jesus to begin with an enigmatic statement, calculated to be pondered deeply by his hearers, but always received with violent contradiction by his vicious adversaries. While John records few of Christ's parables, his words and discourses are marvelously pregnant with profoundest thought. Hence some of the early church fathers called this gospel the spiritual gospel, naming the other three corporeal by contrast.

Although this distinction has been used often to the present day, it is open to serious misunderstanding and should be avoided. It should be remembered that all discourses of our Lord, including those couched in the simplest words, have a high spiritual significance, which cannot be grasped by the heart of man except through the enlightening power of the Holy Spirit.

Summary of contents
   I. Historical introduction, 1:1-37.
   II. Prophetical work of Christ, 1:38–17:26.
   III. Christ's sufferings, death, and resurrection, chapters 18–21.

F. Acts

195. Author

In the introduction, or preface, of this book, we are told that it was written for the same Theophilus to whom Luke had penned the third gospel. Acts, then, is a continuation of the other book, the second volume, as it were. It is not particularly important to decide whether Luke bases his account in part upon oral or written sources of information. There is no reason why he should not have made use of written records or of direct personal testimony about the events of which he was not an eyewitness. On the other hand, he certainly writes from personal experience where he tells his story in the first person (16:10-17; 20:5-15; 21:1-17; 27:1–28:16), because obviously he was there, as Paul's personal attendant.

In the early church, no one ever doubted the authorship of Luke. In fact, from the middle of the second century, we have an unbroken series of witnesses who ascribe the Acts to Luke without hesitation.

The truth and reliability of the account here presented is also apparent because all the discourses and addresses of various persons, delivered at different times, are reported by Luke in perfect accordance with the peculiarities of each speaker and the circumstances under which they were spoken. They must, therefore, be genuine, since no writer could have produced them in this manner simply from his imagination.

196. Purpose

The title of this book, added by a later hand, is misleading, inasmuch as it seems to promise information about the work of all the apostles. It was not the intention of the writer to furnish a complete history of the missionary activities of all apostles. After the list of the Eleven (1:13), he never mentions more than four of them (John, James, Peter, and Paul), and in his detailed historical account, he confines the narrative to the most remarkable doings of Peter and Paul.

Luke himself closely connects this book with his gospel. He can have had no other purpose here than to show how Christ, omnipresent on earth after his ascension, established the church of the New Testament and spread it among Jews and Gentiles from Jerusalem to Rome, the metropolis of the world. The narrative naturally records the sequence of occurrences in the lives of the two greatest apostles, but these men are not at all the chief personages. As everywhere in the Scriptures, our Lord Jesus Christ is understood to be the dominating figure in Acts. It was he who fulfilled his promise to the apostles by endowing them with the gift of his Spirit, and they carried on his work while spreading the Word in the strength that he bestowed. Beginning at Jerusalem, they carried the gospel into the heathen countries. Indeed, Acts tells us how they fully preached the message of Jesus Christ in the very heart, the capital, of the Roman Empire.

In his instructive preface to this book, Luther sets forth its purpose in a manner that cannot be surpassed. He writes:

> With this book Saint Luke teaches the whole Christian church to the end of the world the true chief article of Christian doctrine, that we all must be justified through faith in Jesus Christ alone, without any aid of the law or assistance of our works. . . . This book might well be called a commentary on the epistles of Paul. For what Paul teaches and impresses with words and texts from the Scriptures, that Saint Luke here illustrates and proves with examples and stories, showing that it came to pass, and must come to pass, as Paul teaches, namely, that no law, no work justifies men, but only faith in Christ.

197. Arrangement, date, and completeness

In Galatians 2:9 we are told that Paul entered into an agreement with James, Peter, and John, according to which they were to preach among the Jews while he was to evangelize the heathen countries. Thus Paul became the great apostle of the Gentiles. It is true, nevertheless, that the first church among the heathen was the blessed fruit of Peter's testimony in the house of Cornelius at Caesarea (Acts 10), and it is also true that Paul did not fail to offer the gospel to the Jews wherever he went. But in the story of the Acts, the fact is impressed upon the reader that the two men actually did work along the general lines laid down in their mutual agreement. Thus, after the first, introductory chapter, the book has two distinct parts. The first describes how the church was founded and built up at Jerusalem. The second records the missionary travels of Paul in the gentile world.

Since Luke mentions neither the fall of Jerusalem nor the death of Paul and yet appears to have been the companion of the apostle almost to the last, we may safely assume that he wrote this book before Paul's death, about the year 64, probably at Rome.

It has been said that the narrative of Acts ends too abruptly, lacking a satisfactory literary conclusion, and on that basis it has been suggested that Luke intended to write a third book. This view, however, is a misinterpretation of the writer's plan. His aim was attained when he could record that Paul was finally permitted to preach at Rome unhindered and had thus succeeded in his purpose of carrying the gospel to the city that ruled the world.

Summary of contents

   I. Historical introduction, chapter 1.

  II. Founding and upbuilding of the church at Jerusalem, chapters 2–12.

 III. Spread of the kingdom of Christ among the Gentiles, chapters 13–28.

Chapter 3
The Doctrinal Books of the New Testament

A. General remarks on the apostolic letters

198. Purpose

The apostles had been commissioned to proclaim the gospel of Christ to the whole world and could not, therefore, locate permanently at any one place to serve local churches. But the varying experiences of the new churches soon disclosed the need of further apostolic instruction and admonition. And so it came to pass quite naturally that the apostles, moved and enlightened by the Holy Spirit, wrote letters, or epistles, to various congregations of believers according to their individual needs, instructing them on important points of doctrine and urging them to strive after true holiness of life.

We shall discuss the special occasion for each epistle in subsequent paragraphs. But it should be noted here how closely the apostles kept in touch with the churches, scattered as they were. Paul, for example, says, "Besides everything else, I face daily the pressure of my concern for all the churches" (2 Corinthians 11:28). Periodically he received messages from the churches, both by letter and messenger (1 Corinthians 1:11; 7:1; Romans 1:8; Philippians 4:16,18; Colossians 1:8; 1 Thessalonians 3:6; 2 Thessalonians 3:11). Similarly, Peter, James, and Jude must have been fully informed on conditions prevailing in the churches that they addressed, since they confine their instruction to definite points. And the first epistle of John was certainly prompted by the needs of the churches in Asia Minor, which he knew thoroughly.

199. Number

We have 21 apostolic epistles in the New Testament. For many centuries Christian scholars have debated the question whether all letters of the apostles, especially of Paul, have been preserved. It surely is not improper to assume that Paul may have communicated at times with some churches through letters of which we have no record, for example, to acknowledge the receipt of a gift of money (compare Philippians 4:16). The disagreement, however, is mainly on the significance of 1 Corinthians 5:9, which many scholars understand as implying that the first real letter of Paul to the Corinthians has been lost. Again, it is argued from Colossians 4:16 that Paul wrote a special epistle to the Laodiceans, of which we have no other record.

As far as the Christian doctrine is concerned, it is quite immaterial which of the views mentioned is adopted. In any case, we can be content with the rich treasures of apostolic instruction that have been preserved to us by the providence of God. If he did not consider it necessary to preserve certain writings of the apostles for our use, we feel assured that they were not needed for the continuation of his kingdom on earth.

200. Agreement

In the epistles that we possess, the apostles are in complete harmony on all points of Christian doctrine. Since they wrote at different times, for various reasons, and to churches differing in character and needs, we must not expect them to discuss the same points of doctrine or to express all doctrines in exactly the same terms. A close examination of apparent differences or seeming contradictions will assure us that natural and satisfactory explanations can always be found.

The most serious case of this kind is the apparent glaring contradiction between Paul and James on the doctrine of justification (compare Romans 3:28 and James 2:24), but the contradiction disappears at once if we remember that Paul speaks of justification before God, while James refers to justification before men (see section 250).

For all their fundamental agreement, however, each one of the three major apostles has such an individual way of presenting the Christian truth that Paul has been called the apostle of *faith,* John the apostle of *love,* and Peter the apostle of *hope.* According to 1 Corinthians 13:13, faith, hope, and love are three gifts of the Spirit, the graces that adorn every Christian heart. For good reasons, however, Paul places special emphasis on faith, while John sets forth the real nature of love, and Peter the true character of Christian hope. This observation, however, indicates only the general impression made by the epistles written by these three men. In point of fact, each one has something to say about all three Christian graces.

201. Authors

Thirteen of the 21 epistles were certainly written by Paul. He names himself as their writer, and the early church never raised the question whether any of these epistles might be spurious. In the canon of the New Testament, they formed the second section, so to speak, probably because they were assembled sooner than the remaining epistles and were known simply as "the Apostle." The epistle to the Hebrews was also frequently ascribed to Paul, and the disagreement as to the authorship of this document, which persists to this day, is the reason the number of Pauline epistles is listed differently by different authors.

The remaining seven epistles, two of Peter, three of John, and one each of James and Jude, were commonly called the catholic epistles. As the word *catholic,* that is, *general,* admits of various interpretations, its use in this case has been justified in various ways. The early writers of the church, who introduced the term, probably meant to indicate that these letters were more general in their contents and purpose than those of Paul, who directed his epistles to certain named churches or individuals, while Peter, John, James, and Jude addressed whole groups of churches. According to this view, however, the epistle to the Hebrews would have to be classed with the catholic epistles, while the second and third letters of John, having been written to individuals, could not properly be placed under this heading. But in the latter case, the defense might be found in the common practice to name a collection of things from its chief constituents.

202. Language and authenticity

By far the greater number of these apostolic epistles were so obviously written in the Greek language that this fact has never been called into question. James, however, and the author of Hebrews make it plain that they are addressing Jewish Christians. It would not, then, seem unreasonable to suppose that they wrote in the Hebrew language originally. Careful investigation, however, makes it quite certain that these two epistles were written in the Greek form in which we now have them.

That the 13 epistles of Paul, 1 John, and 1 Peter were actually written by the men whose names they bear has never been disputed successfully. As to the remaining epistles, their divine origin has been acknowledged by the church with fair unanimity. Nevertheless, 2 Peter, 2 and

3 John, James, and Jude belong to the deuterocanonical books because it is a historical fact that they were not unanimously received as apostolic writings. It is easy to see that 2 and 3 John failed to be universally accepted because they were addressed to individuals and are very brief. But the question as to the authorship of Hebrews and the apostolic character of Jude and James is much more complicated and will be discussed in greater detail later on.

B. The epistles of Paul

203. Life story of the apostle

There is no apostle of Jesus Christ whose life story has been given in more detail than that of Paul. In the second part of Acts, his person dominates the narrative to such an extent that we may assume this part was written in order to show the great importance of Paul's work. If we add to this the many glimpses of his personal experiences, which he records incidentally in his epistles, we have ample material for an instructive biography of this great man. In the following sketch, we shall also indicate where and when he wrote each letter, but as some of these statements are based on assumptions, they must not be taken as definitely proved.

Paul was born at Tarsus, a prominent city in the province of Cilicia, on the southeast edge of Asia Minor. His father, a Jew of the tribe of Benjamin, had acquired Roman citizenship, which he transmitted to his son as a birthright. According to a common custom, the boy was given both a Hebrew name, Saul, and a Roman name, Paul. He discarded the former entirely after he set out for Cyprus on his first missionary journey (Acts 13).

Because his father belonged to the sect of the Pharisees (Acts 22:3), he brought up his son in strict accordance with the tenets of his sect and later sent him to Jerusalem, where the youth received a thorough education at the feet of the learned Pharisee Gamaliel (Acts 23:6). During the same period, presumably, and in compliance with an accepted practice, he learned the trade of a tentmaker (Acts 18:3), so that he could support himself in later years without depending upon the gifts of the churches (1 Thessalonians 2:9).

Filled with burning zeal for his pharisaism, he developed a deep hatred against the Christian faith, which grew into active hostility as the first church at Jerusalem prospered. When Stephen was stoned to death, Paul participated as an interested and approving spectator, and soon thereafter he became a violent leader of a bloody persecution. But while on the way to Damascus, to harass the Christians even there, he was overtaken by the saving grace of God. A vision of Jesus, living and exalted in divine glory, demolished the foundations of his pharisaic belief, making room for the gospel to work the fruit of conversion.

On this occasion the Lord called him to be his apostle to the Gentiles (Galatians 1:13-17). But before he took up this new work, he went to Arabia, where he lived in quiet seclusion for probably three years (Galatians 1:18). As soon as he began to preach the salvation of Jesus Christ at Damascus with great power, however, the Jews set the governor under King Aretas against Paul, forcing him to flee. Next he visited Peter at Jerusalem and also preached there after the brethren had gained confidence in him through the testimony of Barnabas (Acts 9:26-30). But his life was threatened there likewise. Therefore the disciples sent him to Tarsus, his native city, by way of Caesarea.

At a later date, Barnabas came to get him and brought him to Antioch, where both served the local church for a year in the ministry (Acts 11:26). Bearing a sum of money, which the Christians of Antioch had collected for their suffering brethren at Jerusalem, Paul and Barnabas journeyed to the Holy City but soon went back to Antioch, accompanied by Mark.

Then Paul set out on his first missionary journey, having been commissioned by the church of Antioch to do this work. Accompanied by Barnabas, Paul first landed on the island of Cyprus, the home of Barnabas, where they labored with great success. Crossing over to Pamphylia, they visited the countries of Pisidia and Lycaonia; established Christian churches, especially at Antioch (Pisidia), Iconium, Lystra, and Derbe; and provided them with elders, who continued to preach the gospel.

When they performed a miracle of healing at Lystra, the heathen populace began to worship them as gods and could scarcely be prevented from carrying out their purpose. Soon, however, the Jews caused them to be persecuted with bitterness and even stoned Paul. These unpleasant experiences failed to impair their profound joy at the blessings that God had laid upon their work, and they returned to Antioch rejoicing.

After a considerable interval (Acts 14:28; it was 14 years after the conversion of Paul, Galatians 2:1), a dissension arose concerning the Mosaic Law. To quiet the disturbance, the first Christian synodical convention was held at Jerusalem. There it was shown that Paul was in perfect harmony with the other apostles in his doctrine of free grace, and the convention announced this result to the churches among the Gentiles through a circular letter.

Soon thereafter Paul set out on his second missionary journey. In preparing for this undertaking, Paul had a serious misunderstanding with Barnabas, when the latter insisted upon taking Mark along. Paul disagreed because Mark had deserted them without good cause on their first journey. The two old friends separated, and Paul went on his way with Silas.

Paul quickly passed over the route of his first journey, strengthening the churches that he had established. In Derbe he added Timothy to the company. As it was God's plan to send Paul to Europe this time, the apostle was not permitted to travel to Phrygia, Mysia, and Bithynia. Instead, he quickly reached Troas, where a vision called him over to Macedonia. In this country he established churches at Philippi (Lydia, the seller of purple; the jailer), Thessalonica, and Berea. There again the persecutions of the Jews forced Paul to flee in haste.

He then preached at Athens, without achieving tangible results, and finally reached Corinth, where he interrupted his long journey with a stay of a year and a half. Timothy and Silas, whom he had left behind in Macedonia, caught up with him at Corinth. Their account about conditions in the northern churches caused Paul to write, in quick succession, the two epistles to the Thessalonians, the earliest writings of Paul that we possess. From Corinth he went to Ephesus for a brief stay and then returned to Antioch by way of Jerusalem (Acts 18:22).

After a period of rest, he entered upon his third missionary journey, which again carried him through the countries of Asia Minor. He stopped for more than two years at Ephesus, where he probably wrote the epistle to the Galatians and the first epistle to the Corinthians. After the uproar raised by Demetrius, the Spirit urged Paul to visit Macedonia, where he wrote the second epistle to the Corinthians, and to Greece, where he wrote the epistle to the Romans, at Corinth.

Paul then planned a visit to Rome but first turned his face toward Jerusalem once more, even though he had been informed by persons inspired with the spirit of prophecy that he would be imprisoned there. Luke was one of his companions on this journey. They touched Troas and Miletus, Rhodes and Cyprus, Tyre and Ptolemais; and everywhere Paul heard prophecies of afflictions that were awaiting him.

Soon after his arrival at Jerusalem, the intrigues of the Jews brought about his arrest by the Roman authorities. As his life was not safe at Jerusalem, he was taken to Caesarea and placed under the protection of Felix, the governor (procurator). This official held Paul for two years without sentencing him, because he expected the prisoner to purchase his freedom with money. Felix was succeeded by Festus. When this man also continued to delay Paul's case, the apostle made use of the last resource at his command: he appealed to the emperor and demanded to be sent to Rome.

After a winter voyage, beset with many dangers, Paul at last stepped ashore in Italy, a prisoner. Before he reached Rome, the news of his approach caused the Christians of the capital city to set out in great numbers to meet him, and they conducted him to the city with great rejoicing. His imprisonment at Rome continued for two years more, but though he was under guard continually during that time, he was permitted to preach the gospel freely. During this period he undoubtedly wrote the epistles to the Ephesians, Philippians, and Colossians and to Philemon, in each of which he mentioned that he was a prisoner.

The narrative of Acts does not carry us beyond that period of two years. We are not told whether Paul's imprisonment ended with his death or with his deliverance. Certain statements, however, which Paul makes in the epistles to Timothy and Titus make it impossible to assign these letters to any period of Paul's life known to us. Furthermore, in writing to the Philippians (1:25; 2:24), Paul is quite certain that he will soon be set free. Besides, there is a persistent tradition that Paul made a missionary journey to Spain. And so it is assumed that Paul, having been delivered from his first imprisonment, made one more trip through Greece, Asia Minor, Crete, and probably Spain and that it was a second imprisonment which resulted in a martyr's death about the year 66, as tradition has it.

204. Order of Paul's epistles

If we were to arrange the Pauline epistles in their historical order as far as we are able to determine it, the series would read as follows: 1 and 2 Thessalonians, Galatians, 1 and 2 Corinthians, Romans, Ephesians, Philippians, Colossians, Philemon, 1 Timothy, Titus, and 2 Timothy. The period during which all these epistles were written lies between the years 52 and 65.

In our Bible the chronological sequence is disregarded. The epistles are arranged partly according to their destination and partly according to their contents. We find them divided into two distinct groups. The first group includes the epistles addressed to churches, and the second those that were written to individuals. The epistles addressed to churches are again arranged according to their apparent importance, as decided either by their contents or by the reputation of the different churches. Consequently, first place was assigned to Romans because it is an elaborate treatise on justification, the doctrine of paramount importance. The Corinthian letters follow because, besides being addressed to one of the largest churches, they are of considerable size and offer thorough discussions of various points of doctrine. Galatians, though comparatively short, ranks next because, like Romans, it treats mainly of justification. Ephesians, Philippians, and Colossians form a natural group, because they were written during Paul's imprisonment. The Thessalonian letters are last in this group because they are not meant primarily to teach doctrine, but to admonish.

205. General character

Paul was both a masterful teacher and a powerful exhorter, and his epistles reveal him in both capacities. Generally he sets out to discuss some doctrinal point or points, but he never fails to add the necessary admonition. In Romans, Galatians, Ephesians, and Colossians, we find the admonitory section set off sharply from the doctrinal section. In Corinthians, Philippians, Thessalonians, Timothy, and Titus, the streams of doctrine and of admonition run fairly side by side.

The entire theology of Paul is based upon the one fundamental truth that man is justified by faith, without the works of the law. But Paul takes occasion to discuss quite a number of important doctrinal questions in his letters, depending on the needs of the churches or individuals addressed. Here is a comprehensive summary: *Romans:* Justification, election, government. *Corinthians:* Ministry of the gospel, church discipline, marriage, Christian liberty, Lord's Supper, spiritual gifts, resurrection. *Galatians:* Justification and the Christian's freedom from the law. *Ephesians:* Election, the church. *Philippians:* The two states of Christ. *Colossians:* Divine glory of Christ, the Sabbath. *Thessalonians:* day of judgment, Antichrist. *2 Timothy:* Efficacy of the Scriptures. *Titus:* Baptism.

206. Paul's manner of writing and transmission

As a rule, Paul used the services of a scribe, to whom he dictated his letters. He notes it as an exception that he wrote the epistle to the Galatians with his own hand (Galatians

6:11). In Romans 16:22 the scribe to whom Paul had dictated added his own greetings. But it is to be assumed that Paul accredited each epistle by adding his signature. Sometimes he did so quite elaborately, as in 1 Corinthians 16:21; Colossians 4:18; and 2 Thessalonians 3:17. The last passage shows that Paul found it necessary to call the attention of the readers to his signature. The reason probably is indicated in 2 Thessalonians 2:2, where Paul indicates that some impostors had been circulating spurious letters in his name. Perhaps the invocation at the end of each epistle was Paul's signature and written in his own hand.

To each epistle of Paul, including Hebrews, we find appended in some translations (such as the KJV) statements giving information about the place of writing and the persons through whom the letters were transmitted. These additions did not originate with the apostle. They are missing in some manuscripts and are differently worded in others, often in such a way that Paul could not have penned them. Thus we are told at the end of 1 Corinthians that this is the first epistle to the Corinthians. In one manuscript it is stated of 1 Thessalonians, "This first epistle of the holy Apostle Paul to the Thessalonians was written at Athens." This statement is erroneous besides, for Paul mentions Silas and Timothy as being present with him at the time of writing (1 Thessalonians 1:1), and they did not join him before he came to Corinth (Acts 18:5).

C. Romans

207. The church at Rome

As far as we know, the church at Rome came into existence without the intervention of any apostle. For obvious reasons the present Roman Catholic Church maintains that Peter the apostle was the founder of the church at Rome and guided its destinies for 25 years as its first bishop. This claim is at variance with all reliable historical information about the beginnings of the church at Rome. Trustworthy tradition tells us no more than that Peter came to Rome in the last years of his life and died there as a martyr.

If Peter had been bishop of Rome for 25 years, he must have been there when Paul wrote to the Romans. This is impossible, because Paul took scrupulous care not to interfere with another apostle's work, a rule of conduct which he voices most emphatically in the epistle to the Romans (15:20). It should also be noted that among the many persons whom Paul greets by name as members of the church at Rome, the name of Peter does not appear, for the very good reason that Peter was not there at the time. So we may conclude that no apostle can be named as founder of the church at Rome.

Yet it is plain from Romans 1:8 and 16:7 that the church had existed for quite some time when Paul wrote this letter. It is a reasonable suggestion that some of the "visitors from Rome" who were present in Jerusalem on the day of Pentecost (Acts 2:10) were among the thousands converted there and carried the gospel back with them to Rome. According to Suetonius, a Roman historian, Emperor Claudius (A.D. 41–54) expelled the Jews from Rome temporarily because they had caused rioting, involving violent disputes about the Messiah (whom Suetonius calls *Chrestus*). This is good evidence that the Word of Christ was preached publicly in Rome at the time. We may also note that Paul mentions Andronicus and Junias as members of the church at Rome, adding that they "were in Christ," that is, they had become Christians, before him (Romans 16:7).

The membership of this church was composite, being in part gentile. This is shown by such passages as

Romans 4:1 and 11:13. This fact caused Paul to launch his powerful and convincing argument that both Jews and Gentiles are alike lost in sin (chapters 1–3) and that the Gentiles have no advantage over the Jews in God's election (chapters 9–11). At the same time, this church was renowned in the whole Christian world for its faith and its obedience to the gospel (1:8; 16:19).

208. Purpose

Having "fully proclaimed the gospel" to Illyricum, so that he had "no more place . . . to work in these regions" (15:19,23), Paul was very hopeful that he could fulfill a wish of long standing, to make a visit to Rome (1:13; 15:24). At the time of writing, however, he was prevented by a divine command from traveling to Jerusalem by way of Macedonia and Achaia (Acts 19:21). He, therefore, decided to get in touch with the church at Rome by letter.

Since the apostle discusses the fundamental article of justification with particular power and thoroughness in the epistle to the Romans, some commentators have thought that he intended to introduce himself to them by presenting most lucidly the central thought of his great message. But surely the Roman church had even less need of information about the person and doctrine of Paul than he had of information about them. It is much more reasonable to suppose that Paul wrote this letter because he had definite knowledge concerning the spiritual needs of the Christians at Rome. In this way the epistle itself furnishes trustworthy information about the conditions in the Roman church that caused Paul to write precisely this letter.

It seems that the members of the church, being in part Jews, in part Gentiles by birth, did not agree among themselves. The Jewish members liked to boast of their descent from Abraham and of their possession of the ancient revelation, while the Gentiles were inclined to despise the Jews, who had so often rejected the grace of God and had finally become hardened in their unbelief. This prompted the apostle to show, in the first place, that there is no difference between Jew and Gentile in the New Testament, neither in regard to their sinful state nor in regard to justification, but that, rather, the blessings of divine grace are granted to all who believe, without any distinction. Then he proceeded to show that the eternal decrees of God are inscrutable and that they are not influenced in any way by human merit. The Gentiles, therefore, are not entitled to gloat because so many of them accepted the gospel, while but a small number of Jews were converted to Christ.

The admonitory section of the epistle indicates that the Christians at Rome, being oppressed by the imperial government, needed an energetic reminder of the requirements of the Fourth Commandment and also that the strong in faith among them did not always exhibit due consideration for their weaker brethren. Luther says:

> This epistle is truly the chief part of the New Testament and the purest gospel, being so valuable altogether that a Christian might well not only memorize it word by word, but keep in touch with it every day, as with the daily bread for his soul. For it can never be read or considered too much or too well, and the more it is handled, the more precious does it become, and the better does it taste.

209. Date, place, and transmission

When Paul wrote to the Romans, he had already preached in Illyricum (Romans 15:19). According to Acts this cannot have taken place until after his stay of nearly three years at Ephesus (Acts 20:1-3). Therefore Paul must have written this letter while on his third great journey, during his stay in Greece for three months. The opportunity for writing came to Paul at Corinth. He indicates this by lauding the hospitality of Gaius (Romans 16:23), whom he had baptized at Corinth (1 Corinthians 1:14), and by sending the letter to Rome along with Phoebe, who had been a servant of the church at Cenchrea, the port of Corinth (Romans 16:1).

Summary of contents

  I. Salutation and introduction, chapter 1:1-17 (the chief theme of the epistle, verses 16,17).

  II. Didactic part, chapters 1:18–11:36.
   1. Sinful corruption of all men, chapters 1:18–3:20.
   2. Justification through grace alone, chapters 3:21–5:21.
   3. The fruits of justification, chapters 6–8.
   4. Predestination, chapters 9–11.

  III. Admonition, chapters 12–15.

  IV. Personal news, greetings, conclusion, chapter 16.

D. 1 and 2 Corinthians

210. Corinth and its church

In the year 146 B.C., the city of Corinth had been captured and razed by Mummirus, a Roman general. It was rebuilt by Caesar, and because of its favorable location between two ports, Cenchrea on the east and Lechaum on the west, it soon regained its former position as the most important center of trade for the world traffic between Rome and the Orient. While it was renowned as a seat of Greek learning, it was also noted for its immorality.

Paul reached this wealthy and thriving city on his second missionary journey. He made the acquaintance of Aquila, a Jew born in Pontus, who with his wife, Priscilla, had been expelled from Rome by an edict of Claudius. Being of the same trade, Paul and Aquila jointly engaged in tentmaking, the way Paul earned his living while he preached in the synagogue of the Jews on every Sabbath Day (Acts 18:4). The Jews, however, met his advances with so much hostility that he separated from them and thereafter taught in the house of Justus, a God-fearing man. In the course of one and a half years, by simply preaching Christ crucified (1 Corinthians 1:17,23), Paul gradually gathered a large congregation, consisting mostly of Gentiles from the lower walks of life (1 Corinthians 1:26-31).

Some time after Paul had departed from Corinth, his work was continued by Apollos. This highly gifted man from Alexandria in Egypt had first come to Ephesus, where he soon became renowned for his eloquence and his knowledge of the Scriptures, though he had until then heard only of the baptism of John. When he met Aquila and Priscilla, who had come to Ephesus with Paul, Apollos was quickly brought to a true knowledge of Jesus Christ. Supplied with a written recommendation from the church at Ephesus, he then went to Achaia (Greece) and devoted his time to the church at Corinth (Acts 18:24-28; 19:1; 1 Corinthians 3:6).

211. Occasion for the first epistle

While Paul was making his stop of nearly three years at Ephesus during his third missionary journey, he dispatched Timothy to Corinth for news of the church there (Acts 19:22; 1 Corinthians 4:17). But before Timothy had reached Greece (1 Corinthians 16:10), Paul received much disquieting information directly from Corinth. He mentions certain members of the household of Chloe, a Corinthian woman, as sources of reliable information about conditions there (1:11). The Corinthians also had written him a letter containing various questions (7:1; 8:1; 11:2; 12:1), which probably had been brought to the apostle by Stephanas, Fortunatus, and Achaicus (16:17). At any rate, Paul would use the testimony of these three Corinthians to verify other reports and to obtain additional knowledge. Without waiting for the report of Timothy, Paul hastened to write the first epistle to the Corinthians.

From 1 Corinthians 5:9 it is sometimes argued that Paul had written to Corinth once before but that this first letter had disappeared. But the words of the apostle do not compel this understanding. They may reasonably be taken as referring to our first epistle to the Corinthians. By a peculiar practice of the Greeks and Romans, the writer of a letter would speak in the past tense of things that were happening at the time of writing, because they would be in the past when his readers received the letter.

212. Causes and contents

By careful reconstruction we can piece together a fairly complete picture of the conditions prevailing at Corinth that had been so disquieting to the apostle. During his absence serious dissensions had arisen among the Corinthians as to the qualifications of the various pastors they had known. The strife was so bitter that it threatened the church with disruption (1:11).

While the factions were carrying on their foolish dispute, church discipline was sorely relaxed, so that even a man guilty of incest went unrebuked (4:19–5:1). It also would happen that Christians went to law against one another in the courts of the heathen (6:1); that various forms of licentiousness were practiced (6:13); that common decency came to be disregarded in the public meetings (11:1); that even the celebration of the Lord's Supper was made the occasion for offensive behavior (11:20); that the gifts of the Spirit were misused (chapters 12–14); and that dangerous errors about the resurrection of the body were tolerated (15:12). Paul discusses all these important matters and thus finds reason to set forth the true doctrine concerning the ministry, church discipline, and various other subjects that are of vital significance for every Christian church. Consequently this epistle is a rich treasure of information concerning the practical side of congregational life.

213. The second epistle

Paul waited in vain at Ephesus for a report from Timothy. Then he sent Titus to Corinth, in order to learn what impression his first epistle had made there (2 Corinthians 7:13,14). Leaving Ephesus, Paul went to Troas, but Titus failed to meet him there. He crossed over to Macedonia, and there Timothy and Titus finally caught up with him (1:1; 2:13; 7:6). From Titus, Paul learned that his letter had produced the desired effect in most members of the Corinthian church, inducing them to admonish the brother who had sinned so grievously (2:5-11).

But at the same time, he was told that some members of the church disparaged his ministry, as though he were inferior to the other apostles, and had thus disturbed the whole church (10:10; 11:5,13-15). In deep anguish of soul, Paul then wrote the second epistle to the Corinthians. After giving instructions as to the further treatment of the person who had been guilty of incest but had responded to Christian admonition with true repentance, Paul first praises the effectiveness and results of his ministry and admonishes his readers to strive after sanctification. Then he takes up the case of those who had blasphemed his work, defends his apostolic calling, and threatens severe measures against the unrepentant. This letter he sent to Corinth with Titus and two other brethren (8:6,16-23).

Summary of 1 Corinthians

    I. Salutation and preface, 1:1-9.

    II. Concerning the ministry of apostles and other preachers, 1:10–4:21.

    III. Concerning church discipline, chapter 5.

    IV. Concerning suits at law, marriage, Christian liberty, spiritual gifts, Christian love, chapters 6–14.

    V. Concerning the resurrection, chapter 15.

    VI. Personal information, greetings, conclusion, chapter 16.

Summary of 2 Corinthians

    I. Salutation and prefatory remarks, chapter 1 (reasons why he had not come to Corinth as yet).

    II. General didactic part, chapters 2–9. (How to proceed with the repentant sinner; true estimation of the holy ministry and of the fruit of the gospel, that it works consolation in affliction and a holy life; admonition to be liberal in contributing to the collection that he was raising for the needy Christians at Jerusalem.)

    III. Special instruction concerning his apostolic office, as a defense against his detractors, 10:1–13:10.

    IV. Conclusion, 13:11-13.

E. Galatians

214. The Galatians

The Galatians had originally come from Gaul, the France of today, and therefore were of Celtic blood

(Galatians = Celts). Since the beginning of the fourth century before Christ, great bands of these people had migrated eastward, threatening to overrun Greece and Asia Minor. After a bloody struggle, they were in part driven back to Thrace. Some of them, however, found a new home in the heart of Asia Minor and settled down there permanently. Their fertile and beautiful country was enclosed by the provinces of Bithynia, Pontus, Cappadocia, Lycaonia, and Phrygia. For a time the new settlers continued their predatory invasions of the neighboring countries, until the entire district fell into the hands of the Romans, who gradually enforced more peaceful habits upon the Galatians.

Paul visited them on the occasion of his second missionary journey, at a time when many of their hereditary customs and institutions may still have survived. But their Celtic mother tongue had long given place to the Greek world language. Paul's first visit in Galatia seems to have been quite brief (Acts 16:6), for it was not part of the divine plan that Paul should labor there extensively, as we learn from Galatians 4:13,14 that a certain bodily illness compelled the apostle to travel slowly. He must have made good use of his leisure by preaching the gospel, for it seems that the Christian church was firmly established in Galatia when he finally turned westward.

215. The church in Galatia

While Jews were scattered throughout the countries of Asia Minor and always furnished a number of converts to Christianity, they seem to have found little foothold in Galatia. At any rate, the letter to the Galatians indicates that the churches of that country consisted of heathen converts almost exclusively (compare, for instance, Galatians 5:2,3).

Paul visited them a second time on his third great journey, as we learn from Acts 18:23 and Galatians 4:13, and found ample reason to strengthen them in knowledge and faith. For the Galatians had even then been greatly troubled by the heretical errors against which Paul afterward directed his attacks in the epistle. He refers to this fact repeatedly in the epistle. Thus he remarks in chapter 1:9 that he had told them "already" what he is about to state; in 4:16 he declares that he *had* told them the truth; in 5:3 he testifies "again" as to circumcision. This instruction and admonition of the apostle had apparently succeeded in quelling the disturbance, so that Paul had left the Galatians with good hopes for the future (5:7).

But during his stay at Ephesus, much sooner than he may have anticipated (1:6), he received the unwelcome news that certain perverters of the truth had gained much influence over the Galatians. They were Judaists, who preached that Christians must keep the Law of Moses in order to be saved (4:21) and that circumcision was necessary for justification (5:2,3). To discredit Paul's doctrine of justification by faith alone, they declared that he was not a true apostle of Jesus Christ, since he had not seen the Lord in the flesh and had not, therefore, received the apostolate from him (1:12; 4:17). According to the reports that Paul received, the Galatians had not only introduced Jewish festivals (4:10) but were also strongly inclined to accept circumcision (5:2,3). It would also seem that some had hoped to escape persecution if they would enter into outward fellowship with the Jews (6:12).

216. The epistle

It must have been about the year 55 that Paul wrote this letter. Since he marvels that they had "so quickly" begun to disbelieve his gospel, he must have written shortly after his visit in Galatia, certainly not later than his stay in Ephesus. Some commentators believe that they have found references indicating that Paul was a prisoner when he wrote this epistle, but their arguments are not convincing. It is quite certain that the postscript at the end of this letter (KJV, "written from Rome") is false.

Paul here opposes all Judaism most decidedly and rebukes the Galatians sharply for having listened to the deceivers. After the usual introduction, he first shows that his apostolate was not from men but had been given directly by God. He then discusses the doctrine of justification with the particular purpose of teaching the Galatians that works of the law are not a second cause of salvation in addition to the merit of Christ. To complete the discomfiture of his opponents, he finally shows that the Christian, though free from the law, is not thereby free to lead an immoral life but that his liberty will result in all manner of good works.

The apostle wrote this letter in great agitation but free from passionate anger, speaking to the Galatians as a father to his children. Together with the epistle to the Romans, Galatians ranks first in doctrinal importance, because in both letters Paul discusses the fundamental doctrine of the Christian faith. The presentation differs inasmuch as in the letter to the Romans, Paul discusses the doctrine of justification in all its phases, while in Galatians he emphasizes the Christian's freedom from the law. Luther wrote a remarkable commentary on this epistle, one of his most valuable books.

Summary of contents

I. Salutation and introduction, chapter 1:1-5.

II. Didactic part, 1:6–4:31. (Paul's divine call to the apostolate, 1:6–2:21; the Christian's freedom from the law, chapters 3,4.)

III. Admonition, 5:1–6:10 (the proper use of Christian liberty).

IV. Conclusion, 6:11-18.

F. Ephesians

217. The city and the church

The place where Ephesus once stood is now only a ruin of its former grandeur. In the days when this city flourished, it was not only important on account of its commercial activity but was renowned far and wide as the chief seat of the worship of the goddess Artemis, that is, Diana (Acts 19:23-30). The magnificent Ephesian temple of Diana was known as one of the seven wonders of the world. Paul visited this great city of the gentile world for the first time when he was hastening from Corinth to Jerusalem at the close of his second apostolic journey (Acts 18:19-21). Apollos also labored there for a season (Acts 18:24-27).

Paul, who seems to have been particularly drawn to the church that he had founded at Ephesus, distinguished it by a stay of more than two years during his third missionary journey. Through his energetic labors, Ephesus became the center of the Christian church in Asia Minor. The gospel spread with great efficiency to quite a number of neighboring cities (Laodicea, Colossae), so that John the Apostle, who moved to Asia Minor after the death of Paul, found it convenient to make Ephesus his home.

During his last visit to Ephesus, Paul wrote to the Corinthians, "A great door for effective work has opened to me, and there are many who oppose me" (1 Corinthians 16:9)—thus giving a twofold reason for his prolonged stay. The spirit and viciousness of his adversaries are well illustrated by the story of the riot raised by Demetrius (Acts 19:23-41; see also 1 Corinthians 15:32 and Acts 20:19).

251

The mutual affection existing between Paul and the Ephesian church prompted the apostle to call the elders of the church to meet him at Miletus when he was on his last journey to Jerusalem. He could not pass by without urging the men who were continuing his work in the great city to devote the most conscientious care to their charge (Acts 20:17-38).

218. Time and place of writing

It is certain that Paul wrote this letter while he was a prisoner (3:1; 4:1; 6:20); hence it is classified as one of the captivity epistles, along with Philippians, Colossians, and Philemon. As Ephesians is remarkably similar to Colossians in thought and expression, these two letters must have been written about the same time. Since Colossians certainly originated in Rome, it would appear also that the postscript at the end of the letter to the Ephesians (cf. KJV) rightly names Rome as the place where Paul wrote and by which he sent this letter to the Christians of Asia Minor. The bearer of the letter was Tychicus (6:21), who was undoubtedly known to the Ephesians as a former companion of the apostle (Acts 20:4).

219. Audience

For certain reasons there has been some doubt as to the correctness of the title of this epistle. Some scholars even deny that Ephesus was its real destination. It is remarkable, for instance, that Paul here departs from his usual practice of closing his letters with greetings to personal friends and greetings of his companions. Again, in 1:15 and 3:2, he seems to imply that he was not acquainted with the church and that its members knew of his apostolate only by hearsay. From 4:20,21, indeed, it might be argued that the persons addressed had never received adequate Christian instruction.

All this seems entirely at odds with the fact that Paul was not only the founder of the Ephesian church but had devoted many months to the thorough instruction of its members.

These apparent discrepancies must have been observed at an early date, because we possess ancient manuscripts of the New Testament that omit the name of Ephesus in the first verse. The idea was that the letter was intended as a circular epistle for a group of churches and that Paul, having prepared a number of copies without inserting the name of the church (or churches) addressed, had left it to his messenger to insert a name in the blank space. But it is hardly credible that Paul should have left it to the discretion of any other person to make so important an addition to any of his letters. Moreover, it is the unanimous testimony of the early church that this letter was actually written to the Ephesians.

The peculiarities referred to may readily be explained by assuming that Paul wrote the epistle for the church at Ephesus and also for all the neighboring churches. Because such churches sometimes sprang up very rapidly in those days, many of their members may indeed have been unknown to Paul. This group most probably included the church at Laodicea, so that the epistle "from Laodicea" referred to in Colossians 4:16 is none other than the epistle to the Ephesians. Tychicus, who carried the letters to their destination, could instruct the Christians in Ephesus and its environments how the letter was to be circulated. He also undoubtedly bore the greetings of Paul to his personal friends.

220. Character

We have no means of determining the particular reasons that prompted Paul to pen this beautiful letter, unless it was the general need of assuring the distant churches that the captivity of the apostle must not give offense to any believer. At any rate, the master pen of Paul has nowhere recorded a more satisfactory demonstration that the gospel and the salvation which it brings is in no way dependent upon human agencies but is altogether and in every case a gracious gift of God. He first sets forth most convincingly that our complete salvation is founded upon the eternal decrees of God's foreordination and election. Then he proceeds to show that because of these decrees, the church has been established on earth as the spiritual body of Jesus, the Lord over all, who builds it upon the foundation of the apostles and prophets through the power of the gospel. Jesus makes the church a living spiritual organism, in which not only the teachers whom he gives but every member works toward the edification of the whole body. On this basis Paul then proceeds to general and special exhortations, closing with an appeal to strenuous warfare against the powers of darkness.

As Paul here strives to convey an idea of the most inscrutable thoughts of God through the imperfect medium of the human language, his diction and style assume an exaltation hardly paralleled in any of his other writings. It may well be, then, that Peter was thinking of Ephesians in particular when he wrote 2 Peter 3:16. In our versions the magnificent sentences for which this letter is specially notable had to be broken up into several parts to ensure proper understanding. To illustrate, it may be noted here that after breaking forth in a wonderful hymn of praise, beginning in 1:3, Paul comes to a complete stop only twice before 2:10, the sections 1:3-14; 1:15-23; and 2:1-10 representing, as it were, three magnificent stanzas of an ode of transcendent power.

Summary of contents

G. Philippians

221. Philippi

When Paul first planted the church at Philippi, this city had had a history extending over many centuries. The ancient Greeks knew it under the name of Krenides (that is, City of the Springs). On account of the gold mines located in its vicinity, King Philip of Macedonia, father of Alexander the Great, had taken possession of it, renaming it after himself and fortifying it to protect his northern boundary (358 B.C.). Three centuries later (42 B.C.), a battle was fought near Philippi, in which Octavius and Antonius gained a decisive victory over Brutus and Cassius, the murderers of Caesar. Then the city was made a Roman colony, blessed with many great privileges, so that it soon became a place of considerable importance and ranked as one of the chief cities of Macedonia in the days of the apostle Paul (Acts 16:12). At present, only ruins mark its location.

222. Church

Paul, having been called to Macedonia by a vision while on his second missionary journey (Acts 16:9), made Philippi his first stop on European soil and preached the gospel with remarkable success. He addressed the women who assembled at a certain place of prayer outside of the city walls and converted Lydia, a seller of purple and a native of Thyatira in Asia Minor. A miracle of healing by Paul involving a female slave who was possessed by the devil roused the ire of the heathen multitude against him, and the apostle was put in prison. During the night the jailer was converted and then secured the deliverance of the apostle. Though Paul had been granted but a few days of labor at Philippi, his gospel had been very effective.

He left behind him a church rejoicing in the faith, which also proved its affectionate gratitude to the apostle by sending him sums of money at various times (Philippians 4:10-18; 2 Corinthians 11:8,9). On his third journey, Paul visited Philippi a second time, but the record merely mentions this visit (Acts 20:6). The affection of the church, however, followed Paul into his captivity at Rome, where Epaphroditus reached him with greetings and a substantial present from the Philippians (Philippians 4:10,18). This man, who stayed with Paul for some time, also became the bearer of the epistle on his return (2:25-30).

223. Epistle

All indications seem to make sure that this epistle was written during Paul's imprisonment at Rome. According to 1:7,13,16, he evidently was a prisoner. That he was at Rome at the time is certain, not only because he mentions members of the imperial household (4:22) but because he writes as from the midst of a Christian congregation (1:12-14). We know of no place but Rome where this could have been the case during Paul's captivity. Moreover, the letter must have been written toward the end of the two years mentioned in

Acts 28:30; for not only would the experiences of Epaphroditus described in Philippians 2:25,26 extend over a considerable period, but Paul also writes as one who is confidently expecting his deliverance (1:25; 2:23,24).

Paul exhorts the Philippians to preserve unity and to practice self-denial, according to the example of Christ (chapter 2). He also warns them against the Judaists, who seem to have disquieted some of the members at Philippi (3:2-4). The dominant thought of the epistle, however, is expressed in the words "Rejoice in the Lord"; hence the theologian Bengel says this is *epistola de gaudio,* "the letter concerning joy."

Summary of contents

I. Salutation and personal information, chapter 1.

II. Exhortation to unity (incidentally: doctrine of the humiliation and exaltation of Christ), with news concerning Timothy and Epaphroditus, chapter 2.

III. Warning against errorists and admonition to holiness, 3:1–4:9.

IV. Personal remarks; greetings; conclusion, 4:10-23.

H. Colossians

224. Colossae

Colossae was a city of Phrygia, located on the banks of the river Lycus, so near to the cities of Laodicea and Hierapolis that a traveler could easily visit the three places in one day. As late as the fourth century, Colossae was a populous trading point, but soon thereafter it was outclassed by its competitors and finally disappeared altogether. Recent excavations near the present hamlet of Khonas have uncovered certain ruins, which have practically been identified as those of ancient Colossae.

257

225. Church

From Colossians 1:4,7,9 and 2:1, it appears that Paul was not the founder of the church at Colossae and never visited it personally. He had passed through Phrygia twice (Acts 16:6; 18:23), but both times his journey took him through the northeastern section of the country, toward the boundaries of Galatia. On the other hand, Paul makes it plain that the church owed its existence to the missionary spirit of Epaphras, who also must have labored successfully in Laodicea and Hierapolis (Colossians 1:7; 4:13).

Epaphras, who had been a pupil of Paul, visited the apostle at Rome and reported upon conditions of his home church. The information thus given to Paul referred not only to the general state of the congregation but told in particular of certain dangerous errorists who had sought to lead the Colossians astray. Without naming them, Paul indicates that they were Judaists, or legalists, who tried to perfect the Christian doctrine by philosophical speculation. They had departed from the truth to such an extent that they denied the divinity of Christ, teaching that the angels are his equals and should be worshiped (2:18). At the same time, they claimed to have attained perfect holiness by leading ascetic lives according to the Mosaic Law. Though they made much of Christ, they did not truly believe in him.

226. Epistle

To counteract the baneful influence of these agitators, Paul wrote Colossians. He was a prisoner at the time (4:3), but scholars disagree as to the place of writing. Some maintain that it was Caesarea, while others feel certain that it was Rome. Definite proof is lacking for either view. But it should be remembered that Paul was kept confined very closely at

Caesarea and could hardly have been privileged to receive visitors or to write letters, whereas he was granted great freedom of movement at Rome.

As far as our Christian faith is concerned, this question is as unimportant as that other one, namely, whether Ephesians and Colossians really were written at the same time. The two letters are so similar in many respects that we may reasonably suppose that Paul sent them simultaneously. But it must also be admitted that Paul might have thought and written along the same lines at different times under the inspiration of the Holy Spirit. The similarity of the two epistles is offset by characteristic differences. While Ephesians is largely constructive and doctrinal, Colossians is written in a polemical spirit. Paul emphasizes the divine glory of Jesus Christ, raises a warning voice against hypocritical sanctimoniousness, and finally shows how the people may walk in true holiness.

Summary of contents

   I. Salutation; declaration of the divine glory of Christ, chapter 1.
  II. Warning against false philosophy; exhortation to continue with Christ, chapter 2.
 III. Rules of true holiness for Christians, chapter 3.
  IV. Greetings, conclusion, chapter 4.

I. Thessalonians

227. Thessalonica

About the year 315 B.C., Cassandros, son-in-law of King Philip of Macedonia, founded a new city near the old colony of Therme and called it Thessalonica, after the name of his wife. This city soon became the chief port of Macedonia, and when the Romans occupied the country in 146 B.C., they recognized the importance of Thessalonica by making it the capital of the province. During the subsequent centuries, the city experienced many stirring events. It changed hands repeatedly, especially during the period of the Crusades, until the Turks finally took possession in 1430 (23 years before the fall of Constantinople). Today it is called Salonika. In the days of Paul, it must have been a city of considerable size.

228. Church

When Paul had left Philippi on his second apostolic journey, he went to Thessalonica by way of Amphipolis and Apollonia (Acts 17:1). We are not certain how long he stayed, but since he preached in the synagogue on three Sabbaths only, his visit may have lasted barely one month. Yet his preaching was immediately successful, because both Jewish and gentile converts in considerable number accepted the Christian faith. In order to escape violence at the hands of hostile Jews, Paul was forced to leave abruptly in the night. But he had the satisfaction of leaving behind him a strong church, whose good report spread far and wide within a few months (1 Thessalonians 1:7,8). On his third journey, Paul paid one more visit to Thessalonica, but again his stay was brief (Acts 20:1-4).

229. First epistle

After his flight from Thessalonica, Paul first came to Berea and from there to Athens. Silas and Timothy, who had remained at Berea when Paul left, were immediately called to Athens by the apostle (Acts 17:14,15). It appears that Paul had heard of certain troubles which had befallen the church at Thessalonica soon after his departure and that he sent both Silas and Timothy back to Macedonia (Acts 18:5). The mes-

sage Timothy carried was especially addressed to the Thessalonians (1 Thessalonians 3:1-5). These messengers returned to
Paul at Corinth (Acts 18:1,5; 1 Thessalonians 3:6), and it was
the information that Timothy brought which caused Paul to
write the first epistle to the Thessalonians.

Though firm in the faith, the young church was in
urgent need of definite instruction on certain points of
doctrine. It seems that a difference of opinion had arisen
among them concerning the second advent of Christ,
which was thought by some to be so near that it was not
necessary to continue in the performance of earthly
duties. On the strength of this information, Paul wrote an
affectionate letter, commending their faith in the gospel
and touching lightly upon the points on which they stood
in need of correction.

This is the first epistle that Paul wrote to any church, as
far as we know. It is probably the earliest New Testament
writing that we possess. Remembering how soon the apostle
had been torn away from the Thessalonians, how much
instruction had necessarily been left unsaid, and how seri-
ously the church was threatened by bitter enemies, we can
well understand why Paul thought it necessary to strengthen
them so soon.

230. Second epistle

The first letter of Paul failed to produce the desired
effect at Thessalonica. As the persecutions continued, some
of the brethren insisted all the more that the day of the Lord
was near at hand, and this misconception caused many to
walk disorderly. It would seem, indeed, that these errors
gained strength because of a forged letter which circulated
under Paul's name (2:2; 3:17). Everything indicates that Paul
wrote the second epistle to the Thessalonians as soon as he

learned of these matters, very shortly after the first letter had been sent, and therefore during his stay at Corinth. Though he still praises their steadfast faith, he proceeds to show them that the day of the Lord will not come before the Antichrist, the man of sin and the child of perdition, has arisen and finished his course. Paul also repeats and amplifies the admonitions contained in the first epistle.

Summary of 1 Thessalonians

  I. On the relation of Paul to the church at Thessalonica, chapters 1–3. Paul acknowledges the grace granted to them through his ministry; he reminds them of his labors among them; he expresses his ardent desire to see them once more.

  II. On the duties and hopes of Christians, chapters 4,5 On sanctification in general; on the hope of Christ's return as a comfort and as an admonition; on the true order of Christian life in the church.

Summary of 2 Thessalonians

  I. Consolation in affliction based upon the return of Christ, chapter 1.

  II. Description of the Antichrist, who must come before the Last Day, 2:1-12.

  III. Exhortation to certain proofs of faith in holy living, 2:13–3:18.

J. The pastoral epistles in general

231. Character and authenticity

The two epistles to Timothy and the epistle to Titus form a distinct group among the Pauline writings, not so much because they are addressed to individuals but, rather, because of their contents. They are obviously meant as letters of instruction concerning the proper way of governing and organizing Christian churches, and they were written to certain men who were laboring as pastors in such churches. And so they have very properly been called pastoral epistles.

Though admittedly we cannot positively place them anywhere during that period of Paul's life with which we are familiar from the Acts and from his other epistles, that is no reason why their Pauline origin should be questioned. The early church is unanimous in declaring that these letters were written by Paul, and it stands to reason that a forger would surely have taken great pains to make these epistles fit into the known biography of Paul. Far from casting doubt upon the authenticity of these epistles, the historical difficulties should rather be considered strong proofs of their Pauline origin.

232. Difficulties

In every one of the three pastoral epistles, we meet statements that refuse to be fitted into the life experiences of Paul as we know them. Since full discussion is out of the question here, it will be sufficient to refer to a few items in each of these epistles.

1 Timothy: In 1:3 we are told that Paul left Timothy behind him in Ephesus when he himself went on to Macedonia. But on the only occasion when Paul traveled to Macedonia from Ephesus according to Acts, he had Timothy with him. Timothy was also in the apostle's company when Paul wrote 2 Corinthians (Acts 19:22; 20:1-4; 2 Corinthians 1:1). Again, we are told that Paul hoped to return to Ephesus (1 Timothy 3:14). But when he went to Macedonia on his third journey, he planned to pass the winter at Corinth and go on from there to Jerusalem. In fact, when he set out on this return trip, he avoided a visit to Ephesus in order to save time (Acts 20:16).

2 Timothy: Second Timothy was written while Paul was a prisoner at Rome (see 1:8,16,17; 2:9), but the details mentioned by Paul about this imprisonment do not agree with what we know of the first imprisonment at Rome. Paul does indeed see the end of his sufferings before him, not with the hope of deliverance, but in the certain expectation of death (2 Timothy 4:7,8). Again, Paul here mentions certain companions of whom we hear nothing in the letters written from the first imprisonment (2 Timothy 1:15; 4:14-18). It is also certain that he was at Troas shortly before this letter was penned (see 4:13), but when he was in his first Roman captivity, he had not been near Troas for years.

Titus: The apostle reminds his disciple Titus that he had left him at Crete for the purpose of perfecting the organization of the churches on that island (Titus 1:5). According to Acts, however, Paul was on Crete but once, and that as a prisoner on his way to Rome (Acts 27:8-13). Luke does not mention that Paul met Christians in Crete on that occasion, nor would the apostle have been granted opportunity to establish churches or even to visit any congregations, if there had been any. It is impossible to discover any opportunity during Paul's journeys to have made a side trip to Crete that had been left unrecorded by Luke in Acts. Besides, the apostle nowhere else mentions a plan to pass the winter at Nicopolis (Titus 3:12).

233. Solution

All difficulties disappear if we adopt the ancient tradition that Paul actually escaped from his first imprisonment with his life, as he had foreseen when he wrote to the Philippians. He then made another journey through his former field of operation and also visited Crete. During this period he also may have carried out his plan of going to Spain (Romans 15:24,28).

The meager details mentioned in the pastoral epistles are not sufficient for us to reconstruct the itinerary of Paul on this occasion, nor can we determine where 1 Timothy and Titus were written. Judging from the similarity of these epistles, we may simply express the opinion that they were written in somewhat close succession. Second Timothy, written during the second and last imprisonment of Paul, is also the last message that he penned, for the second imprisonment ended with Paul's martyrdom.

K. 1 and 2 Timothy

234. Timothy

Born of a heathen father and of a Jewish mother (Acts 16:1), Timothy had been taught the Word of God from his earliest childhood by his grandmother Lois and his mother, Eunice. It is likely that Paul converted him to the Christian faith, together with these two women (Acts 16:1; 1 Timothy 1:2; 2 Timothy 1:5; 3:15). He joined the apostle's company when Paul visited Lystra on his second missionary journey. Before taking Timothy with him, however, Paul circumcised him, lest any Jew be offended by Paul's close association with the son of a Gentile.

From that date Timothy was one of Paul's closest companions, leaving him rarely and for short periods only, as in Acts 17:14. When Paul made his long stay at Ephesus, Timothy went to Corinth as his emissary (Acts 19:22; 1 Corinthians 4:17). Afterward, Timothy met Paul at Corinth and traveled to Jerusalem with the apostle (Acts 20:4). During the first imprisonment of Paul, Timothy was his attendant (Philippians 1:1; Colossians 1:1; Philemon 1), and Paul intended to send him from there to

Philippi as soon as the outcome of his trial was certain (Philippians 2:19-23).

A passing remark in Hebrews 13:23 informs us that Timothy also experienced an imprisonment, presumably at some later date. Various allusions of the apostle would seem to indicate that Timothy was quite youthful when he put himself at the service of the aging apostle (1 Corinthians 16:10,11; Philippians 2:22; 1 Timothy 4:12), but his work was so excellent that Paul found reason for the highest praise (1 Corinthians 16:10). According to the tradition of the church, Timothy finally was made bishop of Ephesus and died a martyr's death under Domitian or Nerva.

235. First epistle

When Paul departed from Ephesus on his journey after his first imprisonment, he left Timothy behind him to be a guide for the church in that great city, teaching the Christians and warning them against dangerous errors that might arise (1 Timothy 1:3). For his guidance the apostle sent him 1 Timothy, instructing him how to deal with those who were in the habit of discussing all manner of profitless questions, ignoring the important issues of evangelical doctrine. Paul gave Timothy proper rules of order for public prayer and worship, taught him how to judge properly those who offered themselves for the ministry of the church, and imparted to him practical suggestions for ministering to the spiritual wants of all classes of people.

236. Second epistle

During his second imprisonment and at the end of his earthly career (2 Timothy 4:7,8), Paul wrote a second letter to Timothy, who, presumably, was still at Ephesus. In this last epistle, Paul, as it were, takes leave from all his labors on earth, bequeathing to Timothy, his faithful helper, this testamentary instruction concerning the work of the ministry.

This letter is much more personal than the first one. For this reason Paul here takes less pains than usual to follow a connected line of thought. Nevertheless, the letter plainly consists of two main sections. In the first Paul exhorts Timothy to be steadfast in affliction and faithful in preaching the gospel. In the second he foretells coming departures from the truth and warns against their destructive influence.

Summary of 1 Timothy

   I. The chief doctrines of the Christian faith, as distinguished from impending errors, chapter 1.

  II. Instructions concerning the order of public worship and the appointment of ministers and deacons, chapters 2,3.

 III. Instructions respecting proper performance of ministerial functions, chapters 4–6. (1) How the minister shall take care of himself and (2) How he shall take care of others.

Summary of 2 Timothy

   I. Exhortation to be steadfast in the faith, notwithstanding all afflictions, chapter 1 and in the ministry, notwithstanding all temptations to error, chapter 2.

  II. Admonition to hold fast to the Word in the coming flood of errorism and to be faithful in the ministry, 3:11–4:8.

 III. Conclusion; personal notes, 4:9-22.

L. Titus

237. Titus

When Paul returned to Jerusalem after his first missionary journey to attend the apostolic convention, he brought with him a youth who had been lately converted, Titus, a Gentile. After due deliberation it was decided that Titus should not be compelled to undergo circumcision, and thus the young man became a living example of that Christian liberty which the apostles then upheld in the public convention mentioned (Galatians 2:3).

Later we meet Titus as Paul's companion during his third journey. After the first epistle had been sent to Corinth, Titus was dispatched to Corinth with instructions to meet the apostle at Troas. The meeting, however, did not take place until Paul reached Macedonia, and from there Titus was sent to Corinth as the bearer of the second epistle (2 Corinthians 2:12,13; 7:6,13; 12:18).

The New Testament gives no further information concerning Titus, until we find him as Paul's appointed representative in Crete (Titus 1:5). This remark of Paul gave rise to the tradition that Titus was bishop of Crete and died there.

238. Epistle

Having been freed from his first imprisonment, Paul had labored on the island of Crete and had established a number of churches (Titus 1:5). When he departed, he put Titus in charge of this great field, with instructions to take care of these churches in the proper manner. To guide Titus in preventing serious mistakes, Paul wrote the epistle to Titus, describing the qualifications for the ministry, denouncing the false teachers and warning against them, extolling the grace that brings salvation, and instructing Titus how to perform his duties toward Christians of all classes and how to exhort all believers to lead decent lives.

Summary of contents

   I. Concerning the qualifications for the ministry and the errors then prevailing in Crete, chapter 1.

   II. Concerning the proper ministration of the Word to all classes of people, particularly to slaves, chapter 2.

   III. How Christians should conduct themselves toward the government and toward the ungodly world; how Titus must guard himself against errorists, chapter 3.

M. Philemon

239. Philemon and Onesimus

Philemon undoubtedly was a member of the church at Colossae, since Onesimus, his slave, is described as belonging to that congregation (Colossians 4:9). According to Paul's testimony, Philemon was a dedicated Christian, probably a person of prominence in the church (Philemon 4-7). The slave Onesimus had run away from his master, seeking refuge and concealment in the crowded precincts of Rome (Philemon 10,11,15,16).

What caused his flight cannot be shown from verse 18; Paul merely offers in general terms to make reparation. Divine providence brought Onesimus to Paul, who converted the slave (verse 10). When Tychicus was sent to Ephesus and Colossae by Paul, the opportunity was ripe to return the fugitive to his master, but not without a letter designed to protect Onesimus against the cruel punishment often meted out to escaped slaves.

240. Epistle

When Paul wrote this brief letter, he was a prisoner (verses 9,10,13,23), and since he sent the epistle to the Colossians at the same time (Colossians 4:7-9), Philemon, like Colossians, must have been written from Rome. It is an urgent appeal, yet circumspect and sane. Paul had not taught the slave that his conversion to the Christian faith freed him from his bonds but had looked upon him still as the personal property of Philemon (verses 13,14). Thus the apostle established the principle that the gospel does not invalidate human ordinances that are not in themselves against the moral law. On the other hand, he reminds Philemon that he must now recognize his slave Onesimus as a brother in Christ, who on his part, though aware of spiritual equality with his master, showed genuine fruits of faith by returning willingly to his master.

N. The catholic epistles

241. General remarks

Why the catholic epistles are called catholic has been explained in section 197. They are seven in number, two of Peter, three of John, and one each of James and Jude. To these should be added Hebrews, which is placed last of all epistles in Luther's German Bible, while it follows immediately after Paul's epistles in the English version. Of these eight letters only two, 1 Peter and 1 John, have been unanimously accepted as canonical.

In regard to the other six, various considerations have caused serious doubts as to their apostolic origin. In the case of 2 and 3 John, it would seem that their brevity, coupled with the fact that they are addressed to private persons, was considered sufficient reason for setting them aside. Second Peter is so plainly based upon Jude that this probably made the church doubtful concerning the Petrine origin. The identity of both James and Jude has always been in dispute, because no one can show convincingly that these two men were apostles. The author of Hebrews does not mention his name, and no attempt to determine his identity has led to satisfactory results. Moreover, certain statements in several of these epistles have led some to doubt their apostolic origin because they seem to be at variance with Paul's theology.

A detailed examination of these various problems will be made in the subsequent paragraphs. It suffices for our present purposes to remember that the six epistles in question belong to the class of antilegomena and are canonical writings of secondary rank, historically.

O. Hebrews

242. Author

The writer of the valuable and instructive epistle to the Hebrews does not give his own name, and the scattered references to his personality are altogether insufficient for his identification. Thus every reader may decide for himself which one of the various hypotheses offered by scholars makes the best sense.

At a very early date, the opinion was voiced that Hebrews was written by Paul. For this reason the manuscripts often place this epistle among the Pauline writings or at least immediately after them, which is the arrangement adopted in the English Bible. Defenders of this view point to the elegance of diction and the argumentative power exhibited by the writer, in which he, indeed, closely approaches Paul. Add to this that the writer proves himself to be intimately acquainted with the Jewish law, that he was a prisoner (10:34), that he speaks of Timothy as his special companion (13:23), and that he closes his letter with greetings and benedictions in the Pauline style, and you will feel that this argument has some force.

Nevertheless, the denial of Pauline origin is just as old and hardly less forceful. Precisely because Pauline authorship cannot be definitely established, this epistle was received with misgivings, and the older church fathers make it a point to remind readers of this fact. There are several weighty reasons for rejecting the idea of Pauline authorship in this case:

(1) Paul otherwise never failed to place his name at the head of his epistles, and he often attested their genuineness by a special signature. There is no trace of this in Hebrews.

(2) In 2:3 the author proves the truth of the gospel by appealing to the testimony of eye-and-ear witnesses of the life and work of Christ and thus indicates that he was a pupil of the apostles and not himself one of their number. Paul, on the other hand, lays particular stress upon the fact that he had not received his gospel from the other apostles but by special revelation (1 Corinthians 11:23; Galatians 1:1,12).

(3) The similarities existing between Hebrews and Pauline writings are counterbalanced by diversities that are just as obvious.

These and other considerations caused Luther to say in his preface to Hebrews:

> That the Epistle to the Hebrews is not from Paul, or any other apostle is proved by the fact that we read in chapter 2:3 that "this doctrine came to us and remained with us through those who have themselves heard it from the Lord." Thus he plainly speaks of the apostles as [if he were] a disciple to whom this doctrine came from the apostles, probably long thereafter. For Paul declares powerfully in Galatians 1:1 that he received his Gospel not of men, nor by men, but of God himself.

Thus it would seem to be fairly certain that this epistle was written by a disciple of the apostles, like the gospels according to Mark and Luke. A diligent and continued search among the younger teachers of the early church, as far as we know them, has failed to reveal a person able to qualify as the author of Hebrews. As Luther says in his preface (written in 1522), "It is unknown who has written it, and will probably remain unknown for some time." Afterward, however, he suggested that Apollos of Alexandria (Acts 18:24-28) may have been the author. In his *Church Postil,* Luther says:

> Some think it [Hebrews] was written by St. Luke, others, by St. Apollo, whom St. Luke praises as being powerful in the Scriptures against the Jews (Acts 18:24). It must be admitted that no epistle uses the Scriptures with such force as this one, so that he must have been an excellent, apostolical man, whoever he was.

In another sermon Luther says, "This Apollos was a highly enlightened man; the Epistle to the Hebrews certainly is his."

Others have surmised that Barnabas, the companion of Paul, might have written this epistle, and it would seem that some of the church fathers directly call it the epistle of Barnabas. The name of Silas (Acts 15:22,32,40) has also been suggested in this connection but with no more conclusive evidence to support the suggestion than in the other cases.

243. Audience

Since the entire epistle was written to show that the Levitical order of worship with all its pomp and ceremony was abolished by the advent of the Son of God in the flesh, who substituted something immeasurably greater, the author must have intended his argument for Jewish Christians, who alone would be directly interested in such a discussion. As evidence we mention that he speaks of "our forefathers" without any modification (1:1). He uses the argument that Christ, being a lineal descendant of Abraham, calls the people of Israel his brothers (2:11,16). He compares the Levitic purification with the purification worked by Christ (9:7-15).

At the same time, it is plain that the author is not addressing the Jewish Christians generally but is speaking to a certain church or at least to a definite circle of readers. He knows what they have learned (5:11,12), what they have suffered (10:32; 12:4), and what they have done (6:10). Finally, he expresses the hope that he will soon be reunited with them (13:19). Moreover, these Christians must have lived in a district where converts from among the Gentiles were unknown or present in small number only. If it had been otherwise, the epistle would undoubtedly have mentioned so, since elsewhere there always seems to have been some amount of friction between the two groups of Christians, especially in regard to the ceremonial law of the Jews and its observance.

Again, it is very plain that the writer seeks to protect his particular readers against the danger of relapsing into Judaism by seeking salvation in the forms of worship of the old covenant which had now been abolished by Christ. The only location where groups of Christians answering this description could possibly be found according to our information was at Jerusalem and in the country immediately surrounding that city. While all churches outside of Palestine consisted to a great extent, if not almost exclusively, of former Gentiles, the church at Jerusalem certainly had very few, if any, gentile members. It was, moreover, the oldest of all churches, had enjoyed the ministry of the apostles in particular measure, had suffered persecution, and, alone of all existing churches, saw the Levitical ceremonies in the temple continued before their eyes as a constant temptation. Thus every indication seems to assure us that this epistle was addressed to the church at Jerusalem or at least to a group of churches in lower Palestine.

244. Original language

Since the purpose of this epistle is obvious, the opinion was voiced at an early date that it had been written in Hebrew originally and had been translated into Greek by Luke or some other inspired writer. As it happens, however, no book of the New Testament is written in such fluent Greek as this one. The periodic style, which is an outstanding characteristic of all its sections, is so entirely foreign to the Hebrew language that it could not have appeared in a translation. Furthermore, we find examples of ingenious plays on the sound of Greek words, which could not have been reproduced from the Hebrew (as in 13:14). Finally, quotations from the Old Testament are not always made from the Hebrew original but from the Septuagint version (1:7; 10:37). Consequently, we haven't the least reason to doubt that we possess this epistle in the form in which it was originally written. As all Jews of Palestine were acquainted with the Greek world language, the epistle was quite intelligible to them in its Greek form.

245. Time of writing

Since the epistle was written to Christians in Palestine by a man who was not an apostle, it should not be difficult to decide upon the time when it must have been written. It was well known at Rome before the end of the first century. Clement of Rome, a pupil of Paul, quotes it in a letter addressed to the Corinthians, though without mentioning it by name. Therefore it surely belongs to the apostolic age.

It was written before the destruction of Jerusalem and of the temple, for the writer speaks of the Levitic worship as going on before the eyes of his readers. In addition, he would surely have used the argument that the fall of the Holy City is the most convincing proof of the abolition of the Jewish ceremonial laws if the catastrophe had already taken place. The visitation of God was at hand, however, and the readers had recognized the signs of its coming (10:25).

A man of less than apostolic rank, however, would surely not have presumed to interfere with the work of the apostles if they had still been present at Jerusalem. Since we know that John was the last of the Twelve to leave the city, arriving in Ephesus before the year 66, it would seem to be definitely established that this epistle was penned in A.D. 66 or 67.

As to the place of writing, we have no information whatever. The mention of Italy in 13:24 furnishes no clue, since the words seem to indicate no more than that the writer was not in Italy at the time.

246. Canonical authority

That Hebrews was not received with unanimous approval by the early church is probably due to those statements which Luther also found troublesome. In his preface he says:

> [This epistle] has a hard knot, since in 6:4-6 and 10:26 it straightway denies and refuses repentance to those who sin after baptism, and says in 12:17 that Esau sought repentance, but did not find it. As it reads, this seems to be opposed to all gospels and all epistles of Paul. And though some explanation may be made, the words are so plain that I doubt whether that be sufficient.

The two passages first referred to by Luther obviously describe the sin of a person who rejects the gospel intentionally and blasphemously, though he has experienced its power. This is the sin against the Holy Spirit, of which Christ also declares that it cannot be forgiven (Matthew 12:31,32; Mark 3:29), surely because such a person rejects the one means by which all forgiveness comes to man, the gospel. As to the difficult passage in 12:17, it is suggested that the word *repentance* (NIV, "change of mind") is here used in its widest sense, as denoting any change of mind. Esau urged his father to change his mind but sought for this change in vain. This eliminates the thought, abhorrent to the ears of most Christians, that God deliberately refused repentance to Esau, though he sought it with tears.

Summary of contents

I. Christ, the eternal Son of God, is our High Priest, in whom we should trust, 1:1–4:13.

II. Christ's priestly ministry is greater than that of Aaron, 4:14–7:28.

III. Christ's expiatory sacrifice excels by far all Levitical sacrifices, 8:1–10:18.

IV. Exhortation to be steadfast in faith and patience and to continue in good works, 10:19–13:25.

P. James

247. Author

The writer of the interesting letter James introduces himself as "James, a servant of God and of the Lord Jesus Christ" (1:1), feeling sure that this description would identify him to his first readers. Nobody, however, thought of handing down that assurance to later readers. There is fairly unanimous agreement that this James is the same man whose influential position in the church at Jerusalem is set forth in Acts and in Galatians (Acts 12:17; 15:13-21; Galatians 1:19; 2:9). But to this day, the question whether this James was one of the twelve apostles remains unsettled.

The writer of this epistle speaks with such consciousness of authority that we must necessarily look for him among the most respected teachers of the apostolic age. James the Elder, son of Zebedee and brother of John, certainly did not write this letter, for he died a martyr in the year 44 (Acts 12:2), at a time when the church had not yet grown beyond the reach of apostolic voice. The younger James, however, who was considered a pillar of the church side by side with Peter and John, who also was entitled to speak authoritatively, could expect to be recognized by such a brief introductory word. According to ancient tradition, this James continued his labors in the church at Jerusalem until his death.

Old historians tell us that he was surnamed "the Just," even among unbelieving Jews, because of his righteous life or because of his strict observance of Jewish ritualistic laws. But when the vengeful schemes of the Jews against Paul had been frustrated—so the story continues—their ire turned against James. They demanded that he testify against Jesus during the Easter festival, from the roof of the temple, before the multitudes there assembled. But when he fearlessly proclaimed Jesus as the Messiah, the Son of God, they cast him down from the pinnacle. While he lay on the ground, sorely wounded but still alive, the mob began to stone him. Finally, a tanner killed the martyr with a club while his lips still moved in an intercession for his murderers. According to this story, James achieved the crown of martyrdom about A.D. 69.

Who was this James the Just? The lists of the twelve apostles chosen by Jesus (Matthew 10:2-4; Mark 3:16-19;

Acts 1:13) mention two Jameses, one the son of Zebedee *(Jacobus major),* the other the son of Alphaeus *(Jacobus minor).* The unsettled question is whether James the Just is the same person as James the son of Alphaeus. Though the epistle of James furnishes no clue, the dispute would most probably never have arisen had not Paul called James the Just a brother of the Lord (Galatians 1:19). This instantly reminds us of John's remark that the brothers of Jesus did not believe in him (John 7:3,5), which seems to make it certain that no brother of the Lord was chosen as an apostle, even though he may have turned to Christ later.

A complete presentation of the problem would lead us too far in this connection. Here we present (according to a theologian named Guericke) the reasons for identifying James the son of Alphaeus with James the Just, the author of this epistle:

(1) Acts does not mention an early death of James the son of Alphaeus, whereas, being an apostle and a person of no little importance, his death would not have been passed over in silence.

(2) It is not easy to understand how any man not an apostle could have risen at such an early date to a position of such authority in the church of Jerusalem. Also, it would then have been very peculiar that Paul should have placed his name before the names of two apostles (Galatians 2:9).

(3) According to the only natural understanding of Galatians 1:19, Paul means to say that James, the brother of the Lord, was also an apostle. The same is probably true of 1 Corinthians 15:7.

(4) This view has been adopted by several cautious writers of the early church, such as Clement of Alexandria, Jerome, and Chrysostom, as a result of their investigations.

279

In reference to the objections based upon John 7:3,5, Guericke says:

> It is not here said in so many words that not one of the four brethren of the Lord believed in him at the time. But even if John had meant to include the younger James, he does not say that all four brothers remained unbelievers until the death of Jesus. James may have been persuaded to believe before Christ had definitely designated his apostles.

248. Date and audience

There seems to be small cause for doubting that James is addressing Jewish Christians. He calls them "the twelve tribes scattered among the nations" (or, of the Dispersion, 1:1). The term *diaspora* was otherwise used as a collective name for all the Jews who lived abroad among the heathen nations. Some of them may have been converted as a result of the Pentecostal miracle, before Paul began his journeys. Here, however, the name seems to be applied differently, for James is certainly speaking to Christians belonging to well-established churches. Add to this that he plainly alludes to the gospel according to Saint Matthew (as in 1:22, compared with Matthew 7:21; 2:13, with Matthew 5:7 and 18:30,34; and 4:12, with Matthew 7:1) and even to certain epistles of Paul (compare 1:12 and 2 Timothy 4:8; 2:5 and 1 Corinthians 1:26; especially 4:5 and Galatians 5:17). All this seems to make it certain that James directed his admonitions to the Jewish Christians of the older churches in and near Palestine and that he wrote from Jerusalem after Paul had been removed from the scene of his labors but before the destruction of Jerusalem, which James did not live to see.

249. Character

The purpose of the writer is not so much to instruct as to exhort and admonish. He found ample reasons to write about the many faults that everywhere impeded the proper growth of holiness in the churches. His readers clearly were in great danger of backsliding, under the constant pressure exerted by the unbelieving members of their race (1:2-4; 5:7-11). They were beset with doubts about the fulfillment of sincere prayers (1:5-8; 5:15-18). The wealthy men among them had become influential because of their riches, while the poor were pushed aside (1:9,10; 2:1-13; 5:1-6, though in this last passage James may be referring to non-Christian Jews). Sins of the tongue were common (chapter 3; 4:11; 5:12). Most dangerous of all was the illusion that true faith might well exist without good works (2:14-26). James handles all these questions in a manner peculiar to himself. His style is incisive, strong, and pithy, reminding the reader of the rhythm of ancient Hebrew poetry.

250. Canonicity

The epistle of James was not unanimously accepted as part of the canon by the ancient church, and the doubts then entertained by Christian teachers have never been entirely quieted. They are due, in part, to the difference of opinion about the person of the writer, who some believe never was an apostle. The main reason, however, for objecting to this epistle is found in the undeniable difficulty of harmonizing some statements of James on justification with the clear and unmistakable doctrine of Paul on this point.

Luther refused to accept this epistle as "an apostle's writing." In his preface, written in 1522, he gives his reasons as follows:

In the first place, because, straightway in opposition to St. Paul and all other Scripture, it ascribes righteousness to works, saying that Abraham was justified by his works when he offered up his son, whereas St. Paul (Romans 4:2,3) teaches contrarily that Abraham was justified without works, by faith alone, before he offered up his son, and proves it from Moses (Genesis 15:6). Though some help might be found for this epistle, and also some explanation for such righteousness by works, yet no excuse can be found for this, that in 2:23 the statement of Moses from Genesis 15:6 is quoted as speaking of works, whereas it speaks only of Abraham's faith, and not of his works, as St. Paul applies it in Romans 4:3. This defect, therefore, proves that it was not written by an apostle.

The objection thus voiced by Luther will never quite lose its force as sustaining the ancient doubt about the origin of this epistle, and for this reason it will always rank as a book of secondary canonical authority.

At the same time, there will always be those who believe that the apparent contradiction between Paul and James may be removed in a satisfactory manner by observing that the two inspired writers speak of justification from different points of view. While both describe the saving faith, Paul emphasizes the truth that works cannot earn justification before God, whereas James lays particular stress upon the need of proving inward faith by outward works. Thus, according to James, Abraham was justified before the eyes of all men by his works, since his works were evidence of the faith that justified him before God. Likewise, on the Last Day, God will show from the works of his children that they were righteous through justification by faith.

The Weimar Bible paraphrases James 2:23 as follows: "[In this manner] Scripture makes a complete statement, saying (two things, first): Abraham believed God, and it was imputed unto him for righteousness (he was justified before God); and (secondly, how this righteousness was witnessed publicly in that) he was called the friend of God (Isaiah 41:8)."

Summary of contents

I. Exhortations pertaining chiefly to the first table of the Ten Commandments, chapters 1,2.

II. Exhortations pertaining chiefly to the second table of the Ten Commandments, chapters 3–5.

Q. 1 and 2 Peter

251. Apostle

In the four Gospels and in Acts, we find abundant material for describing the life and character of Peter and, likewise, his position among the chosen heralds of the Lord, up to the period when Paul stepped into the foreground. From that point onward, Peter is rarely mentioned in the biblical record, so that we have no reliable record of his later labors and experience except that of church tradition.

Peter was the son of a certain Jonah (Matthew 16:17; John 21:15, "John"), a man otherwise unknown to us. His brother was Andrew the Apostle. Peter was originally called Simon, but at his first meeting with Jesus, the Master surnamed him Cephas, or Peter, that is, the Rock, to denote the firmness of his character (John 1:42). Afterward Jesus always called him Simon, except on the memorable occasion recorded in Matthew 16:18, where the name of Peter was to remind him of that first meeting and that he was called a rock because of his faith, which was built upon the true

Rock. To the churches of the later biblical days, the apostle seems to have been known only as Peter; for Luke feels the need of explaining the use of the name Simon, as in Acts 10:5. Paul always calls him Peter, or Cephas.

When Jesus began his ministry, Peter lived in Capernaum and was married (Mark 1:21,29,30). We also know that his wife traveled with him when he was engaged in missionary work in later years (1 Corinthians 9:5). We do not hear that he had any children. Although he calls Mark his son (1 Peter 5:13), this term is plainly used in a spiritual sense. Like James and John, the sons of Zebedee, Peter with Andrew, his brother, gained his livelihood by fishing in the Sea of Galilee. These four men were busy with their day's work when Jesus called them as apostles (Matthew 4:18-22). Obedient in faith, Peter at once dropped his business and thereafter followed Jesus in all his wanderings.

He was one of the three intimates of the Lord, being granted the privilege of witnessing both the glory of Jesus revealed on the Mount of Transfiguration and the deepest humiliation of the Savior in Gethsemane. As Peter was of an impulsive character, it happened quite without design that he often appeared as spokesman of the disciples when Christ addressed important questions to them all (Matthew 16:16; 19:27). For this reason he also had to bear the brunt of serious rebukes that were meant for all the disciples (Matthew 16:23; Luke 22:31). The same quickness of temper caused Peter to attempt that ill-advised defense of the Lord in the garden (John 18:10), and his sinful self-confidence carried him into the house of the high priest, despite the faithful warnings of Christ, and led to his grievous downfall, when he renounced his Master in threefold denial. The Lord, however, fulfilling his gracious promise (Luke 22:32), called him to repentance at once.

When the report of Christ's resurrection reached the disciples, Peter was among the first who hurried to the tomb (Luke 24:12). The risen Lord also remembered him particularly (Mark 16:7), visited him and the other disciples, and finally confirmed him in the apostolate by special instruction (John 21:15-19). After the ascension of Christ, we again find Peter at the head of the disciples. He arranged for the election of Matthias (Acts 1:15-26), and on the Day of Pentecost, he delivered the sermon that resulted in the establishment of the first Christian church (Acts 2).

Together with the other apostles, he ministered to this congregation (Acts 6:2) and continued to preach without fear, though persecution soon befell the believers and especially the apostles. Twice Peter was delivered from the hands of his enemies in a miraculous manner, once in company with all the other apostles (Acts 5:17-21) and again after Herod had imprisoned him and had appointed the day of his execution (Acts 12). Before this second deliverance, however, Peter had received a special revelation in a vision, instructing him to spread the gospel among the Gentiles. In response to this call, he traveled to Caesarea, where Cornelius and his household became members of the Christian church through the ministry of Peter.

Later, when Paul and Barnabas came to Jerusalem to confer with the other apostles on the important question of Christian liberty, Peter spoke the words that settled all dispute and frankly sided with Paul (Acts 15). On this occasion the apostles also discussed the missionary outlook and agreed among themselves that, while Paul was to work chiefly among the Gentiles, Peter and John should continue their labors among the Jews (Galatians 2:9). In the biblical record, Peter is last mentioned in Galatians 2:11-16, where we are told that Paul was compelled to take him to task for certain acts of hypocrisy.

No one can say with certainty where Peter labored in his latter years. From the history of Paul, however (see section 204), we know with certainty that Peter did not reach Rome before Paul and that he was neither the founder nor the first bishop of the Roman church. As to the place and manner of his death, tradition is definite and unanimous, making it certain that Peter died at Rome as a martyr of Christ. (The legend: Peter seeks safety in flight. Christ meets him on the way and asks the question, *Quo vadis?* ["Where are you going?"] Peter turns about and submits to crucifixion, being fastened to the cross head downward, at his special request.)

It is quite unscriptural and smacks of Romanism to call Peter the prince of the apostles or the supreme shepherd, as some Protestant writers have done. It is true that Peter excelled among his companions by personal gifts and tireless willingness to work, so that they probably conceded him a certain leadership. But this privilege of Peter, if it existed, was not by divine appointment. On the contrary, Christ forestalled all ambitions of church supremacy by abolishing all differences of rank among his followers, including the apostles (see Matthew 23:8, and compare Luke 22:24-30). Add to this that Paul, suffering under the blasphemies of errorists, felt constrained to claim almost in as many words that his apostleship was equal to that of Peter (2 Corinthians 11:5). It is true that Peter is always named first in the list of apostles (Matthew 10:2; Mark 3:16; Acts 1:13), but this is merely a historical record that Peter was one of the first apostles called by Christ.

252. Peter as a letter writer

Our Bible contains two epistles that bear the name of Peter. No person of unbiased mind has ever expressed a doubt as to the genuineness of 1 Peter, in which the apostle names himself as the writer. Christian writers of the earliest days of the church quote it under the apostle's name. The oldest witness is the author of 2 Peter 3:1, for even though someone might decide that this second epistle is not genuine, its age surely brings it very near to the days when Peter lived. In the course of the second century, almost all church fathers referred to Peter's first epistle, and they were writing at a time when a forgery could, and would, have been detected.

The case is different with regard to 2 Peter. None of the writers of the second century mention it directly, and it is not contained in the earliest version, the Syriac Peshito. In the third century, Origen is the first author to quote it by name. But though he makes use of some statements from 2 Peter, he remarks that its Petrine origin was doubted. These are historical facts that cannot be set aside, and thus the epistle will always belong to the class of the antilegomena, with secondary canonical rank.

At the same time, however, all the facts mentioned above do not prove that this epistle is a forgery. On the contrary, there is strong evidence that Peter the Apostle actually did write this letter.

(1) Although the writers of the second century do not name this epistle, they nevertheless allude to it unmistakably, showing that they were familiar with it. As the letter was written shortly before the death of Peter, this may have been a reason why it was distributed slowly. Each month of delay made it more doubtful, apparently, that it had been written during the apostle's lifetime. This merely shows the caution with which the church scrutinized the origin of inspired writings.

(2) The vague doubt thus engendered may have been strengthened because this letter of Peter and the epistle of

Jude are very closely related. Not only does the second chapter of 2 Peter refer to the same errors that Jude combats, but Peter obviously copies many phrases, comparisons, and so on from the smaller letter. No reader can escape the impression that Jude's epistle lay before the eyes of Peter when he wrote his second letter. Still, this fact should not shake our confidence, since Peter nowhere simply copies Jude but attacks the errorists in his own peculiar way. Peter plainly received his first definite information concerning the dangers threatening the churches of Asia Minor through Jude and considered it his duty to endorse what Jude had written, in order to make the needed warning doubly impressive. Surely this undertaking was not unworthy of an apostle.

(3) A forger setting out to write under the name of Peter would certainly have taken pains to imitate the first epistle of that apostle rather than the brief letter of Jude.

(4) Second Peter contains no statement that is not in full accord with the well-known doctrine of Peter and the other apostles.

253. First Epistle

The apostle writes "to God's elect, strangers in the world, scattered throughout [or, "of the Dispersion in"] Pontus, Galatia, Cappadocia, Asia [the province of that name] and Bithynia" (1:1). As he employs the term *diaspora*, which was commonly used for the Jews living in the heathen countries, it has been supposed that the churches so addressed by Peter consisted exclusively of Jewish Christians. If that were true, the letter must have been sent out before Paul traveled through the countries named, for after his visits there, all the churches had gentile members. It might be admitted that in those districts, as probably in Rome, the first seeds of the gospel were planted effectively as a result of the great Pentecost sermon (Acts 2:9). In any case, the description of 1 Peter 4:3 is sufficient to demonstrate that the churches addressed actually had many gentile members, who may even have been in the majority.

According to the description of the apostle, the Christians of those districts were in great need of consolation because of persecutions that had sorely tried their faith. For this reason his chief topic is the hope of Christians. He adds the exhortation not only to hold fast to the truth but also to adorn it with a godly life.

Peter says that he wrote this epistle at Babylon (5:13). The name reminds us of the ancient Chaldean city of that name, which had a large Jewish colony in those days, where Peter might have found a promising field of labor. But it seems highly improbable otherwise that Peter ever traveled as far east as the real Babylon. On the other hand, we know from Revelation 18:2 that the name of Babylon was commonly used by Christians to designate Rome, and it was suggested at a very early date that Peter uses the same allegory. His readers certainly were not misled by the use of the term. But if written at Rome, the letter must have been sent out shortly before the death of Peter, since it is the constant tradition that he became a martyr soon after he reached the metropolis, about A.D. 65.

There still remains one point of doubt, however. The churches that Peter addresses belonged to the field of Paul. How could Peter presume to act as their teacher without interfering with the prerogatives of his fellow apostle? But this doubt disappears if we remember that Paul firmly intended to make a missionary journey to Spain (Romans 15:24). And so we suggest the following reasonable explanation: when Paul had been freed from his first imprisonment, he made that trip eastward, during which he left Timothy at Ephesus and Titus in Crete. Then he turned westward and labored in Spain. In the meantime Peter came to Rome and there heard of the sufferings and tribulations of the Christians of Asia Minor. As they were in immediate need of spiritual care, Peter did not wait for Paul's return but acted in full accordance with his own apostolic authority.

254. Second epistle

Second Peter was addressed to the same churches that had received the first communication (3:1). In some manner, probably through information contained in Jude, Peter had learned that false teachers and dangerous sects threatened the very existence of the Christian churches of Asia Minor. In particular, he had discovered that scoffers had raised their voices against the Christian hope of Christ's return to judgment. In strong, convincing words, he first demonstrates that the Word which had been preached in Asia rested upon divine revelation. Then he proceeds to teach the proper Christian point of view in regard to errorists and scoffers.

According to his own testimony, Peter knew that his death was near at hand when he wrote this letter (1:14). Therefore he must have sent it soon after the first epistle.

Summary of 1 Peter

    I. Introduction; salutation, 1:1,2.

   II. The sure salvation of Jesus Christ, which the tribulations of this earth cannot render doubtful, 1:3-12.

  III. The knowledge of this salvation as a constant impulse to increasing holiness, 1:13–3:16.

IV. On their way with Christ through sufferings to glory, Christians should fight against sin and bear their afflictions patiently, 3:17–4:19.

V. Particular admonitions; conclusion, chapter 5.

Summary of 2 Peter

I. Salutation; exhortation to lead a godly life, based upon the divine origin of Scripture revelation, chapter 1.

II. The punishment of errorists; their character, chapter 2.

III. The certainty of the day of judgment; concluding exhortation, chapter 3.

R. The three epistles of John

255. First epistle

First John has always been received by the church as written by John the Apostle and Evangelist, though he mentions his name as little as he does in his gospel. Here, as there, he furnishes ample means of identification. In 1:2 and 4:14, he declares himself to be an eye-and-ear witness of the revelation of the Son of God in the flesh and to belong to the group of the original messengers of the gospel. Even a casual comparison will also show that the greatest similarity exists between the fourth gospel and this letter, in subject matter as well as style, which absolutely discloses the identity of the author.

Accordingly, it is generally supposed that the letter was written about the same time as the fourth gospel, during John's stay at Ephesus (see section 193). It is impossible, however, to determine whether the epistle was written before the gospel or after it. It was meant as a letter, not as a mere addition to the gospel, as its style and the direct addresses demonstrate, though John does not follow the usual form of salutation and conclusion familiar to us from the Pauline writings.

John makes it clear that his readers were not beginners in the Christian faith, who needed fundamental instruction, but persons of some spiritual experience, who had long been in the faith (2:13,14,20,21). Such were the members of the churches in Ephesus and its environs, where Paul had labored most diligently and intensively. These people, who were well versed in the doctrine of faith, needed to be reminded that true faith must necessarily be followed by true love. John extols the love of God and insists that it should be the real cause for sincere love toward God and toward our fellow Christians.

In his preface to this epistle, Luther says:

> Having discussed faith in his gospel, so John in the epistle takes those to task who boasted of faith without works and teaches in various ways that works will not remain undone where there is faith. If they fail, however, then faith is not sincere, but is a lie and darkness. . . . Thus the epistle argues against both errors, as much against those who intend to be believers without works as against those who think to be righteous by works. It holds us to the proper middle way, that through faith we become righteous and without sin and then, after we are righteous, practice good works and love for God's sake, freely, without any requirement.

256. Second and third epistles

Second and 3 John are personal letters, the former being addressed to a certain "chosen lady and her children," the latter to a certain Gaius. Undoubtedly for this reason, together with their brevity and seeming unimportance, these letters were distributed slowly and were not universally accepted as written by John. Yet their authenticity should not be called into question, even though John here simply calls himself "the elder."

There is an old legend to the effect that there lived in Asia Minor another John, in addition to the apostle of that name, who held an influential position in the church and was known as "John the Presbyter," that is, "the elder." Some investigators have suggested that the two smaller Johannine letters were really written by this alleged presbyter and that this was the reason why they were rejected by some churches.

However, a comparison of the language used in these letters with that of 1 John leaves no room for doubt that they were all written by the same man. Again, it should be plain that only John the Apostle could have been entitled to call himself the elder without further explanation, since this title would naturally belong to him as the one surviving representative of the first Christian generation. Any other person bearing the title of elder by virtue of his official position in the church would have had to identify himself by adding his name. In fact, there is good reason to believe that there never was a presbyter John in Asia Minor other than the apostle.

These letters were certainly sent out from Ephesus, but we do not know where the chosen lady and Gaius lived. The name of Gaius was very common at the time. The man here addressed may have been of some prominence, but he was not among the public ministers of any church. As to 2 John, some commentators believe that it was addressed to a church, which the apostle honors with the title "chosen lady," the children mentioned being the individual members. It is more reasonable, however, to understand a Christian woman, to whom John makes suggestions about the proper exercise of Christian love and the necessary caution against deceivers. In 3 John, Gaius is praised for his hospitality and is warned against the evil example of Diotrephes. In both letters the apostle promises an early visit.

Summary of 1 John

I. The great blessing extended to us by the incarnation and death of Christ, chapter 1.

II. How we should show our gratitude to Christ for his blessing, chapters 2,3.

III. A warning not to be turned from this gratitude by false teachers, chapters 4,5.

Summary of 2 John

I. Greetings; command to walk in love, verses 1-6.

II. Warning against deceivers, verses 7-13.

Summary of 3 John

I. Commendation for Gaius' love and hospitality, verses 1-8.

II. Concern for the mean spirit of Diotrephes, verses 9-11.

III. Closing, verses 12,13.

S. Jude

257. Author

The author of the brief letter Jude calls himself "brother of James," viewing this as quite sufficient to identify himself, and it seems to be his intention to indicate that he himself was not an apostle. But he must have been a well-known, highly gifted man of some prominence in the apostolic church. The mere naming of James would also have been insufficient unless this James was a very prominent man. Hence there is very good reason to identify him with the author of the epistle of James, whom we recognize as an apostolic leader of the church at Jerusalem, a man known as James the Righteous. This James, a brother of the Lord, actually had a brother called Jude (Matthew 13:55; Mark 6:3); hence the writer of this letter also was among the brothers of Jesus.

He plainly shows in verse 17 that he was not an apostle, otherwise he surely would not have introduced himself merely as the brother of James. This agrees with the record of the gospels. There was an apostle named Judas (besides the betrayer, also called Thaddaeus). But in the two lists in which the brothers among the apostles are named as such (Matthew 10:2-4; Luke 6:14-16), the apostles James and Judas are not named together. Judas is described as the son of one James (compare Acts 1:13). Perhaps the writer of our letter was that Judas Barsabbas mentioned in Acts 15:22. At any rate, he held a position at Jerusalem that entitled him to a respectful hearing by other churches.

258. Epistle

The age and genuineness of this short sketch is evidenced in a unique manner by the endorsement that Peter gave it in his second epistle. It is the most satisfactory way of accounting for the close correspondence between the two epistles to assume that the short, compact treatise of Jude reached Peter the apostle. He then was moved by the Spirit to take up the message, emphasizing and broadening the warnings voiced by Jude, so that the Christians to whom they were directed might take them to heart more readily.

Because the letter of Peter itself was received with a certain measure of doubt, its endorsement did not secure full acceptance for the epistle of Jude. Furthermore, not only was Jude obviously not an apostle, but some surely took offense because Jude supports his testimony by quoting a prophecy of Enoch, which is not included in the canonical books of the Old Testament.

For us neither of these objections is serious. The first falls to the ground when we consider that Mark and Luke also were not men of apostolic rank. The second is outweighed by the fact that Paul even quotes from heathen writers (Acts 17:28; Titus 1:12). The prophecy of Enoch may have been correctly recorded outside of inspired Scripture, and the witness here of Jude through the Holy Spirit establishes its truth.

As the epistle contains no other objectionable feature, it has held its position in the canon throughout the centuries. Even the early writings of the church contain strong testimonies to its genuineness, and its very brevity and simplicity are arguments in its favor. The final evidence regarding the age of this letter is derived from the fact that Jude does not mention the destruction of Jerusalem. Since he supports his warnings by references to other judgments of God, he certainly would not have failed to emphasize the fate of Jerusalem if this catastrophe had already taken place. Thus the writing of this letter must be placed in the period immediately preceding the year 70.

According to Peter's testimony, Jude wrote chiefly for the churches of Asia Minor, which had been endangered by the appearance of lascivious, heretical, vicious deceivers. He denounces them briefly but sharply, prophesying the sure visitations of God's wrath upon them.

Summary of contents
  I. Greetings; introduction, verses 1-4.
  II. Warnings and judgments, verses 5-16.
  III. Admonitions, verses 17-23.
  IV. Doxology, verses 24,25.

Chapter 4
The Prophetic Book, Revelation

259. Author

The writer of Revelation mentions his name, John, on several occasions (1:1,4,9; 22:8) but does not call himself an apostle. This omission is of no significance in itself, as John does not even mention his own name in his gospel. But since the apostolic origin of Revelation has actually been doubted by Christian investigators, it is good to remember that Revelation contains the following unmistakable evidences concerning the person of its author:

(1) In the opening words, he declares that he received a direct revelation from God, one of great extent and supreme importance at that. Recalling that Paul points to the direct revelations he received as proof of his apostolic authority (Galatians 1:12), we must surely admit the force of this argument in the case of John's Revelation.

(2) In chapter 1:2 the author obviously speaks of the testimony that he gives as an eyewitness of the life of Jesus Christ, precisely as in John 1:14; 19:35; and 1 John 1:1-4.

(3) In chapter 1:9 John mentions his banishment to Patmos. It is the firm tradition of the early church that it was John the Apostle who was banished to Patmos.

(4) Only an apostle would have been entitled to address great Christian churches in the authoritative manner used by the writer in the first four chapters.

(5) In chapter 22:9 the angel calls John a brother of the prophets, thus declaring his apostolic rank, which is the same as that of the prophets.

Some of these arguments would not be decisive when standing alone. Taken together, they show convincingly that the writer claimed to be John the Apostle. That settles the question of the authorship, for it would have been morally impossible for a deliberate forger to fabricate the sublime visions recorded here. In fact, the book itself is the strongest argument for its inspired character.

One of the most skillful opponents of the Johannine origin of this book is forced to confess that he could not assemble a convincing argument for his view from Revelation itself. The critics then take refuge in certain statements, more or less clear, in which some church fathers are said to have spoken of a certain John the Presbyter, who was supposed to have existed in Asia Minor at the same time as John the Apostle. This presbyter is then hailed as the author of Revelation. But even if it should ever be demonstrated that such a presbyter actually existed, it would never follow that an unknown elder would have dared to write in the style of the first four chapters.

In his preface to Revelation, written in 1522, Luther directly denied the apostolic origin of this book, and he retained this opinion as late as 1545. But he was far from imposing his arguments, which are based on doctrine, as binding upon the consciences of others, for he writes (1545): "As far as we are concerned, these doubts remain to this day; but this is not intended as preventing anybody from believing the book to be St. John the Apostle's, or whatever he pleases."

260. Canonicity

Revelation belongs to the group of deuterocanonical writings (antilegomena), since it was not universally received from the beginning as a work of John the apostle or even as an inspired book. The reason for this is to be found in the peculiar arrangement, contents, and diction of Revelation, which closely resemble the apocalyptic prophecies of Ezekiel and Daniel and are without parallel in apostolic writings.

A book of such unique character naturally was received with great caution and made friends very slowly. We must also remember that the church was much troubled with the false doctrine about the millennium as early as the second century and that chiliasts from the beginning confidently claimed Revelation 20:1-8 as their great and invincible proof text. And so it is not surprising that Christians should have looked with some misgivings and uncertainty upon a book that could so easily be used by errorists.

Yet it happens that we have direct testimony of prominent teachers of the church as to the Johannine origin of Revelation, both from Asia Minor, where reliable information concerning the author was most easily available, and from the Alexandrian school of theology, whose members were recognized as most careful and cautious investigators.

261. Where written

John records that he received this remarkable revelation on the island of Patmos. Ancient tradition adds the information that the apostle had been banished there during a persecution. It is a rocky island of scarcely 60 square miles, one of the Sporades, which lie scattered in the Aegean Sea off the coast of Asia Minor. Slightly to the northeast of Patmos, on the mainland, was the Ionian city of Miletus, which, in turn, lay about 30 miles almost due south of Ephesus. When John was on Patmos, the island may have been covered with forests. Today the rocky cliffs rise bare and cold before the eye of the traveler, with only a group of trees here and there to break the bleak monotony.

In the beginning of the Middle Ages, the island had been uninhabited for a time because of the pirates who infested the Mediterranean. In 1088, however, the Monastery of Saint John was built, which stands to this day as the central feature of the city of Patmos. From the port of La Scala, a paved road leads steeply upward toward Patmos. About halfway up the traveler is shown a small cave, the Grotto of the Apocalypse, where John is said to have received the Revelation.

According to the statement of John, he experienced the entire vision in all its voluminous complexity on a single Sunday (1:10). But he does not inform us whether he wrote the record of this vision immediately or upon his return to Ephesus.

262. Time

We do not know with certainty when John suffered his banishment to Patmos, because the ancient writers do not agree on this point. Some claim that Nero (A.D. 54–68) was the emperor whose edict brought John to Patmos; others declare that Claudius (A.D. 41–54) was responsible, while a third group has decided that it happened under Domitian (A.D. 81–96). Since the period of Claudius is quite certainly out of the question, because it is much too early, one must decide between Nero and Domitian. Irenaeus, the chief witness for Domitian in this case, may have been misunderstood. His statements may actually refer to Nero, who was surnamed Domitius, so that his name might easily be confused with that of Domitian. Thus, strong evidence points to those witnesses who claim that John was banished during the Neronian persecution.

This also agrees with the allusions of those writers who name no emperor when speaking of the date for Revelation. Furthermore, it would seem from Revelation 11:1,2,8,13 that the destruction of Jerusalem still lay in the future when John wrote. Many commentators also assume that Revelation

17:7-12 indicates the number of Roman emperors who had completed their reign. We are then fairly sure that this book was written about the year 68 of the Christian era.

263. Original language

The language that John uses in this book is strongly tinged with Hebraisms. Yet he undoubtedly wrote in Greek, or else he would not have called Christ the Alpha and Omega (1:8), the first and the last letters of the Greek, not of the Hebrew, alphabet. Nor would he have named the jewels in chapter 21 by their genuine Greek names. It must also be remembered that the book was primarily intended for the churches of Asia Minor, whose members were chiefly of Greek extraction.

The surprising difference between the style of Revelation on the one hand and that of the gospel and epistles on the other hand is easily explained by the early date of Revelation. This book is surely the oldest document that we have from the pen of the apostle and was written before he had acquired the purer Greek spoken by the Christians at Ephesus.

264. Structure

A very short prologue (1:1-3) introduces the first larger section of the book, a special message of the Lord to the seven churches of Asia (that is, Asia Minor). These seven churches were grouped around the great city of Ephesus. Smyrna, 35 miles to the northward; Pergamos, 80 miles north; Thyatira, 70 miles to the northeast, between Pergamos and Sardis; Sardis, 55 miles to the northeast; Philadelphia, about 35 miles southeast of Sardis; Laodicea, which lay farthest away, nearly 100 miles to the east of Ephesus. Each of these churches is addressed by name and spoken to with the authority of him who had been their spiritual bishop and advisor since he had come to Ephesus from Jerusalem. The exhortation, adapted in each case to the particular needs of the church, is directed to the angel of that church, that is, to its bishop, whose duty it would be to impress upon his people the message of the apostle. Incidentally, some of these admonitions contain prophetic references to the future that are in keeping with the apocalyptic character of the whole book. Since each message ends with a solemn pronouncement of general importance, exhorting everyone to take to heart the words of God spoken to these churches (2:7,11,17,29; 3:6,13,22), it is plain that the Lord intended these messages for the instruction of his church throughout the ages.

Without further introduction, chapter 4 opens the second and chief section of Revelation proper. It is a series of powerful, tremendous visions, presented in symbolical language throughout, which presents an almost insurmountable task to the commentator. But it has been understood in the church from the beginning that the Lord here offers prophecy concerning the fate of the New Testament church during the world period that is to end on the day of his second advent.

The book closes with a solemn epilogue (22:6-21), in which the inspired character of Revelation is emphatically asserted.

265. Symbolism and prophecy

Throughout the book of Revelation, the symbolical character of the number 7 is a dominating feature. It may be that the selection of just seven churches was unintentional, but in the Revelation proper, the entire arrangement is in groups of sevens. Seven seals are opened by the lamb (6:1–8:1). After the opening of the seventh seal, seven trumpets are sounded in succession (8:2–15:8), and during the period of the seventh trumpet, seven bowls of wrath are poured out upon the earth (chapters 16–19). During all these portentous happenings, the growth of the church continues under sufferings and struggles, until the church's final triumph in glory.

In its form the prophecy of this book is similar to the apocalyptic writings contained in the second part of Ezekiel's book and in the visions of Daniel. Because of its symbolical nature this prophecy is much more difficult to understand than prophecies such as Paul's concerning the Antichrist (2 Thessalonians 2). Consequently, commentators disagree even as to the general intention of Revelation. Some believe that everything written in Revelation refers merely to the period immediately following the visions. But this is untenable, since John speaks too plainly of the day of judgment. Others, falling into the opposite extreme, would have us believe that no reference whatever is made to apostolic days. But this is surely wrong, because 17:9,10 clearly refers to the Roman emperors of that period.

It appears advisable, therefore, to adopt the suggestion of those commentators who say that the prophet paints into one grand picture the near and the distant future, setting side by side events that may be separated by great lapses of time. This lack of perspective is not unusual in biblical prophecy. In the same manner, for instance, Christ combined his statements concerning the approaching doom of Jerusalem and the final judgment of the world into one magnificent picture (Matthew 24:14-31). As the disciples surely were unable to separate the two groups of items until the prophecy had been fulfilled in part, so we cannot hope to decipher all the marvelous imagery of the book of Revelation before fulfillment has come.

Thus it need not trouble us that no explanation of Revelation so far offered enjoys the approval of all readers. Every commentator will choose his point of view without being able to offer convincing proof that he is right.

The Lutheran church, however, feels quite assured that Revelation 14:6-12 is a prophecy of Luther's Reformation. All true Lutherans also agree that Revelation 20:1-7 is not a promise of a visible kingdom of Christ to be established on earth (the millennium), since it is the universal and continuous doctrine of Christ and his apostles that his church on earth will never be without trouble and sore affliction as long as this earth shall stand. John did not contradict Christ and Paul and the evangelists. Every reader of Revelation should be warned not to arrive at any conclusion from this symbolical book that disagrees with outright statements of the other books of the New Testament.

Summary of contents

Addendum to the New Testament

A. Miracles and parables of the Lord

266. Source of miracles

When Jesus wept at the tomb of Lazarus, the Jews said, "See how he loved him!" (John 11:36). What they recognized in this one case is easily observable in all the miracles of Christ. They had their source in his loving compassion. His divine hand was always ready to deliver the afflicted and oppressed from their burdens. "He went around doing good" (Acts 10:38) is a proper description of Christ's great works. Only one miracle, the chastisement of the barren fig tree (Matthew 21:19), seemed to have been done in anger, but even in that case, Jesus was thinking of his disciples and intended to strengthen their faith (verses 20-22).

It was but natural that these miracles were performed upon, or on behalf of, such persons as believed in Jesus. The others did not seek his help or his miracles with sincere hearts (read Matthew 12:38,39; Luke 23:8). Jesus took notice of faith (Matthew 9:2), required it (Mark 9:23), nurtured it through his Word (John 5:8,9), and praised it where it was revealed in its strength (Matthew 8:10; 15:28). Among the thousands whom Jesus fed in the wilderness on two occasions, there must have been many believers. The only exception to this rule seems to be the healing of Malchus, who surely was not a believer (Luke 22:50,51). In this case the miracle intervened, lest the course of events, decreed by God, be hindered by the untimely zeal of Peter.

267. Purpose

Though Jesus conferred many temporary benefits by his miracles, his purpose was greater than the bestowal of passing gifts. The miracles were not performed against nature but went beyond nature and its laws. They were not unnatural but supernatural. They differed from similar works of prophets and apostles in that these men performed miracles with power specially granted by God in each particular instance (Acts 4:10), while Jesus even as man always acted in his own power and according to his free decision (Matthew 8:3; Mark 5:41; Luke 7:14; and so on).

Since only God, the independent Lord of creation, can go beyond the laws of nature, which he established in the beginning, the miracles of Jesus are so many proofs of the truth that in him the fullness of the Godhead dwelled bodily (John 5:17; 10:37,38). He likewise intended them as undeniable evidences of his messiahship (Luke 7:20-23), and the Jews acknowledged the force of this argument (John 7:31). Again, Jesus demanded that his miracles should be recognized as true evidence of the divine origin of his teaching (John 12:49; and so on). For these several reasons, the miracles are often called signs.

Rationalists make the sweeping statement that real miracles are impossible. Though they admit the historical character of the gospel record, they seek to eliminate all miracles by various tricks of interpretation. But they always end by denying the true divinity of Christ, the vicarious atonement, and the divine character of Christian doctrine.

268. Season

Christ performed no miracles before he entered upon his public ministry. This seemed unsatisfactory to certain imaginative persons of an earlier period, and they proceeded to write apocryphal supplements to the gospel story, filling out the apparent omissions. Among their inventions are various puerile tales concerning miracles that Jesus is said to have performed long before his 30th year, while still a child at play and a youth at work.

All these stories are branded as fiction by the plain statement that the making of wine at the marriage feast at Cana was the first sign that Jesus did, the beginning of his miracles (John 2:11). Miracles were not needed prior to the public ministry of Jesus, so none were performed. But as soon as the Lord began to preach, the people were granted miraculous proofs of his divine glory. The evangelists indicate repeatedly that they record but a part of that which Jesus did (Matthew 8:16; 9:35; Mark 1:32; and so on). John declares that innumerable books would be needed to record all the miracles of Jesus (John 21:25). The record provided for us by God contains only what we need for the strengthening of our faith.

269. Classes

It would be quite proper to include in the miracles of Christ all evidences of his divinity recorded in the gospels, as, for instance, his omniscience demonstrated in the meeting with Nathanael (John 1:47,48), in several disputes with the Jews (for example, Luke 5:21,22), in the foretelling of his betrayal (Matthew 26:21-25), and on many other occasions. Usage has determined, however, that the name miracle be confined to the evidences of Christ's omnipotence, which are most spectacular and certainly produced a most powerful effect upon the witnesses.

It is difficult to group these miracles of omnipotence as we know them from the New Testament, but Christ himself seems to suggest an arrangement based upon Isaiah 35:5,6 (Matthew 11:5):

(1) *The blind see* (the man blind from birth, John 9; two blind men, Matthew 9:27-30; the blind man of Bethsaida, Mark 8:22-26; the two blind men of Jericho, one of whom was called Bartimaeus, Matthew 20:29-34 and Mark 10:46-52).

(2) *The lame walk* (the servant of the captain at Capernaum, Matthew 8:5-13; the paralytic, Matthew 9:2-7; the lame man of Bethesda, John 5:1-15).

(3) *The lepers are cleansed* (the leper, Matthew 8:1-4; ten lepers, Luke 17:11-19).

(4) *The deaf hear* (the deaf-mute, Mark 7:31-35).

(5) *The dead are raised up* (the daughter of Jairus, Mark 5:22-43; the youth of Nain, Luke 7:11-15; Lazarus, John 11:1-44).

But this list far from exhausts the wealth of the wonders of Christ's omnipotence. *He delivered many who were possessed by the devil bodily* (Matthew 8:28-32; 9:32,33; 12:22; 15:22-28; 17:14-18; Mark 1:23-26). *He healed all kinds of sicknesses* (the mother-in-law of Peter, who was sick with a fever, Mark 1:30,31; the son of the ruler, John 4:47-53; the woman with a spirit of infirmity, Luke 13:11-13; the woman with the issue of blood, Mark 5:25-34; the man with the withered hand, Luke 6:6-10; the man with dropsy, Luke 14:2-4; Malchus, Luke 22:50,51). *He fed the hungry and refreshed the thirsty* (the two multitudes, Mark 6:30-44; 8:1-13; wedding at Cana, John 2:1-11). *He demonstrated his supreme control over nature* (quieted the tempest, Matthew 8:23-26; walked on the sea, Matthew 14:22-32; blessed Peter's fishing on two occasions, Luke 5:1-11 and John 21:1-14; provided the tax penny, Matthew 17:24-27; cursed the fruitless fig tree, Mark 11:12-21).

It should not be forgotten that the resurrection of Christ is not only one of his miracles but the very greatest miracle of all (Matthew 12:40; John 2:19; Romans 1:4).

270. Parables—character

According to the language of the Bible, we designate as parables the discourses of Jesus that are clothed in the figurative language of metaphors. In a wider sense of the word, all similes and metaphors, even if they consist of a single word or statement, might be classed as parables (for example, the keys of the kingdom of heaven, Matthew 16:19; salt of the earth and light of the world, Matthew 5:13,14; "destroy this temple," John 2:19; Herod, the fox, Luke 13:32; the great harvest, Matthew 9:37; the lost sheep of Israel, Matthew 10:6; the Bread of Life, John 6:35). The biblical writers, however, confine the use of this term to such discourses in which the metaphor is elaborated and often developed into a complete story. The shorter parables are sometimes called allegories. Thus the brief comparisons in Matthew 13:31-35,44-52 figure as allegories, while the story of the weeds in Matthew 13:24-30,36-43 is a parable.

271. Material

It is obvious that a parable must describe things that actually occur, even though the particular occurrences are invented. In this manner a parable differs, on the one hand, from a fairy tale, which delights in the impossible and unreal, and, on the other hand, from a fable, which is an instructive tale, introducing animals, plants, and lifeless objects as thinking, speaking, and acting like human beings.

The purpose of the parable also requires that its material be familiar to the reader or listener. Otherwise he would not be able to see the point of comparison. All those who heard Jesus were familiar with the Pharisee and the publican, Oriental wedding customs (as in the parable of the ten virgins), the fig tree, and the mustard seed, while we frequently must first study the meaning of the story before we can understand the point of the parable.

Every parable of Jesus is designed to present some heavenly truth clothed in a simple story. His one great subject is the kingdom of heaven, that is, his church. As it was his purpose to save his listeners through his sermons, his parables center on this one theme, which is developed from a great variety of viewpoints.

272. Purpose

It was the aim of our Lord to bring his listeners into close touch with the heavenly truths of the gospel. Parables were peculiarly fitted for this purpose, since they present the divine mysteries in the most tangible form possible. To the simple minded, the parable opens up the gate of understanding, and yet the advanced Christian student finds ample food for reflection in the lines of thought suggested by the story.

There was also another side to this matter. For the greater number of his listeners, Jesus used parables as a means of concealing the saving truth. They were to hear and to see without understanding. He explains that this was in the nature of a judgment of God upon the Jews, who resisted the message of the Lord in unbelief (Matthew 13:10-15). All spiritual knowledge is a free gift of God's grace.

273. Interpretation

In each parable the Lord aims to develop one chief thought, which determined the wording of the story. Since the divine truths are closely interrelated, several doctrines are often touched upon in one parable. But of these one is dominant and must be made the basis of interpretation.

In the parable of the good Samaritan, for instance, conversion is plainly demonstrated as the one true source of neighborly love, but the true purpose of the parable is indicated in Christ's question, "Which of these three do you think was a neighbor to the man who fell into the hands of robbers?" There the Lord teaches the scribe that the question which this man had used as an excuse should rather have been worded thus, Am I his neighbor? (Luke 10:36).

In the parable of the weeds, the Lord teaches incidentally that hypocrites will always be concealed among the external membership of the church. But the real aim of the parable is to show us that we must not expect to establish on this earth a church made up only of believers (Matthew 13:24-30).

Another reason why the purpose of each parable must be carefully observed is that the story sometimes fails to convey an important thought otherwise connected with the doctrine. Thus the first part of the parable of the wicked servant (Matthew 18:23-35) teaches that God forgives sin freely, out of pure grace. Not a word is said, however, that might be understood as referring to the atoning work of Christ. And yet that work is surely the cause of God's free grace in the forgiveness of sins. The parable was not intended to dwell on the underlying, meritorious cause of forgiveness but to show the uncharitable wickedness of the servant in the strongest light.

Often the Lord indicates the purpose of his parables, sometimes by means of lengthy explanations (Matthew 13:37-43; 20:16; 21:42-44; and so on). In other cases he simply speaks the parable, leaving it to the listener to discover the proper key (Matthew 13:44-46; Luke 6:41,42). In all cases the interpretation of a parable is wrong if its aim has been misunderstood.

On the other hand, an interpreter who understands Christ's aim will be protected against that other serious error of trying to force every single feature of the parable into the parameters of strict interpretation. In explaining a parable, one should not go beyond the point of comparison. Details that are given merely to give body to the story may safely be left to take care of themselves.

B. Some people mentioned in the New Testament

274. Mary, the mother of Jesus

What little we know of the life of the mother of our Lord is found in the brief notices scattered through the historical books of the New Testament. The two genealogies that exhibit the lineage of Jesus (Matthew 1:1-16; Luke 3:23-38) seem to refer only to Joseph, the lawful head of the family, and even in Luke 1:27, there is some doubt whether the words "a descendant of David" are meant to describe Mary. But since the genealogy of Luke contains many names differing from the list of Matthew, our Lutheran fathers have suggested with good reason that Luke records the genealogy of Mary, which would mean that Heli, who appears here as the father of Joseph, was really the father of Mary and Joseph's father-in-law. Other commentators suggest that the words "He was the son, so it was thought, of Joseph" (Luke 3:23), are to be taken as a parenthetical note. In that case, Heli would be directly designated as the grandfather of Jesus, according to the flesh. In Luke 1:32 Jesus, son of Mary, is at the same time called the son of David, which obviously implies the Davidic descent of Mary (compare Romans 1:3). Mary was a relative of Elizabeth, the aged wife of Zacharias the priest, but we do not know how close this relationship was (the word translated "cousin" in Luke 1:36 KJV is the general term for "relative").

At the time when Mary's history begins in the New Testament, she was the promised wife of Joseph, who then took her to his home in obedience to divine revelation

(Matthew 1:24). The child Jesus was the object of Mary's most motherly care (see the story of Jesus' first visit to the temple at the age of 12 years), and it seems that she accompanied her beloved Son at various times during the journeys of his public ministry (Luke 23:49,55).

From the beginning she received with a believing heart whatever was told her concerning her son (Luke 1:38; 2:19) and surely did not fail to receive his own words in the same spirit at all times (Luke 2:51). At the wedding feast in Cana, she disclosed a deep understanding of the divine nature of Christ, and this knowledge must have served to mitigate her grief when the sword pierced her soul under the cross of Christ (Luke 2:35; John 19:25).

On that occasion the Lord entrusted the care of his mother to John the Apostle, who received her into his own house (John 19:26,27). In the days intervening between Christ's ascension and the outpouring of the Holy Spirit, Mary remained with the disciples at Jerusalem (Acts 1:14). This is the last we hear of her in the Bible. Christian tradition has it that she died at Jerusalem about the year 47.

In a later period, many imaginative minds busied themselves with the mother of our Lord, who became a figure of romantic interest. A great number of fanciful tales became current. Parents named Joachim and Anna were invented for her. The apocryphal gospels busily recount many items descriptive of Mary's family life, of which there is no historical record.

When the great theological disputes about the divine nature of Jesus Christ were going on during the fourth century, overzealous minds raised the mother of Jesus Christ to an unwarranted position of honor. Having rightly determined that she was entitled to be called the mother of God, it soon became an accepted practice to honor her with idolatrous worship. In the Roman Catholic Church, this idolatry continues to this day in the most extreme form, the mother of Jesus being considered of rather greater importance and power than the Son of God himself.

This horrible error gave rise to the lie of the immaculate conception and birth of Mary, which was proclaimed as an accepted dogma of the Roman Church by Pope Pius IX on December 8, 1854. Its companion doctrine is the fiction of the ascension of Mary into heaven.

275. Joseph, the husband of Mary

In acknowledgment of the honored position belonging to Joseph as the foster father of Jesus, his genealogy is quoted as the civil and legal lineage of Christ (Matthew 1:1-16). This table informs us that Joseph's father was called Jacob and that he was a direct descendant of David (compare Luke 2:4).

Joseph proved his fear of God by accepting without protest the amazing information revealed to him about the son who was to be born of Mary (Matthew 1:20-24), and his faith participated in the wonderful gospel preached of the young child thereafter (Luke 2:33). From the story of the boy Jesus, it appears that Joseph conscientiously performed his duties in respect to the proper training of the holy child. Under his guidance and instruction, Jesus learned the trade of a carpenter and pursued it for a time (Matthew 13:55; Mark 6:3).

Since only the mother of Jesus is mentioned after the Lord began his public ministry, it would seem that Joseph died before Jesus was 30 years old. At any rate, Joseph was no more among the living when Christ was crucified, otherwise the Lord would hardly have entrusted his mother to the care of John.

Many fanciful legends concerning Joseph have been invented, and in the Roman Church, Joseph is a person of high rank among the saints to whom idolatrous worship is extended. It is unnecessary to say that all this is contrary to the simplicity and divine truthfulness of the gospel record.

276. The brothers of the Lord

It is an article of faith that Jesus was born of the virgin Mary in a supernatural manner (Isaiah 7:14; Matthew 1:23; Luke 1:27,34). It is true, however, that there is no statement of the Scriptures that teaches the perpetual virginity of Mary. That the New Testament speaks freely of the brothers of Christ has been considered by many as ample cause to assume that after the birth of Jesus the marriage of Mary and Joseph was blessed with several natural sons, whose names are recorded in Matthew 13:55.

Although this view is not against the Scriptures and certainly is not derogatory to the honor of either Mary or Jesus, the doctrine of the perpetual virginity of Mary has found widespread sanction among Christians. This assumes that the brothers of Jesus were not bodily sons of Mary. It has been suggested these persons were either children of Joseph by an earlier marriage or sons of a sister of Mary, who is supposed to have been the wife of Alphaeus, or Clopas. In the latter case, the word *brother* would be used in the wider sense to include cousins (compare Genesis 13:8).

277. The apostles

After the Lord began his public ministry, he soon assembled, by personal call, a group of 12 men who were to be his companions thereafter. They were to be taught by him with divine care, while at the same time they became eyewitnesses of his works and earwitnesses of his discourses.

This training was to prepare them for the time after his ascension, when they were to go forth into the world as his messengers to establish his church among all nations.

We do not know at what time Christ began to call these men, and we are told just how only a few were called. But since they were to become witnesses of his *entire* ministry, he surely did not delay their calling very long.

By miracles and instruction, he imbued them with faith in his divine nature and mission (Matthew 16:16; John 6:68,69). But he did not succeed in making them understand these matters correctly until their eyes were finally opened by his resurrection (Matthew 16:21-23; Luke 18:31-34; 24:25-27,44-49). Then, indeed, a new light shone upon all that they had seen and heard, and they never failed thereafter to emphasize that they were witnesses of the Lord (Acts 2:32; 3:15; 4:20; 5:32; etc.). They certainly paid due attention to this require-ment when they prepared to elect Matthias (Acts 1:21-23).

During the period of Christ's ministry, they were once sent forth to preach but were distinctly forbidden to seek out Gentiles and Samaritans (Matthew 10; Mark 6:7-12; Luke 9:1-6). Shortly before his ascension, however, Jesus commis-sioned them to preach in all the world and thus made the whole earth their field of labor. On the Day of Pentecost, he endowed them with extraordinary gifts of his spirit to make them fit for their great mission.

Christ himself tells us that there is a symbolical signifi-cance in the appointment of just *twelve* apostles (Matthew 19:28). This symbolism was not destroyed by the subse-quent addition of Paul, since he was appointed the apostle to the Gentiles from his birth (Galatians 1:15,16).

The Twelve whom Christ called were Simon Peter and Andrew, the sons of Jonas; James the Elder and John, the sons of Zebedee and Salome; Philip; Bartholomew; Matthew (formerly called Levi); Thomas (surnamed Didymus, that is, the Twin); James the Younger, son of Alphaeus; Simon the Canaanite (called the Zealot); Judas Lebbaeus (also known as Thaddaeus and as Judas, son of James); Judas Iscariot (that is, the man from Kerioth), the traitor, in whose place Matthias was chosen after the ascension of Christ (Matthew 10:1-4; Mark 3:16-19; Luke 6:14-16; Acts 1:13). Finally Saul, afterward named Paul, was called in a vision and was endowed with the same authority as the other apostles. Having sketched the life of Matthew, Paul, Peter, John, and James the Younger earlier (see sections 177, 190, 203, 247, 251), it remains for us to assemble what information we may gather about the other apostles, chiefly from the Scriptures and, to some extent, from church tradition.

Andrew, brother of Simon Peter and a disciple of John the Baptist, accepted John's testimony of Jesus and followed him. Together with John the son of Zebedee, Andrew was the first of the apostles to speak with the Lord (John 1:40,41). He brought his brother Simon to the Savior, accompanied Jesus to Cana, and then returned to his fisherman's work with Simon. On the shores of the Sea of Galilee, the call of the Lord came to him, and he cheerfully obeyed (Matthew 4:18-20).

He seems to have enjoyed the intimacy of Jesus nearly to the same extent as Peter, James, and John (Mark 13:3-37). When the multitude was to be fed, he felt himself entitled to express his opinion (John 6:8,9), and it was Andrew who, with Philip, approached Jesus on behalf of the Greeks (John 12:20-22).

After this the biblical record has no more to say of Andrew. It was reported, however, that Thrace and Greece afterward became the field of his apostolic work and that he died as a martyr at Patrai in Greece, being nailed to a cross of the form X, which thereafter was called Saint Andrew's cross.

James the Elder (Jacobus Major), son of Zebedee and Salome, the brother of John and probably older than he, since he is always mentioned before John in the lists, was called on the shore of Lake Gennesaret at the same time as John, Peter, and Andrew (Matthew 4:21). Jesus called the two sons of Zebedee Boanerges, that is, the Sons of Thunder, perhaps in memory of the incident related in Luke 9:54.

This James was among the most intimate associates of Jesus. With Peter and John, he was permitted to see the glory of the Lord both at the deathbed of the daughter of Jairus and on the Mount of Transfiguration, and he likewise witnessed the deepest agony of the Savior in Gethsemane.

It was his privilege to be the first martyr among the apostles; Herod Agrippa I ordered him to be executed with the sword (Acts 12:2). The legend has it that his accuser, being converted by the heroic testimony of the apostle, was converted to the Christian faith and was immediately led away to be executed, not, however, before he had asked and received the apostle's pardon.

Philip (not to be confused with the deacon and evangelist of the same name, Acts 6:5; 8:5; 21:8) was a native of Bethsaida in Galilee (John 1:43,44). After being called by Jesus, he brought Nathanael to the Lord (John 1:45-51). On the occasion of the feeding of the multitude, he was put to a test by Jesus (John 6:5-7). He led the Greeks to Jesus (John 12:21) and afterward gave Jesus occasion to declare his essential unity with the Father (John 14:8).

More the Scriptures do not tell us concerning Philip. Christian legend records that he labored in the Phrygian city of Hierapolis and has much to say concerning his

God-fearing daughters. He is said to have been crucified, head downward.

Bartholomew, most probably, is none other than Nathanael of Cana, whom Philip brought to Jesus, for John speaks of Nathanael precisely as though he belonged to the apostles (John 1:45-51; 21:2). Except for these remarks, the Scriptures are silent concerning this apostle. There is a tradition to the effect that a missionary laboring among the Indians at the close of the second century found there the gospel according to Matthew, which had been brought there by Bartholomew. This apostle is said to have been skinned alive before being nailed to a cross, head downward.

Thomas, or Didymus (both names mean "Twin"), is mentioned only four times outside of the lists of the apostles (John 11:16; 14:5; 20:24-29; 21:2). He was a faithful disciple of the Lord, ready to follow Jesus into death but likewise very persistent in his doubts, so that only a personal view of the Savior could persuade him to believe in the resurrection.

Christian legend sought to supplement the biblical record by inventing both a twin brother and a twin sister of Thomas, as well as the names of his parents and his native place. On the other hand, the report may be true that Thomas preached in Parthia, then in Edessa of Syria, and finally in far-off India. Even to this day, there exist native Christians along the coast of Malabar, on Ceylon, and near Madras who venerate Thomas as the founder of their church. The explorer Cosmas Indicopleustes met such "Thomas Christians" in those regions in the sixth century.

Lebbaeus also bore the name Thaddaeus (Matthew 10:3; Mark 3:18). He was likewise called Judas, being distinguished from other men of the same name as Judas son of Jacob. On the only occasion when his name is mentioned in the Bible outside of the lists, he asks the Lord, "But Lord, why do you intend to show yourself to us and not to the world?" (John 14:22).

Simon, surnamed the Zealot, was a native of Cana in Galilee. He is said to have lived longest of all apostles, dying as a martyr in the year 107. His calendar day, like that of Lebbaeus, is October 28.

Judas Iscariot probably was the only apostle who was not a native of Galilee, if it is true that his surname really means "the man of Kerioth" *(ishkarioth)*. Kerioth was a city of Judea (Joshua 15:25). His father's name was Simon.

This unfortunate man obviously never believed in the Lord with true faith. Having charge of the common treasury of Jesus and the apostles, he abused his trust by stealing. When Jesus was anointed at Bethany, he grumbled at what he considered a wanton waste of the costly ointment (John 12:4-6). He offered to deliver Jesus into the hands of the Jews for money (Matthew 26:14-16; Mark 14:10) and persisted in his treachery in spite of the many faithful and pointed warnings of the Lord (John 13:18; Matthew 26:25; John 13:21-30). In Gethsemane he betrayed the Lord with a kiss but soon thereafter returned the blood money, being tortured by vain regrets. Because his protests went unheeded, he hanged himself and burst asunder (Matthew 27:3-5; Acts 1:18). The tainted money was used for the purchase of a potter's field in which to bury strangers, which was thereafter called the Field of Blood (*Akeldama;* Matthew 27:6-10; Acts 1:18,19). Speaking through the inspired writers, the Holy Spirit declares that the horrible deed and the fearful end of Judas were foretold in the following words of prophecy: Psalms 41:10 (John 13:18); 69:26; and 109:8 (Acts 1:20).

Matthias stepped into the place of Judas Iscariot. His election took place under the supervision of the other apos-

tles in such manner that the Lord, answering the prayer of
the congregation, decided by lot to whom the office should
be given (Acts 1:15-26).

278. Jewish courts and officials

When Jesus was born, the scepter had departed from
Judah (Genesis 49:10), for even the highest Jewish court, the
Sanhedrin, had lost the power of life and death. Yet these
officials retained a certain authority, especially in religious
matters, though the office of the high priest had lost much
of its dignity and influence because of the frequent changes
of its incumbents.

The Sanhedrin (KJV, "Council") consisted of 71 members (former high priests, scribes, and elders, Mark 14:53;
15:1) and was always presided over by the acting high
priest. Originally this was the court of last appeal among
the Jews (see Matthew 5:22: "[He] is answerable to the
Sanhedrin," that is, he is guilty of being condemned to
death), but it had been deprived of this supreme dignity
as soon as Roman procurators (governors) began to rule
the land. This they themselves were compelled to admit
when they planned to kill Jesus (John 18:31), and thus
they became unwilling witnesses that the day of the Messiah was at hand.

The Roman officials, however, did not interfere with the
religious authority of the Sanhedrin, for it was always the
policy of the Romans to respect the religions of subjugated
nations. This is why the Sanhedrin sent messengers to
inquire concerning the work of John the Baptist (John 1:19);
they questioned Jesus concerning his claim of being the Son
of God; they called the apostles to account for their preaching (Acts 4:5-7), and so on. The stoning of Stephen (Acts
7:57,58) was a deed of mob violence, without a show of

right. Neither did Herod act within his rights when he executed James the Elder.

Attentive readers of the Bible will have noticed that the writers of the New Testament frequently speak of several high priests living at the same time. According to Mosaic law, there could be only one high priest at any time, who also retained the office as long as he lived. The departure from this divine ordinance began in the days of Herod the Great, when the political leaders assumed the right to depose and to install high priests at pleasure. Thus Quirinius had raised Annas to the office of the high priest, while Valerius Gratus granted the dignity to Caiaphas, son-in-law of Annas. It was customary, however, to take the high priest from certain privileged families, so that it became possible to speak of a "high priest's family" in this sense (Acts 4:6).

In their control of Jewish religious customs, the Romans went so far as to keep locked away during the year the costly garments worn by the high priest on the Day of Atonement. Seven days before the feast, they were delivered to the priest, who then purified them for sacred use from the defilement inflicted by the touch of heathen hands. Under these conditions the office of the high priest could not retain the respect of the people. When Christ entered upon his sufferings, the aged Annas, though deposed from the office, was a man of much greater influence than Caiaphas, the real high priest; this explains why Jesus was first taken to Annas (John 18:13).

279. Roman officials

Roman control was felt as a burden at all times and in all respects by the Jews. But their special hatred and contempt was directed against the publicans, the collectors of taxes, whose shameless extortion made the yoke of the conquerors all the more onerous. Roman taxation, inescapable as it was under the circumstances, had become particularly offensive because the governors had incautiously imposed the payment of tithes from certain products. Since the tithes were the ancient and sacred privilege of the temple and the priesthood, the Roman demand was deeply resented as an interference with the religion of the Jews. Accordingly, it was a popular subject for heated discussion at the time of Christ whether it was lawful, that is, in accordance with divine law, to give tribute to Caesar (Matthew 22:17). But aside from all alleged conscientious scruples, the taxes were truly oppressive and almost unbearably burdensome.

Judea shared the fate of all Roman provinces. In order to simplify the system of taxation, the government at Rome would sell the taxes of an entire province to some nobleman, who then paid the entire sum into the imperial treasury at once. Such buyers of taxes were called *publicani*. Dividing his province into several districts, the original publican sublet each district, and this division of districts was continued until finally the collection of taxes in definite small precincts lay in the hands of those publicans (NIV, tax collectors) who are mentioned so often in the New Testament.

As each buyer of tax rights naturally was not satisfied with a mere return of his purchase money but demanded as much profit as possible, the taxes as finally collected were unreasonably high. The farmer had to pay the tenth part of all grain and the fifth part of wine and oil. To this were added tolls for the use of streets and bridges, as well as import duties collected at the boundaries of each district and at the gates of cities. Everywhere the publicans found opportunities for extortion, and as the *publicani* at Rome were men of the highest rank, all complaints of the oppressed remained unheard.

For this reason the Jews classed tax collectors with the heathen and criminals (Matthew 11:19; 18:17; and so on), and John touched the real sore spot in his exhortation of tax collectors (Luke 3:12,13), while Zacchaeus proved the truth of his repentance by returning his unrighteous gains (Luke 19:8).

Archelaus, the last Jewish king, lost his throne in the year 6, after Christ's birth. From that date, with one brief interruption only, Roman procurators governed the province of Judea and used Roman legions to repress the rebellious tendencies of the people. The castle of Antonia at Jerusalem always held a Roman garrison, and Roman swords dripped with Jewish blood whenever the mob of the city rose in tumult. Roman legionaries participated in the torture and crucifixion of Christ and guarded his tomb. Roman soldiers saved Paul from the wrath of the Jews and then escorted him to Caesarea (Acts 21:32; 23:23,24). A Roman centurion whose servant was ill approached Christ and found help.

Of the Roman governors and general officials who ruled over Judea, the New Testament mentions only those who became important as participants in the history of Christ and the apostles. Sulpicius Quirinius (KJV, "Cyrenius") was governor for the first time when that decree went forth which was to make Bethlehem the birthplace of Jesus.

After the deposition of Archelaus (A.D. 6), when Quirinius became governor for the second time, he enforced a second decree of taxation, demanding the tenth part of grain and a double tenth part of wine and fruit. Joazer, the high priest, advised the people to submit in patience, but he could not prevent the formation of a new party of patriots, who called themselves Zealots and took their motto from 1 Maccabees 2:50: "And now, children, be ye zealots for the Law and give your souls for the covenant of your fathers!"

One of these Zealots was Judas of Gamala in Galilee, of whose revolt and fate Gamaliel spoke (Acts 5:37). This revolutionary party attracted youths of the best blood among the people. It seems that even two of the apostles originally belonged to it (Simon the Zealot, Acts 1:13, and Paul, Acts 22:3; Galatians 1:14). Among the Zealots there was never a lack of fanatical agitators, who began here and there to make war against the Romans. Property and life became such insecure possessions that Jesus did not exaggerate in the parable when he described as a matter of daily occurrence robbery and deadly assault committed on the short and frequently traveled road between Jerusalem and Jericho.

Once, probably while Quirinius still was governor, the Samaritans found opportunity to play a nasty trick upon the Jews. According to custom the gates of the temple were opened immediately after midnight on the day of Passover. Sneaking in, some Samaritans scattered human bones on the floor of the Sanctuary, necessitating a solemn purification and rededication before sacrifices could once more be made.

Pontius Pilate was made governor by Emperor Tiberius and continued in the office for ten years (A.D. 26–36). From the beginning he displayed that wanton cruelty which is familiar to us from the history of Christ's passion. Following the suggestions of the emperors, Pilate's predecessors had hesitated to offend the religious feelings of the Jews, even to the extent of forbidding the display of military standards by the legions garrisoned at Jerusalem. These standards exhibited not only the Roman eagle but also a medallion with the bust of the emperor, which had become an object of heathen worship. Pilate, however, ordered the garrison to carry its standards from the headquarters at Caesarea to Jerusalem and to raise them in the Castle of Antonia, facing the temple.

Immediately a large multitude set out for Caesarea and made a great, but peaceful, demonstration before the palace of the governor, fairly besieging him with their petitions for five days and nights, urging him to have the obnoxious images removed. When, on the sixth day, Pilate called them into the Circus and surrounded them unexpectedly with soldiers, the Jews, falling upon their knees, offered their naked throats to the swords, declaring that they would rather die than break the law of their God. Pilate could not afford to carry the outrage to a bloody climax, for the emperor would surely have called him to account for any massacre. He yielded and removed the images, and the Jews remembered the weak spot in his authority.

At a later date, he ordered certain small golden shields, dedicated to the emperor, to be fastened to the exterior of Herod's palace at Jerusalem, merely to bait the Jews in childish vindictiveness. Again the populace assembled, pressing him with their petitions and adding the challenge "Tiberius certainly does not desire that our customs be destroyed, but if you affirm that it is so, show us an order or an epistle or the like, in order that we may cease to trouble you and proceed to choose messengers who may carry our prayers before our lord." This threat was very embarrassing, because Pilate had reason to fear that a Jewish embassy to the emperor would also complain of his corruption, extortions, and many executions, which often were a mockery of justice. Yet he stubbornly refused to yield. So the Jews sent an urgent petition to the emperor Caesar, who immediately responded by writing a letter of flaming wrath to Pilate. This experience was decisive. During the trial of Jesus, the mere mention of Caesar's name sufficed to make the stubborn autocrat a pliant instrument of murder for the Jews (John 19:12).

At last Pilate got his just desserts. After a massacre that he arranged on Mount Gerizim against the Samaritans who really had done nothing wrong, Pilate was deposed by the governor of Syria and was sent to Rome to answer to the emperor for his innumerable evil acts. Tiberius, indeed, had died before Pilate set foot on the Italian shore, but it is credibly reported that Emperor Caius Caligula passed judgment upon the miscreant, compelling him to execute judgment against himself by committing suicide.

Antonius Felix, a former slave whom Emperor Claudius had freed, became procurator of Judea, Galilee, Samaria, and Perea in A.D. 52 or 53. Tacitus, a Roman historian, describes him as a cruel profligate, who dared the utmost in all kinds of wickedness, relying on the favor of the court.

During his term of office, Paul became a prisoner and was sent to Caesarea by Lysias, the chief captain (Acts 23:24-35). From the mouth of the apostle, Felix heard solemn words of warning on justice, chastity, and the future judgment (Acts 24:24,25), and every word was a direct arraignment. The Jewess Drusilla, his third wife, had previously been married to King Azizus of Emesa. Felix had induced her to leave her lawful husband and to marry him, a heathen, thus causing her twice to transgress the law of God. (Drusilla, with Agrippa, her son by Felix, died a victim of the Vesuvian eruption of the year 79.)

While Felix was procurator, the final catastrophe was set in motion. He hired assassins to murder the high priest in the temple, which was the signal for innumerable assassinations, many committed in the public streets and often in the temple. Murders occurred daily, so that peaceful citizens hardly dared to leave their houses. Outside of the city, great bands of robbers assembled, the largest one (four thousand men) under the leadership of "the Egyptian" referred to by the chief captain when he examined Paul (Acts 21:38).

Felix dispersed this band but was unable to restore order. Everywhere similar leaders arose, who passed through the land with their adherents, robbing and murdering and excusing their wicked deeds as being done in the interest of Jewish liberty. In the year 60 Felix was at length recalled to Rome, and the insistent accusations of the Jews would have cost him his life if it had not been for the intercession of his brother, who had almost unlimited influence with Emperor Nero.

Porcius Festus succeeded Felix as governor of Judea. The testimony of Acts (chapters 25,26) that he was a temperate and just ruler is borne out by other historical records. He would undoubtedly have dismissed the case against Paul, who had been held against all evidence by the corrupt Felix (Acts 24:26,27), if Paul had been willing to submit to another trial before the Jews and had not already appealed to the emperor. Festus bent all his energies toward the extermination of the bandits but soon came to his death somewhere in Judea in an unexplained manner. (King Agrippa, who is mentioned together with Festus [Acts 25:23–26:32] was Herod Agrippa II, son of Herod Agrippa I, who is mentioned in Acts chapter 12. Herod Agrippa II ruled a portion of Galilee and Perea during the governorship of Festus. Imitating the customs of the heathen, he maintained an incestuous relation with his sister Bernice. During the Jewish war, he sided with Vespasianus, though he himself was a Jew. He lived to the year 100.)

Gessius Florus, who is not mentioned in the Bible, deserves a place here because it was during his administration that Jerusalem was overwhelmed by the final catastrophe. As soon as he had entered upon his office in the year 64, he oppressed the Jews more shamelessly than any of his predecessors. Josephus declares: "It seemed small to him to gain profits from individuals; he preferred to pillage entire cities and ruined entire districts. He stopped just short of proclaiming throughout the land: 'Robbery is permitted, provided only that I receive my share of the booty.'"

An investigation conducted by Cestius Gallus barely resulted in a reproof for Florus, but he believed that the only way for him to escape the punishment of the emperor would be to incite the Jews to open rebellion. And so he deliberately provoked the unfortunate people to rebel. He robbed the treasury of the temple, massacred those who assembled to soften his wicked heart, and finally accomplished what he desired. The war party among the Jews gained the ascendancy and began to wreak bloody vengeance upon the Romans. This was the final struggle, which ended with the destruction of Jerusalem and the dispersion of the Jewish nation by Titus, who became the next emperor of Rome.

C. The apostolic fathers—
Apocrypha of the New Testament

280. Fathers

Among the leaders of the early church who became its instructors after the death of the apostles were those men who had been tutored by the apostles personally and were for that reason supposed to be endowed with special theological knowledge and naturally were looked up to with particular reverence. Seven of these men achieved remarkable prominence, and their writings were held in such high esteem that they were not only distributed very widely but were even read side by side with the apostolic writings in the public meetings of the churches. These were the apostolic fathers: Clement of Rome, Barnabas (the companion of Paul), Hermas, Ignatius of Antioch, Polycarpus of Smyrna, Papias of Hierapolis, and an unknown man who simply recorded that he was a disciple of the apostles. The books purported to have been written by these men all date from the earliest time of the Christian church. But in several cases, it is doubtful whether they were actually penned by those whose names they bear. They are all written in Greek.

According to tradition, Clement was the third bishop of the church at Rome (A.D. 93–101). Some very late and doubtful witnesses declare that he died a martyr. Some also claim to know that he is the Clement mentioned by Paul in Philippians 4:3. An epistle written to the Corinthians by the church at Rome is ascribed to him. The letter itself discloses no more than that the writer must have been a man of high authority in the Roman congregation. Tradition, however, states directly that Clement was the author.

An incomplete copy of this epistle was discovered appended to one of our most ancient Bible manuscripts, verifying the report that it was often read in public for the edification of the congregation. It consists of a rather rambling exhortation to preserve peace among the members of the church.

In a later period, two other documents were falsely passed along under the name of Clement. The one, *Clementine Homilies,* is a baseless fiction, claiming to be a factual account of the successful fight of Peter against all false developments of the church. The other, the so-called *Apostolic Constitutions,* is a series of ordinances respecting the external government of the church, purporting to be derived from the apostles but really a fabrication of the third century.

Barnabas, the companion of Paul (Acts 9:27; etc.), is declared by many witnesses of Christian antiquity to have written the letter that is called the epistle of Barnabas. This document discusses the Law of Moses, but its argumentation is so extremely peculiar that there is every reason to doubt the authorship of Barnabas. The writer declares that the Jews never kept the Law rightly because it was meant to be interpreted spiritually throughout. Occasionally he also betrays an ignorance concerning the Levitical ceremonies that would have been impossible in a person of the training and experience possessed by Barnabas. At any rate, the epistle dates at least from the beginning of the second century and was rated so highly that it was frequently read in the churches.

A certain Hermas is named by the ancients as the writer of a book that has been handed down to us under the title *The Shepherd of Hermas (Pastor Hennae)*. The ancient records suggest that this was the Hermas mentioned by Paul as a member of the church at Rome (Romans 16:14). Some even claim to know that he was a brother of Pius I, the tenth bishop of Rome. There is no proof whatever for either of these assertions.

The book presumably was called *The Shepherd* because it states that a person dressed in shepherd's clothing appeared to Hermas as a messenger of God to convey the visions, precepts, and parables there recorded. Its chief subject is the doctrine of repentance. Though some of the early teachers of the church even believed the book to be inspired, this view was widely contradicted, and that with good reason, for the writer does not even mention the name of Jesus and speaks only incidentally of the Son of God. Nevertheless, it was long considered an edifying book and was widely read.

Ignatius was bishop of Antioch in Syria from A.D. 70 to 107. Among the many legends that clustered around his memory, one says that he was sentenced to death after a trial held by the Emperor Trajan at Antioch. He was supposedly carried to Rome by imperial order to be cast before the wild beasts. On the long journey, the indomitable martyr used the leisure time to write a number of letters to various churches and one to Polycarp, then bishop of Smyrna.

The seven epistles of Ignatius are still extant. The churches addressed are those of Ephesus, Magnesia, Tralles, Rome, Philadelphia, and Smyrna. Ignatius inveighs with great fervor against all heresies and declares the divinity of Christ. But he also defends the view that the episcopal form of church government is necessary as a representation of Christ.

Polycarp was bishop of Smyrna for many years. He had known John the Apostle personally and often had conversed with him. It is said that John appointed him bishop of Smyrna. A bond of friendship connected him with Bishop Anicetus of Rome, whom Polycarp even visited on one occasion.

Under Marcus Aurelius the violence of heathen hatred against the Christian faith broke forth in an even more bloody persecution than before and threatened to engulf the church at Smyrna. Polycarp was apprehended, and the judge demanded that he deny Jesus. In the course of his defense, the steadfast witness said, "Should I deny my Lord, whom I have served for 86 years, and from whom I have received nothing but good?" He was condemned to be burned and died in the year 166. He wrote an epistle to the Philippians, in which he chiefly discusses rules for a God-fearing life and warns against heresies.

Papias, another disciple of John, was bishop of Hierapolis in Phrygia and is said to have suffered a martyr's death at

Pergamos, in the same year as Polycarp. Of his chief work, entitled *Exposition of the Words of Jesus,* only fragments have been preserved as quoted by other writers. According to his own declaration, he made it his business to visit such persons as had personally seen and heard Jesus and to put in writing the words of the Lord as they quoted them.

Eusebius, a historian, judges that Papias was "of a very small judgment," so it is not unfair to presume that his *Exposition* suffered a just fate by disappearing. We have certain information that he was a zealous defender of chiliasm and certainly departed from the doctrine of the apostles on this question.

The epistle to Diognetus was formerly believed to have been composed by Justin Martyr, but it was quite certainly written at a much earlier date. The writer attempts to convince the heathen Diognetus that his prejudices against the Christian faith are unreasonable. But in his arguments he speaks of the ordinances of the Old Testament as though they were of human invention and even foolish in part.

The writings of the apostolic fathers have little value except in a historical way. They rank high, however, as witnesses for the early existence of the books of the New Testament, from which they often quote.

281. Apocrypha

While the writings of the apostolic fathers may be classed as apocryphal in a certain sense, it has become customary to designate as Apocrypha of the New Testament a definite class of books that are much less valuable than the former. It is certain that none of these Apocrypha date earlier than the year 150, and many were certainly written much later. Generally speaking, their theme is the life of Christ, together with related facts.

Viewed from the point of origin, they fall into two distinct groups. In the first we find the gospel story written from the viewpoint of heretical communities, who were not in agreement with the canonical gospels or even rejected them outright. We know of these books only from the writings of Christian authors. None of them have been handed down to us intact.

It seems that the heretical sects, after developing their particular errors, naturally could not continue to use the canonical books of the New Testament in the form given to them by the inspired writers. Consequently, they either falsified or rewrote them entirely, with the result that all statements disappeared that were not in agreement with their heresies.

To this class, doubtless, belonged the gospel of the Hebrews. It may have been based upon the gospel according to Matthew, but from all indications it seems to have been the religious book of the Ebionites, who held Jesus to have been no more than a great teacher of morality and insisted that observance of the Mosaic ceremonial law was necessary to salvation.

We have more definite information concerning the gospel of Marcion, a remarkable leader of the Gnostic sect, who maintained that Paul's epistles alone contained the true doctrine, rejecting all other apostolic writings. As a matter of course, he could not follow Paul's teachings but mutilated the apostle's letters to make them agree with the antinomistic (opposed to law) views of the Gnostics. Since Luke was a pupil of Paul, Marcion adopted his gospel but "purified it of doctrinal misrepresentations," as he blasphemously put it, and rejected the other gospels entirely.

Besides these two documents, Christian writers also mention a gospel of Peter and a gospel of the Egyptians, without, however, describing them definitely.

The second group of Apocrypha owed its existence to the unwarranted desire to know more of certain phases of the Savior's life than the Holy Spirit has seen proper to record. The authors were plainly actuated by the belief that a pious fraud was permissible if perpetrated in the interest of the church. It was an unholy curiosity, which tried to supply spicy information concerning such matters as the youth of Mary, the life of Jesus from the return out of Egypt to his 12th year, and his experiences from that time to his 30th year.

These fraudulent stories were doubtless read eagerly, especially among the heretical sects. The fabrications clearly betray the spirit from which they sprang. Highly colored miracle stories, together with indecent and immoral episodes, brand them as productions of a spirit that had nothing in common with the Spirit of holiness and of truth prevailing in the canonical gospels. It can, moreover, be proved that not one of them existed before the year 190.

The *Protevangelium of James* (the brother of the Lord), written in Greek, is considered the oldest and, comparatively, the best of these doubtful books. Its complete title fairly characterizes its contents: "Historical exposition how the most holy Mother of God was born for our salvation." Of course, it was not written by James, the brother of the Lord. Among other things, it relates that Mary was born to Joachim and Anna after many years of childlessness, that she was educated in the temple from her third year, that in her 12th year she was by lot given into the care of the aged Joseph, and that in her 15th year she became the mother of our Lord.

The Greek gospel of Thomas claims to disclose unknown facts from the life of Jesus from age 5 to age 12, but the account consists of such fanciful and unhealthy vagaries that it is justly believed to be of heretical origin. Its tales about the child Jesus are intended to glorify his miraculous powers. They are so entirely at variance with the holy character of the Christ Child, however, that they become repulsive to the Christian mind.

The gospel of Nicodemus, also written in Greek, has for its first part an itemized report concerning the trial of the Lord before Pilate, together with an account of the crucifixion and resurrection. The second part contains a fantastic account of Christ's descent into hell and the statement that after the resurrection of Christ, Annas and Caiaphas declared under oath before Pilate that Jesus is truly the Son of God.

In the Arabic history *Joseph the Carpenter,* Christ is represented as relating to his apostles whatever was remarkable in the life of his foster father. The style is romantically fanciful, trivial, and insipid.

The Arabic *Gospel of the Childhood of the Savior* is much like the gospel of Thomas in contents and style of presentation. Its peculiarity is the stories of miracles said to have been performed by the child Jesus through his mother.

Probably the youngest of all these Apocrypha are two written in Latin, the *Gospel of the Birth of Saint Mary* and the *History of the Birth of Mary and of the Childhood of Jesus.*

To this group also belong a number of writings imitating either Acts or Revelation or certain stories of the Old Testament. They form a part of what is called Christian apocalyptic literature and are written in various languages. We merely mention some of the titles: *Apocalypse of Paul, Apocalypse of Peter, Apocalypse of Mary, Revelation of Bartholomew, Ascension and Vision of Isaiah,* and *Testaments of the Twelve Patriarchs.* They move in a sphere quite outside of scriptural thought and, in part, originated as late as the Middle Ages.

Some of these Apocrypha were known and read in Europe as late as the period of the Reformation, but others were entirely unknown in Luther's day and were discovered through modern research among the vast store of ancient manuscripts. But even those which Luther knew were disregarded by him entirely when he translated the Bible, for their religious value was immeasurably below that of the Old Testament Apocrypha. Even the Roman Church found them unworthy of consideration.

D. Manuscripts of the New Testament

282. Materials

The materials that the writers of the New Testament used are named by John: ink and paper (2 John 12; 3 John 13). The pens were cut from the stems of reeds; the ink used was black, as its Greek name indicates. The paper used at that time was manufactured from the pith of the papyrus plant, chiefly found in Egypt. The pith was cut into thin strips, which were then pressed or glued together in two layers laid crosswise. This material was quite fragile and therefore perishable. No book made of papyrus endured for a century, even if used only occasionally.

By mere accident alone, a number of papyrus rolls have been preserved intact to our days in the sheltered interiors of Egyptian tombs and Palestinian caves. Paul, indeed, on one occasion refers to "parchments" (2 Timothy 4:13). It is reasonably certain, however, that the term here signifies a book, probably a copy of the Old Testament, because parchment was by far too expensive to be employed for purposes of correspondence. At any rate, certain remarks of the early writers of the church indicate that the original manuscripts of the apostolic writings had disappeared before the year 150, for by that date nobody even knew where they had been seen last.

For use in the Jewish synagogues, however, the Old Testament had for centuries been copied upon parchment, in order to secure reasonable permanency for the precious volume under constant usage. Since the Christian congregations almost immediately made the public reading of the Scriptures a part of their liturgy, we can assume that they also began to use parchment copies in their churches almost at once. In addition, wealthy individuals doubtless permitted themselves the luxury of such costly books for personal use in their homes.

Parchment got its name from the city of Pergamos in Asia Minor, where King Eumenes (197–159 B.C.) is said to have invented the process of working up the skins of animals into smooth writing material. But it is certain that the skins of sheep and other domestic beasts were employed in this manner many centuries before that date. This expensive material was chiefly used for manuscript copies of the Bible until the process of making paper from cotton (called Damascus paper) was invented in the ninth century. Linen paper was added some three centuries later.

Those who made a business of producing copies of the Bible ordinarily used the cheaper and more abundant material available. In fact, good parchment was often so rare that a copyist would erase the writing of some old manuscript and use the same parchment for his new work. Such manuscripts are called palimpsests (codices, rescripti, that is, rewritten codices). On these it is sometimes possible to decipher the first writing under the second. It is plain that the writing material used for a manuscript may serve to indicate its date, at least in a general way.

338

In the early days, Romans and Greeks made up their "books" by gluing the leaves together along the edges so as to form one long strip, which was then wound around a stick of wood. The Jews also used this process of binding. (See Luke 4:17; Jesus unrolled the book!) They prepare the rolls, or scrolls, for their synagogues in this form to this day. We do not possess a single complete manuscript copy of the New Testament in this form. Before the fourth century, it must have become common practice to bind the manuscript leaves together in the book form with which we are familiar, because all the major manuscripts now known have this form and are called codices.

283. Number

Since every large city of the Roman Empire readily became a center of literary activity, in which the copying of books was a recognized branch of industry, any person who really desired to possess the New Testament and had the necessary means could procure a copy. Because the sum involved was considerable, many Christians had to content themselves with copies of parts of the precious book, such as the four gospels or the Pauline epistles. The lectionaries designed for use in divine worship contained only the appointed Scripture lessons. Some were *evangelistaries,* that is, they comprised the gospel lessons, while those offering selections from Acts and the epistles were *praxapostoli.*

It is certainly evidence of God's providence that an amazing number of valuable codices of the New Testament have been preserved in spite of the confusion of the turbulent centuries. Of all the Greek and Roman writers of old combined, we do not have nearly as many ancient copies as we have of the New Testament and parts thereof. For the study of the most renowned philosophers, historians, and poets of the heathen world, a scant half-dozen copies are at our disposal in any single case. But the students of the text set down by the inspired evangelists and apostles have available more than 2,300 manuscripts of the New Testament or its parts. It is not at all improbable that some valuable additions may still be found in the great libraries of Europe and Asia, which have not yet been exhaustively investigated.

284. Character

According to the style of writing, all codices fall into two great classes, called *uncials* and cursives, respectively. The uncials, also known as *majuscule* codices, the most ancient manuscripts in our possession, are written in capital letters throughout. (Hence the name: the Latin word *uncia,* that is, one-twelfth, signifies an inch and thus came to be used as a name for the capital letters of the alphabet, which also were called *majuscules,* "big ones.") The ancient copyists separated neither words nor sentences, broke off the words at the ends of lines with no regard to syllabication, and knew nothing of punctuation. Patiently they outlined one letter after another, producing one or two, rarely three, columns to each page. Such books were not easy to read, though the writing usually was plain enough. What a puzzle each page of our Bibles would be if they were printed in this style:

ONEOFTHEMTHEDISCIPLEWHOMJESUS
LOVEDWASRECLININGNEXTTOHIMSIMON
PETERMOTIONEDTOTHISDISCIPLEAND
SAIDASKHIMWHICHONEHEMEANS
(John 13:23,24)

With such manuscripts the early churches appointed special readers, called anagnosts, who were trained to read the lessons in the services. It also happened quite naturally that learned men disagreed on the proper division of words and sentences. In some passages the discussion is going on to this day.

The copyists never learned to know and apply the rules for punctuation invented by some old Greek scholars. Matters were but little improved by the invention of Euthalius of Alexandria to let every line of the manuscript contain only those words which should be spoken together (called stichometry, from *stichos,* "a line"), for even then the words remained unseparated. To save space, the word groups forming the lines were later merely separated by dots, and as various kinds of dots were gradually introduced, to which other marks were added, a system of punctuation slowly developed.

The second group of codices, called cursives, or *minuscules,* were written in a kind of script in which the forms of the uncial letters were rounded off and thus became easier to write. As they also looked smaller, comparatively, than the uncials, they were naturally called *minuscules,* "little ones." In codices of this class, the words were also written separately, and gradually all Greek marks of punctuation were applied.

The oldest cursive manuscripts that we now have date from the ninth century, while some of the uncials reach back to the fourth century.

E. Variant readings of the Greek New Testament
285. Origin

While the Jews have always insisted upon the most punctilious care in the production of their Bible manuscripts, so that the Hebrew codices of the Old Testament show remarkably few variant readings, the copyists of the New Testament worked without any accepted rules and probably performed their work, in general, according to their own personal ideas and desires.

In our day nobody expects to find a printed book without some mistakes. Somewhere you will find a misplaced or false letter or punctuation mark and even a word entirely out of place. Yet the conscientious printer subjects his pages to the most anxious scrutiny over and over before going to press.

The work of copying by hand is even more mechanical, and mistakes are much more easily made, because the mind is often concerned with other thoughts while the hand outlines the letter. Moreover, it may have rarely occurred to have someone carefully look over a new copy to correct mistakes. Thus it happened quite naturally that a great number of differing readings gradually appeared, as the copyists changed the text either inadvertently or intentionally.

An unintentional change might have happened to a copyist when he misread the text or when, writing from dictation, he misunderstood the person dictating. He might even make some alteration unconsciously while writing, even though he had received the dictated words correctly.

Intentional alterations almost without exception came about in an honest endeavor either to correct what to the copyist seemed wrong or to add what appeared to be missing or to harmonize seeming contradictions. It is very rare to find that the text of a manuscript has been falsified intentionally in the interest of some heresy. If such things happened among the heretical sects, the orthodox church was scandalized by such sacrilegious violation of the divine Word.

Most variant readings developed during the first three centuries. In the year 240 the learned scholar Origen already found reason to deplore that the various manuscripts differed so greatly. After that, greater care was taken with the codices used in the churches, and in this manner the text gradually assumed a definite form.

286. Character

All variants of the New Testament text fall into three groups, according to their origin, since they arise either from omissions or from additions or from misunderstandings.

Omissions were very apt to happen when two lines of the codex from which the writer was copying ended with the same word. His eye would glide past the ending of the second line to the third line, and thus his copy would show a break.

Additions arose from various causes. It happened very easily, for instance, that in parallel texts of the gospels, words taken from one gospel were inserted in another. Sometimes the possessor of a manuscript would write these additions between the lines or on the margin, and the next copyist would embody them in the text. Sometimes the copyists quoted texts of the Old Testament more completely than the original writer had done. Since the first words of the Sunday lessons in the lectionaries were often changed slightly, as, for instance, by writing the name of Jesus in place of the pronoun *he,* these alterations sometimes crept into the text of complete copies. More important are those additions that entered the text from other sources and were translated in the early versions.

Thus the earliest manuscripts omit the doxology at the end of the Lord's Prayer (Matthew 6:13), as do several ancient versions. Since no manuscript contains this doxology in the parallel passage (Luke 11:4), it has been suggested that it was first used to close the prayer in public worship and from there was added to the text of Matthew. Similarly, the words of 1 John 5:7 ("There are three that testify: . . .") are missing in all the earlier Greek manuscripts. They are found only in some Latin copies and in two Greek codices of very late date. Luther did not translate these words; they were added to his version after his death. The revised versions of the English Bible have also omitted them.

Misunderstandings of the text placed before the eye of the copyist were possible not only because certain Greek letters are very similar in form, but more so because certain words were usually written in an abbreviated form and the abbreviations were not always readily distinguishable.

An example of the first kind is found in Romans 5:1, where some manuscripts read, "We have peace with God," while others have, "Let us have peace with God." In the Greek text, the difference lies in a single letter of the word meaning "have"; the Greek alphabet has one letter for the short sound of *o* and another for the long sound, and these two sounds are used to distinguish the moods of the verbs in the manner indicated by the English translations given above.

Examples of the second kind occur, for instance, when the copyist confused the abbreviations for the words *God* and *Son.* Thus in John 1:18 some codices read, "the only begotten *Son,*" while others say, "the only begotten *God.*" Similarly, the words "church of *God*" in Acts 20:28 were sometimes read as "church of the Lord," and in 1 Timothy 3:16, it was possible to mistake the words "*God* appeared" for "*who* appeared."

287. Number and importance

Because each manuscript exhibits its own peculiar errors, a comparison of the numerous codices has resulted in a vast accumulation of variant readings. At present they have reached the total of 150,000. But this number includes all differences found in the manuscripts, even such minute ones as mistakes in spelling, different order of words, and various spellings of the same words. These trifling differences form the great bulk of the variant readings, and they are mostly so insignificant that they are not considered even in the most exhaustive critical editions of the New Testament and certainly could never be traced in any translation.

Competent investigators assure us that of all the 150,000 readings, not more than 400 appreciably affect the meaning of the passage in which they occur, and only 50 of the 400 are of notable importance for one reason or another. But even these 50 readings make no change whatever in the doctrinal content of the Scriptures. Not one article of faith and not one exhortation to godliness of life is changed or eliminated.

Far from justifying any anxiety on our part, the multitude of variant readings, properly considered, serves to emphasize that God took special precautions to preserve his precious Word by causing so many copies to be made that they could not possibly be all destroyed, even in the days when fierce enemies of the Christian faith tried to do so. The works of no Greek or Latin writer provide so many different readings as the New Testament because no book of ancient days was ever distributed in so many copies as this one. As the copies multiplied, though, the number of readings naturally increased.

Moreover, the very character of the variant readings is an evidence of divine providence. Whereas the copyists mostly did their work as a matter of business, the text of the New Testament nevertheless remained practically unaltered under their hands. We may thus feel assured that we really have the true text of the New Testament. If only a *single* manuscript of this book had been preserved from all the centuries before the invention of printing, no amount of reasoning could quiet the fear that the text so preserved might be adulterated. But as the hundreds of manuscripts all show practically the same text, they testify with a loud voice that we still have the words of the evangelists and apostles precisely as they were first written.

F. Versions of the New Testament and of the entire Bible

288. Necessity

During the days of the apostles and for a long time thereafter, the Greek language was spoken and understood in the whole Roman Empire. Nevertheless the need was soon felt in certain regions to translate the Bible, especially the New Testament, into the language that was most familiar to the common people. In this manner a number of translations were made between the second and the fifth centuries, which are of great value for examining the original text.

As every translation is, in a way, a commentary of the Bible, these ancient versions furnish very interesting data concerning the understanding of the Scriptures prevailing among certain groups of Christians. They are much more important, however, as aids to the restoration of the original text. Since some of them were made long before our oldest manuscripts were written, a retranslation into Greek brings us close to the earliest form of the text. The better such a translation rendered the sense of the original into the idioms of the language, the less its value for textual criticism. If the version attempted a slavish reproduction of the original, the latter may be reconstructed quite readily. One service every version is sure to perform—it will show what was missing or added in the text that the translator used.

289. Latin versions

The first Latin Bible was called *Itala* because it was presumed to have been produced in Italy. However, since the church at Rome employed the Greek language in its public services for two centuries, while the Christians in Northern Africa primarily used Latin, it is more probable that the Itala is of African origin. We have no complete text of this version, but only such fragments as occur in the writings of the Latin fathers. It seems, moreover, that the Itala never enjoyed great authority, for those who used it habitually referred to the Greek original. This explains the remarkable fact that everybody considered himself free to make what changes he pleased in this version, until a thorough revision became obviously necessary.

Bishop Damasus of Rome took this matter in hand in 383 and appointed the scholarly Jerome for the task. The choice was a happy one, for Jerome was not only a highly gifted man but had acquired an excellent working knowledge of both Greek and Hebrew. He began his difficult labors immediately and first produced an entirely new translation of the Old Testament. In the New Testament he wisely resisted the temptation to set the Itala aside and followed it as closely as possible in order not to offend the ignorant. Though his cautious circumspection failed to prevent a storm of criticism, the undeniable value of his translation secured its rapid spread, and in the eighth century it became known as the *Vulgate,* that is, the version generally used.

The subsequent history of this version is highly interesting. At the time of Charlemagne, it had become infested with many errors, due to the carelessness of copyists, and the great emperor ordered Alcuin, in 802, to revise and correct it. But as far as we know, this measure produced no lasting results. The Vulgate was the very first book ever printed in Europe. It was published in 1455 by Gütenberg and Faust at Mayence. This rare edition is called the Mazarin Bible, because the first copy still existing was located in the library of Cardinal Mazarin.

When the invention of the printing press made the rapid multiplication of copies possible, the defects of the version became altogether unbearable. The Council of Trent (1545–1563), which dared to make the Vulgate the basis of all its theology, set aside the original text and advised a revision. But this did not appear until 1590, under Pope Sixtus V. In a boastful bull, Sixtus ordered that this edition of the Vulgate should be considered the only standard of faith and morals, cursing anyone who would dare to change it or to publish another text of the Bible.

Hardly had a hundred copies been issued, when it appeared that this "infallible" edition was sadly disfigured by numerous errors of all kinds. Some had been corrected with pen and ink, others had been pasted over with strips of paper. As more people read the book, the number of discovered errors assumed frightful proportions. In great haste the adjutants of the Pope sought to regain possession of all copies that had been sold and nearly succeeded in destroying the entire edition. To save face for the Pope, the printer was held responsible, and a new edition was quickly prepared, which was published in 1592, under Clement VIII. From that time this *Clementina* became the official version printed in the Roman Church.

290. Syriac versions

The earliest Syriac version is known as the *Peshito,* the "plain one," because of its simple, plain language and style. It probably originated near the end of the third century and is used to this day in the public services of the Syrian church, though the language of the people has changed greatly in the course of the centuries. All scholars are unanimous in considering the Peshito the best of all ancient versions. Not only does it reproduce the sense of the text with great fidelity, but it also speaks in purest Syriac. Notwithstanding its age, it did not become known in Europe until 1522. It was printed at Vienna for the first time in 1555, at the expense of Emperor Ferdinand I.

A second Syriac version, the *Philoxeniana,* dates from the year 508. It was prepared at the suggestion of Bishop Philoxenus of Mabug, Syria. As a translation it is much inferior to the Peshito, because it reproduces the Greek text with slavish exactness.

291. Versions in Coptic, Ethiopic, and Armenian

In the second century, Coptic translations appeared in Egypt in three dialects, Sahidic (or Thebaic), Memphitic, and Bashmuric. We know very little about their histories.

Ethiopia was Christianized at the beginning of the fourth century. The crew of a ship that had landed on the coast of Abyssinia was massacred by the savage natives. Two Christian youths, Frumentius and Aedesius, alone were spared, and Frumentius made excellent use of his opportunities to preach the gospel. He was afterward ordained bishop of the Ethiopians by the patriarch of Alexandria and was known as Abba Salama. His memory is still preserved among the Christians of Abyssinia.

According to tradition he also was the author of the Ethiopic version of the Bible, which is highly prized by scholars for its fidelity and beauty. The dialect in which it was written has been supplanted by another, but the ancient version is still used by the Abyssinians in public worship.

Until the fifth century the Armenians used the Syriac alphabet and probably the Syriac Bible. But when Izaac was made patriarch in 388, he caused his friend Miesrob to become an ardent missionary, and this man produced an alphabet for the Armenian language. Both men then collaborated in the work of translating the Bible, Izaac undertaking the Old Testament, while Miesrob became responsible for the New Testament.

292. Gothic version

The Germanic tribe called the West Goths (Visigoths) had settled along the lower course of the Danube in the third century and there came under the influence of Christianity. The honor of being their apostle has been ascribed to Ulfilas (or, rather, Wulfilas, "Little Wolf"), whose ancestors had been carried away from Cappadocia as prisoners by the Goths. Since Ulfilas' parents gave him an education according to Greek standards, he was well qualified to become a teacher of the Christian faith. Unfortunately he belonged to the sect of the Arians, who denied the divinity of Christ. In 313 he was ordained as bishop of the Goths and served in that capacity among them till 383. Having devised an alphabet for the Gothic language, he translated the entire Bible for his people. It is said, however, that he omitted the books of Kings because they were filled with stories of war and would make his warlike kinsmen still more ungovernable. This version has been preserved only in fragments.

293. Old versions of later date

A number of versions were made just before the beginning of the Middle Ages. They are of little value for textual criticism because none of them are based upon very early manuscripts. The Georgians, who adopted an alphabet after the Armenians, received their Bible version at the beginning of the sixth century. The first Arabic versions, like the Persian ones, owe their existence to the spread of Islam. In Arabia, Syria, and Egypt, the Muhammadan conquerors forced their language upon all their victims, so that they soon lost the use of their former Bibles. In Persia, however, where Christians had until then used the Syriac version, the Persian language began to flourish under the influence of Muhammadanism, and this development caused the Christians to translate the Bible into their native tongue. The Slavic version was made in the ninth century by two brothers, Cyrillus and Methodius, who had labored among the Slavs as missionaries from Thessalonica.

294. Pre-Reformation versions

During the period when Europe lay under the thralldom of popery, the work of spreading the Bible gradually ceased. As the rubbish of man-made doctrines grew, it served to stifle all desire to make the common people familiar with the Bible in their mother tongue. It was not in the interest of the defenders of papal claims to dispel the ignorance of the ordinary people by giving the Bible into their hands. From the first, Romanism was animated by the spirit that later produced decrees against Bible reading.

Since priests and monks were practically the only learned persons during the Middle Ages, the Bible naturally disappeared from the knowledge of the common people. Such translations as were made with consent of the priesthood were either confined to small portions of the Bible, as the book of Psalms and so on, or they rendered the historical content of the Bible in poetic paraphrase. All real efforts at making the Bible accessible to the laity were made in pronounced opposition to the hierarchy.

The most interesting of the poetic paraphrases is the *Heliand,* the "Savior," written in old Saxon. It owes its origin to a distinct missionary effort of Louis the Pious, son and successor of Charlemagne. By force of arms, the great emperor had compelled the Saxon tribes to adopt the outward semblance of Christianity. But while they spoke the names of Christ and the saints, their hearts were filled with thoughts of their ancient gods, Wotan and Thor, and their old heathen songs were still perpetuated. Louis had gained the confidence of the Saxons because of his mild government, and he determined to use his influence in the interest of religion. Probably soon after 830, he set his learned men to work to put the biblical stories into poetic form, hoping that the Heliand so produced would take the place of the heathen songs. Almost two hundred years before that date, Caedmon of England, known as the father of English song, had written a similar poem in Anglo-Saxon.

Throughout the Middle Ages, wherever a decided opposition to the hierarchy arose, and the so-called forerunners of the Reformation gained a following, the Bible was generally used as the basis of attack and was translated into the vernacular. Even the sect of the Cathari (also known as the Albigenses), who flourished greatly during the 12th century, possessed at least the New Testament in a Provencial translation. And though the doctrines of the sect were a complete departure from the Christian faith, their New Testament shows no trace of falsification. The Cathari have disappeared without a trace. Their Bible version was discovered during the last century.

In the second half of the 12th century, the sect of the Waldenses was founded by a man named Waldez, a pious citizen of Lyons, who became eager to search the Scriptures after hearing the gospel lessons read in public services.

Though the Waldenses did not gain a clear knowledge of the gospel, the Bible showed them the error of many Romanist dogmas. They were zealous in distributing the Scriptures and therefore translated them into the language of their people.

How greatly the hierarchy feared these undertakings of the Waldenses was shown by its mighty efforts to snatch the Bible from the hands of the laity again. In 1229 the Council of Toulouse forbade laypeople to read the Scriptures in any language whatsoever. In 1234 the Council of Tarragona decreed that neither priest nor layman should read the Bible in the Romance dialect. These are the first two prohibitions of the Bible issued by the Antichrist! Though persecuted without mercy, the Waldensian sect persisted. To this day churches of this denomination are found among the Piedmontese of Italy.

In England, where kings and Parliament had for some time chafed under the yoke of the hierarchy, the scholar John Wycliffe, of Oxford, began to raise his voice against popery in 1360. He learned to see quite clearly why Rome was the Church of the Antichrist. He had to suffer bitter persecution from the defenders of Romanism and died in 1384 as a defamed and dishonored man, stigmatized as a heretic. He translated the entire Bible into English, but from the Vulgate, not the original language.

295. German versions

It would be erroneous to believe that there were no German translations of the Bible before Luther's. In the quiet seclusion of monasteries, quite a number of pious men spent their leisure hours in translating the Holy Book. When printing was introduced, publishers dared to disregard the prohibitions of church councils and put German

Bibles on the market. At present we possess 17 German Bibles (14 in High and 3 in Low German), which were printed between the years 1466 and 1522.

These translations, however, failed to become popular and made no lasting impression upon the people. The language used by the translators was extremely awkward, and all their work had, moreover, been concentrated upon the Vulgate instead of on the original text. The many mistranslations of the Vulgate were not only reproduced but added to by the unskilled translators.

Thus there was ample room for the masterwork of Luther. While he was kept in safe concealment against his deadly enemies in the Wartburg, the restless activity of his mind found leisure to devote itself entirely to that effort through which the Reformer still continues to be a living influence in the Christian church, more than through any other phase of his many labors. On December 18, 1521, he informed a friend, "I am going to translate the Bible into German." He undoubtedly went to work at once and labored incessantly upon the great task, for when he returned to Wittenberg three months later, he brought with him the German New Testament and published it in September 1522.

Many other tasks then claimed the attention of the great man, and the translation progressed more slowly. In 1523 the books of Moses were printed; the book of Psalms followed in 1524 and the Prophets in 1532. The remaining portions of the Bible were printed for the first time in the first complete edition of the German Bible in 1534.

Since then the German people have possessed a Bible that is in a class by itself among all versions ever made in any language. All competent critics admit that it is unsurpassed. This magnificent result was due in part to Luther's linguistic gifts and scholarly endowment but most of all, however, to his strict adherence to sound rules of interpretation. On the one hand, he declared, "I did not set aside the literal meaning too freely, but saw to it with great care, as did my helpers, that, where a word is of special significance, I retained it to the letter and did not depart from it so freely." On the other hand, however, he was guided by the following considerations:

> One must not ask the letters of the Latin tongue how to speak German, as these asses [his malicious Romanist critics] do, but one must inquire about it from the mother at home, the children in the street, the unlettered man in the marketplace; one must observe their mouth, how they talk, and translate accordingly. Then they will understand and know that one is speaking to them in German.

To show how strictly he adhered to this sound principle, we are told that he caused a butcher to slaughter and dress a number of sheep in his presence, in order that he might learn how the tradesman named the different parts of the animal. He did not intend to furnish a literal translation, which no German would have understood. His aim was to render the true meaning of the sacred text in the corresponding German idioms.

By the exercise of his remarkable judgment, he also escaped the danger of choosing one of the many German dialects as the medium of expression. With a sure sense of fitness, he chose the diction employed by the German chancelleries, in the form used in the Electorate of Saxony, the central province of Germany. This idiom had been developed because the various courts needed a medium of expression free from the peculiarities of the many dialects.

In his *Table-talk* Luther says: "I speak after the manner of the Saxon chancellery, which is followed by all princes and kings of Germany. All imperial cities, all courts, write as does the chancellery of our Saxon ruler; therefore it is the most universal German tongue."

This does not mean that Luther found this idiom spoken by the people. His genius rather made it the common language of Germans, by ennobling and perfecting it in his translation of the Bible. He is justly called the creator of modern High German, and his Bible is to this day an unsurpassed model of the language. In the performance of this great work, Luther exhibited tireless perseverance and minute accuracy. He says: "It happened to us frequently that we looked and inquired for some one word for fourteen days, three, four weeks; and sometimes we did not find it even so. In Job we, Magister Philip [Melanchthon], Aurogallus and I, labored with such difficulty that we barely could complete three lines in four days."

Afterward Luther worked unceasingly to improve and beautify his version. Though burdened with many demands upon his time, he succeeded in putting forth eight more editions (in 1535, 1536, 1538, 1539, 1540, 1541, 1543, and 1545), each of which bore plain marks of his indefatigable pen. For the preparation of the first edition, Luther had accepted the help of Melanchthon. In 1539 he enlisted the aid of a number of learned men for a thorough revision. Among his advisers were such men as John Bugenhagen, Justus Jonas, Cruciger, Matthew Aurogallus, and Philip Melanchthon. George Roerer served as proofreader. Occasionally some scholar from a foreign land who visited Wittenberg would lend a hand in passing. But the final decision always rested with Luther, so that the chief honors, as far as they belong to man, are Luther's.

The dates of the Luther editions given previously show conclusively that the German Bible rapidly became the most popular book of Germany. In further proof it may be stated that the three thousand first copies of the New Testament were sold in three months, that not fewer than 17 editions of this portion of the Bible were issued by the various printers before 1534, and that 52 other reprints appeared in various cities, showing that the publishers did not overlook this opportunity for certain and quick profit. Thus it is not astonishing that the German of Luther spread and was adopted rapidly.

296. English versions

The history of William Tyndale (1484–1536) is a record of the close relation between Luther's Reformation and the work of the English Bible translation. Tyndale came to be suspected of heresy because he accepted and defended the fundamental truths underlying the Reformation. After he had begun to translate the New Testament into English, he was threatened by the Inquisition, and he fled from London to the continent.

The story of his stay in Germany is not quite clear, but he certainly visited Wittenberg and there both saw and heard the man whose discourses had served to open his eyes in England. It cannot be doubted that he profited thereby in regard to his Bible translation. We know that he translated many marginal notes of Luther together with a portion of Luther's preface to the New Testament and published these fragments in the first edition of his New Testament.

Tyndale entrusted his manuscript to a printer at Cologne. But after the first ten sheets had left the press, his enemies once more beset him so that he barely escaped with his life and his property. Finally he succeeded in having the New

Testament printed at Worms (1525). Six thousand copies were shipped to England and were purchased eagerly, though not without strong opposition, since Henry VIII, a violent enemy of Luther, could not but detest a book which so obviously owed its existence to the influence of the great Reformer. Nevertheless, five editions of Tyndale's New Testament appeared within four years, and he also completed a translation of the Pentateuch in 1530.

When Tyndale openly admitted his authorship in a new edition of the New Testament, which was published at Antwerp in 1534, he was arrested and imprisoned at Antwerp upon the demand of the English government. After 18 months of prison life, he was strangled, and his body was burned.

Tyndale's version remained the basis of all subsequent English translations of the Bible. In 1535 the first complete English Bible was published from the translation of Miles Coverdale, who had before aided Tyndale in his labors. Coverdale's Bible forms the basis of the Great Bible, published in 1540 at the suggestion of Thomas Cranmer, the first Protestant archbishop of Canterbury.

In opposition to these Bibles, the Geneva Bible appeared in 1560. Its authors were certain English Protestants who had fled to the continent during the reign (1553–1558) of Queen Mary ("Bloody Mary," a daughter of Henry VIII). They had found a refuge in Switzerland, where they enjoyed the hospitality of Protestants of their own kind. Calvin and Beza, the ruling men of the Reformed church, supported the new translation with their authority. The notes added to the Geneva Bible breathe the spirit of the leaders. This version was printed in 117 editions and was used in many churches far into the 17th century.

When James I ascended the English throne, he immediately (1604) convened the leaders of the various parties and took counsel with them concerning the welfare of the commonwealth. This was the Hampton Court Conference. Their most important decision was to the effect that a new version of the Bible should be made. In consequence of this agreement and as the head of the Church of England, James entrusted the momentous task to a company of 55 scholars, who distributed the work among themselves. They met whenever some portion had been completed, to discuss and approve it. They consulted the existing English translations and also a number of versions in other languages.

Thus the *Authorized Version,* or *King James's Bible,* came into being. The name is not exactly well chosen, however, since it cannot be shown that the translation was ever officially authorized by the king or any competent court. It was printed in 1611, and though it was criticized with some violence, especially by the friends of the Geneva version, it finally outlived all opposition and was accepted universally. In point of perfection, it ranks alongside Luther's masterpiece and has for years remained the paramount standard of excellence in English diction, like Luther's version for the German language.

The undisputed worth of the Authorized Version, however, did not prevent a determined attempt, made during the 19th century, to modernize it by eliminating a number of archaic expressions and by changing the translation wherever the results of modern language study would seem to require such a procedure.

A considerable number of English and American scholars, working together in committee, produced the Revised Version, which was published in May 1881. This edition, however, presents the text according to the decision of the

English revisers, to whom their American collaborators conceded the right of ultimate decision wherever the two sections of the joint committee disagreed. The Americans also pledged themselves not to permit the publication of any other revision for a period of 14 years. After this period had elapsed, the American committee published an edition embodying all the emendations that had been rejected by the English committee, together with many other changes. This American Revised Bible appeared in 1900.

Though we must admit that the revisers in many instances offer a more faithful rendering of the original text than the Authorized Version (the American revision being even more successful in this respect than the English), the popular verdict among English Christians seemed to prevail that the old Authorized Version was still to be preferred for public and private use. This is due not only to a conservative preference for the accustomed text but to the observation that the revisers belonged to the school of modern liberal theology and were frequently influenced in their translation by the alleged results of "higher criticism." This creates a reasonable distrust in their ability to interpret the original text. As an example of the tendency to liberalism, which offended many Christians, we mention that the Revised Version replaces the word *hell* by the word *Hades* in ten passages, with the obvious purpose of emphasizing the difference between the place of eternal punishment and the state of death, as in Luke 16:23.

297. Other modern versions

It is due chiefly to the concerted efforts of many Bible societies that the Bible has been made accessible to almost all people on the face of the globe. It may be read, complete or in part, in more than 350 languages and dialects. In many cases, missionaries performed the laborious task of first learning the difficult language of some primitive society, then expressing the unfamiliar words in alphabetical signs, and finally translating the Scriptures, or important parts of it, in the new tongue. This is one of the blessed fruits of the Reformation. Under the dominion of the papacy, such a wide distribution of the Bible would have been unthinkable. In fact, the Roman Catholic hierarchy has resisted all efforts of this kind to the utmost in those countries where they control the government.

The Dead Sea Scrolls and the Bible

John F. Brug

What are they?

The Dead Sea Scrolls are a collection of ancient manuscripts found near the northwest shore of the Dead Sea beginning in 1947. They are widely considered to be the most important find of biblical archaeology in the 20th century. Most of them can be dated from the second century B.C. to the first century A.D. Very few of them are actually intact scrolls. Most are scraps. Many are very difficult to read. The scrolls have been a source of much discussion and controversy from the time of their discovery right down to the present. Though they have been greatly hyped, their contribution to our understanding of the Bible is quite modest.

Where were they found?

Most of the scrolls were found in caves near the ruins of Qumran, close to the shore of the Dead Sea. A smaller number were found at other sites in the Judean wilderness west of the Dead Sea or at the fortress Masada on the southwestern shore of the Dead Sea. The first manuscript finds can be called *archaeological finds* only in a loose sense because they were discovered accidentally by Bedouin shepherds, not by archaeologists. They came to the attention of scholars only after they appeared on the antiquities market in Jerusalem. Some of them were obtained by Israeli archaeologists and found a home in the Shrine of the Book at the Israel Museum. Others were placed in the Rockefeller/Palestine Museum, which was under Jordanian control until 1967 when it came under Israeli control. Additional manuscripts were found by archaeologists making a systematic search of caves in the area, but the majority of the most important finds were by the Bedouin.

What do the scrolls contain?

It is generally agreed that the manuscripts found in the caves near Qumran were placed there by the inhabitants of Qumran around the time of the destruction of Jerusalem by the Romans in A.D. 70. They may have been placed there for safekeeping during the war. It is generally believed that Qumran was occupied by members of a Jewish sect known as the Essenes. Both of these beliefs have been challenged, but there is no convincing evidence to overturn either of these conclusions.

The manuscripts can be divided into four categories:

Biblical manuscripts: Portions of almost every book of the Old Testament have been found. Only one of these, however, is complete, the Great Isaiah Scroll.

Apocryphal writings and *pseudepigraphic writings:* Apocryphal writings are religious or devotional texts that are not part of the biblical canon but are generally recognized as valuable by mainstream Judaism and Christianity. Pseudepigraphic writings are one step further removed from the Bible. They are more like religious novels or fiction. These texts give us interesting insights into the literary tastes and religious attitudes of Judaism at the turn of the era, but they have little direct relevance to understanding the Bible.

Sectarian texts: These could be called denominational writings of the Qumran sect. They include such things as worship materials and the rules of the community. If these are, in fact, documents of the Essenes, they give us valuable information about that sect but do little to increase our understanding of the Bible.

Why are they important?

For biblical studies the most important contribution of the Dead Sea Scrolls is the evidence they provide for the reliable transmission of the text of the Hebrew Bible through the centuries. Before the Dead Sea Scrolls were found, the oldest manuscripts available for the Hebrew text were only about one thousand years old. Then suddenly there were texts that were twice as old. Some scholars were quick to assume that this would show how much the Bible had changed over the years during which it was copied by hand. On the contrary, texts like the Great Isaiah Scroll showed how faithfully the text has been transmitted. Contemporary translations of Isaiah that make use of the Great Isaiah Scroll generally have from 8 to 15 places in which they adopt readings that differ from older translations, which had only the medieval Hebrew manuscripts as their source. These variants are minor matters that do not affect the teachings of the Bible.

The opportunity to study these ancient texts gives scholars much valuable information about how ancient manuscripts were produced and about the techniques the scribes used. This is helpful in understanding the history of the biblical text and how textual variants arose.

As mentioned previously, the texts provided a wealth of information about Jewish literature from the turn of the era and insight into the sect of the Essenes.

Speculative theories based on the texts

Although the actual contribution of the scrolls to the understanding of the Bible is small, many speculative theories based on the scrolls have created concern or confusion.

An open canon at the turn of the era: Because, in addition to the biblical book of Psalms, the scrolls also contain another book of psalms that has the psalms in different order than the biblical psalms and contains additional hymns, some have speculated that the canon of the Bible was not yet determined at the time of Jesus. This is contrary to abundant historical evidence that it was. The second psalter at Qumran was very likely a simple worship resource like our hymnals.

The nature of the text of the Hebrew Bible: Some of the biblical texts from Qumran show greater variation from the standard biblical texts that we use as the basis for our translations. Some have speculated that at the time of Christ, there was not much concern about precise copying of the Bible. But these looser texts were not official copies of the Bible as were the texts at the temple. They were for private study, like our Bible history books or amplified Bibles in which greater freedom of wording is allowed.

Degree of diversity of 1st-century Judaism: Some use the diversity of the texts to argue that there was no such thing as "orthodoxy" at the time of Christ. Remember that the group at Qumran was a breakaway sect. Their existence does not disprove the existence of a Jewish orthodoxy any more than the existence of the Mormons at Salt Lake City disproves the existence of orthodox or mainstream Christianity.

Unfounded theories on the origins of Christianity: Some have suggested that Jesus or John the Baptist got many of their ideas from the Qumran sect. The similarity between Christianity and the Qumran sect is no more than would be expected between any two groups that had their roots in the Old Testament. They shared many things, even though they were moving in different directions.

Hidden secrets: There have been many claims that there were secrets in the texts which were harmful to Christianity that were suppressed by the Catholic Church, whose scholars were in control of many of the manuscripts. There were shameful delays in the full and formal publication of the scrolls, but this was due to ineptitude and to the hoarding of the scrolls by an academic clique rather than to any conspiracy. Reports of hundreds or even thousands of unpublished "manuscripts" refer to scraps and fragments that hardly deserve the name scroll. The major manuscripts are all available now, and they do not reveal any startling new information about Christianity.

APPENDIX TWO

*Eight English Versions of the Bible Evaluated**

Abbreviations
AAT — An American Translation (Beck)
CEV — Contemporary English Version
GW — God's Word
KJV — King James Version (or Authorized Version—AV)
LB — Living Bible
NASB— New American Standard Bible
NIV — New International Version
NKJV — New King James Version
NLT — New Living Translation
RSV — Revised Standard Version
TEV — Today's English Version (or Good News Bible)

King James Version

Armin J. Panning

The number of modern translations available today is eloquent testimony to the fact that we have passed the day

---

* Originally prepared by the WELS Commission on Christian Literature and published in 1980 under the title *Bible Translations*, revised for this publication.

when one version is accepted by all English-speaking people as the authorized version. Regardless of what one may think of the modern translations, they emphasize the important truth that God's Word, written originally in Hebrew and Greek, comes to us today via translation. Even the venerable King James Version (KJV) is a translation—one in a long line of translations.

When King James I in 1604 called the conference that suggested a new translation, there were at the time two English Bibles in general use. The *Geneva Bible* was the Scripture of the Puritans. The Anglicans favored the *Bishops' Bible*, a version that had already passed through numerous revisions since the days of Wycliffe's first complete English Bible in the 1380s.

Under the direction of King James I, a group of 47 translators, over a period of four years, produced the translation that in 1611 was dedicated to the king and, thus, came to bear his name. It was authorized only in the sense that it was the official successor to the *Bishops' Bible,* which had been "appointed to be read in all the churches."

Basically the KJV was a revision of the *Bishops' Bible,* though it incorporated many superior renderings from the *Geneva Bible* while avoiding its Calvinistic notes. By royal decree, notes in the KJV were limited to giving information on Hebrew or Greek words and indicating parallel passages. Subsequent editions have varied in format, ranging from no notes at all to elaborate expanded editions. Generally standard today is a center column of number references indicating alternate translations and letter references indicating parallel passages.

The text has traditionally been printed in verse form—not grouped together into paragraphs—though paragraphs are indicated with printer's marks (§). For some reason these marks are discontinued after Acts 20:36. There are no introductions or outlines to the individual books, but chapter headings and page headlines give a general indication of the content. Italics indicate words that are not in the original Greek and Hebrew but have been supplied for sense.

Old Testament quotations and allusions are not indicated, nor is direct discourse. While the lack of quotation marks is something of a disadvantage for the reader, it does occasionally save the translator from becoming an interpreter. For example, the use of quotation marks would make the translator commit himself as to whether he thinks Jesus or John spoke the words of John 3:16. A system of dating, reflecting basically the chronology of Bishop Ussher, was added in 1701. Over the years, spellings have been modernized, though some still lag, such as "musick" (Luke 15:25) and "plaister" (Daniel 5:5).

Among the reasons given for producing modern translations, there is invariably included some reference to the difficulty of the KJV English. To be sure, there are words that have passed out of our vocabulary. Some are *amerce* in Deuteronomy 22:19 (fine); *daysman* in Job 9:33 (umpire); and *bruit* in Nahum 3:19 (report). Equally troublesome are words that remain in usage but with a changed meaning. Such include *suffer* in Mark 10:14 (permit), *carriages* in Acts 21:15 (baggage), *let* in Romans 1:13 (prevented), *prevent* in 1 Thessalonians 4:15 (get ahead of), and numerous others.

Another claim made for modern translations is that they reflect an updated text. Particularly for the New Testament, a great number of Greek manuscripts have been discovered since 1611. Generally, where the manuscripts differ, the more recently discovered texts tend to be shorter than the Received Text (*textus receptus*), which underlies the KJV. Hence some passages included in the KJV may not appear

371

in the modern translations, for example, Mark 16:9-20; John 5:3,4; John 7:53–8:1; 1 John 5:7,8; and others.

Also, there has been progress in understanding the original languages. The meanings of some difficult words and expressions have come to light. Grammar and syntax studies have advanced. It has been learned that the Greek word that is translated as three times *that* in Mark 6:14,15 is actually a sign of direct discourse. Replace *that* with quotation marks and the construction becomes clear. Similarly, strides have been made in understanding the Greek way of thinking. The translation in Philemon 20 is literally correct, in which the KJV has Saint Paul saying, "Refresh my bowels in the Lord." The equivalent thought in English, however, might better be expressed, "Cheer my heart."

Fortunately the weaknesses in translation that the KJV displays do not affect its doctrinal content, an area that is absolutely critical in any Bible translation. Consistently the KJV gives Christ his due place in Scripture. That is particularly gratifying in the Old Testament messianic prophecies, where some modern translations are decidedly weak.

Finally, a subjective matter—the literary quality of the KJV. It is generally conceded that the translators of the KJV were masters of English style. Its prose rhythms have a solemnity that lends itself admirably to public and private reading and also memorizing.

Revised Standard Version

Harold E. Wicke

The Revised Standard Version (RSV) is copyrighted by the Division of Christian Education of the National Council of the Churches of Christ in the United States of America. The New Testament was first copyrighted in 1946, a second edition in

1972. The Old Testament was copyrighted in 1952. Since the RSV has been accepted and used by most denominations in America, we are including a brief review of it here.

The RSV is an authorized revision of the American Standard Version of 1901, which in turn was a revision of the King James Version of 1611. Both revisions were initiated because of the great increase in the knowledge of Hebrew and Greek, the two original languages of Scripture, because of the discovery of many ancient manuscripts, and especially because of the great change that had taken place in the English language since the days of King James I. Since the RSV is one of the earlier of the many new translations, its language and style retain much of the flavor of the KJV. The RSV did not wholly succeed in eliminating all archaic expressions.

In the areas of historical geography, recovery of place names, identification of religious and secular objects used in Hebrew worship and life, standardization of weights and measures, and clarification of official names and titles, the RSV has done yeoman service in the cause of promoting a better understanding of Holy Writ.

Nevertheless, the RSV should not be used indiscriminately. A reading of the Preface and a study of the text of the translation reveals that the translators of the RSV were not guided by the same principles that guided the translators of 1611. The translators of the KJV were committed to the plenary and verbal inspiration of the Scripture. Though the translators of the RSV admit, "The Bible is more than a historical document to be preserved," they do not, as a group, subscribe to the verbal inspiration of the Scripture. Rather, they state, "[The Bible] is a record of God's dealing with men, of God's revelation of Himself and His will." That "inspiration" and "record" are not synonymous becomes evident from the translation.

373

The RSV has been severely criticized by many. Some criticisms are justified; others are not. Some have criticized the RSV for downgrading the deity of Christ. They have cited passages such as Romans 9:5; 2 Thessalonians 1:12; and Hebrews 7:28. The teaching that Jesus is the Son of God is, however, clearly set forth in passages such as Matthew 14:33; Mark 1:1; Luke 1:35; John 1:34,49; 10:36; 20:31. Though in Micah 5:2 the RSV, contrary to the Hebrew, does not ascribe eternal existence to the Lord Jesus Christ, that truth is brought out in passages such as John 1:1; 8:58; and 17:5.

Justified is the criticism that many of the messianic passages in the Old Testament have been mistranslated. This has resulted in an indefensible tension between the prophecies recorded in the Old Testament and their fulfillment in the New Testament. The following may serve as examples: Genesis 22:18 compared with Galatians 3:16; Isaiah 7:14 compared with Matthew 1:23; Psalm 45:6 compared with Hebrews 1:8, and Zechariah 11:13 compared with Matthew 27:9.

In introducing changes in the text of the Old Testament, the RSV often prefers the Septuagint and other ancient versions over the Hebrew Masoretic text. Most, but not all, of these changes are indicated in the footnotes. Whenever a footnote is marked *Cn* (Correction), the reconstruction does not even have the support of an ancient version but is based solely on the judgment of the translators. Consequently the text of Scripture has often been treated with a freedom incompatible with a high regard for its trustworthiness.

In translating the covenant name of God (YHWH) with the word *LORD* in capitals, the RSV follows the lead of the KJV and of the Greek New Testament itself. It might be wished that the translators of the RSV had also followed the

lead of the KJV in italicizing all words added by the translators. They have, however, led the way in recognizing poetry
as an element employed by the writers of Scripture and
have printed it accordingly.

New American Standard Bible

Hogey W. Birkholz

The New American Standard Bible (NASB) was produced by 58 scholars for the Lockman Foundation of
La Habra, California. Their fourfold aim was (1) These publi-
cations shall be true to the original languages. (2) They shall
be grammatically correct. (3) They shall be understandable
to the masses. (4) They shall give the Lord Jesus Christ his
proper place, which the Word gives him, and no work will
ever be personalized.

The New Testament was first published in 1963. The
entire Bible came out in 1970. It is a careful and conservative revision of the American Standard Version of 1901.

The order of books is normal. While there are no
introductions to individual books, there is a general introduction to the entire Bible, giving a history of this version
and citing the principles of revision as well as of the
translation of tenses.

The text is printed in verse form. Paragraphs are designated by bold-faced numbers or letters. There are running
headlines at the top of each page in boldface. In margins set
on the side of each page, notes are numbered, and cross-
references are lettered. Included in the notes are literal
renderings, alternate translations, readings of variant manuscripts, and explanatory equivalents of the text.

Quotations from the Old Testament are set in small caps.
Direct speech is indicated by quotation marks. Emphatic

words and phrases are not generally indicated. Italics are employed in the text to indicate words not found in the original and in the margin to signify alternate readings.

For the Old Testament, the latest edition of Rudolph Kittel's *Biblia Hebraica* was employed, together with the most recent information from lexicography, cognate languages, and the Dead Sea Scrolls. For the New Testament, the 23rd edition of the Nestle Greek New Testament was followed in most instances, although the latest available manuscripts were taken into consideration.

The NASB is recommended for its accuracy in the translation of various terms, synonyms, and tenses, for its use of articles, and for its treatment of passages that speak of Christ. A few examples suffice. In Matthew 1:23, we read "*the* virgin shall be with child"; in John 18:27, "*a* rooster crowed"; in Acts 17:23, "*an* unknown god"; in 1 Timothy 6:10, "*a* root of all sorts of evil." It properly translates in Philippians 3:20, "our *citizenship* is in heaven"; in Revelation 1:12, "seven golden *lampstands*"; and in chapter 19:12, "on His head are many *diadems*." John 13:10 reads, "He who has *bathed*"; and Acts 19:15, "I *recognize* Jesus, and I know about Paul." Matthew 25:8 has "lamps *are going out*"; Luke 5:7, "[boats] *began to sink*"; Hebrews 11:10, "*was looking for* the city." Of the Savior, we read in John 1:1, "the *Word* was God"; in Philippians 2:7, "emptied *Himself*"; and in Hebrews 1:3, "exact representation of *His* nature."

Many Bible students feel that the NASB is a bit wooden in style. If, however, we remember its purpose—to revise the American Standard Version of 1901, we have to say that the translators achieved their objective. While avoiding archaisms, the NASB retains much of the quality of its predecessor. Even though it may not be the most readable version, it is a useful tool for the study of Holy Scripture.

An American Translation

Paul E. Eickmann

William F. Beck was a conservative scholar who served as a parish pastor and seminary professor of the Lutheran Church—Missouri Synod. His translation of the New Testament was published in 1963. An American Translation (AAT), including Beck's version of the Old Testament, appeared in 1976, ten years after the translator's death.

Unlike many modern Bible scholars, Beck strongly defended the inspiration of the Scriptures and the divinity of Jesus Christ. "In His Word the Spirit of the living God is talking to us, and His book is the book of life," Beck wrote. His translation capitalizes all nouns and pronouns referring to Jesus, even when unbelievers are speaking to or about him.

The text is printed in paragraph form; poetry is set in poetic lines. Old Testament passages quoted in the New Testament are italicized in both places. Cross-references appear in the center margins.

The translator supplied every section of text with a brief topical heading. The Old Testament has a few footnotes on textual and other matters. Chronological notes are added at the foot of the page in the gospels and at the beginning of every epistle. A few footnotes explain the translator's choice of Greek text in the New Testament (for example, 1 John 5:7,8), such a term as *righteous* (Romans 3:20), and even the original author's line of thought (see especially Galatians).

Because the New Testament was written in the everyday Greek of the people, Beck tried to give his translation a simple, informal "coffee and doughnuts" flavor. "So, don't worry about tomorrow," Jesus says. "Tomorrow will take care of itself. Each day has enough trouble of its own" (Matthew 6:34). "And when I have gone and prepared a place for you, I'll come again and take you home with Me so you'll be where I am. You know the way to the place where I'm going" (John 14:3,4).

Beck was a conservative Lutheran, but he intentionally avoided using theological terms like *reconcile* and *justify.* "In Christ, God was getting rid of the enmity between Himself and the people of the world by not counting their sins against them" (2 Corinthians 5:19). "All have sinned and are without God's glory. They become righteous by a gift of His love, by the ransom Christ Jesus paid to free them" (Romans 3:23,24). Here the reader must keep in mind the footnote on Romans 3:20: "God . . . as a judge declares us righteous."

In the Old Testament, where some translators strive for majestic style, Beck's main concern was simplicity. "As rain and snow come down from heaven / and don't go back again but water the ground / and make it produce and grow / and give seed to the sower and bread to the eater, / so will My word be that I speak. / It will not come back to me with nothing done / but do what I want it to do / and accomplish what I sent it for" (Isaiah 55:10,11). In the following translation, the prophet clearly testifies to the Messiah: "Look, the virgin will conceive and have a Son, and His name will be Immanuel" (Isaiah 7:14).

Briefly characterized, the AAT is informal, plainspoken, and doctrinally sound. The Bible student who is looking for a version in plain English will find a reliable guide in William Beck. He was a Christian who loved the inerrant Word of God, and the purpose of his life and translation work was to glorify the Lord Jesus Christ by "letting God speak the living language of today."

378

New International Version

John C. Jeske

The New International Version (NIV) is a fresh translation of the Bible from Hebrew, Aramaic, and Greek. The New Testament was published in 1973; the complete Bible, in 1978.

The beginnings of the NIV go back to 1965, when a group of Bible scholars met in Chicago and concurred in the need for a new translation of the Scriptures. They were convinced that the archaic language of the King James Version was making it unacceptable for communicating the gospel in the 20th century. The following year more than three hundred pastors and laymen from many denominations met and endorsed the need for a new translation, delegating final responsibility to a body of 15 known as the Committee on Bible Translation.

In 1967 the New York International Bible Society (founded in 1809) agreed to provide financial support for the project, and the work of translation began. More than one hundred translators and editors were active on the NIV, the largest number ever to work on any version of the English Bible. Although they came from different denominations and from half a dozen different countries, they were all committed to the divine inspiration and the full authority of the Scriptures.

What makes the NIV distinctive is the working procedure of the translators. The translation of each Bible book was assigned to an Initial Translation Team. This team translation was then given to an Intermediate Editorial Committee, which rechecked the translation with the original text for accuracy, reviewed it for style, and reworked it. This translation was then given to a third committee, the General Editorial Committee, which again

379

reviewed and revised the translation verse by verse. During the second and third phases of editorial work, copies of the two latter translations were sent to numerous pastors, scholars, English stylists, and laypeople for criticisms and suggestions. The last revision, in turn, was carefully reviewed by the 15-man Committee on Bible Translation, which again made changes and issued the final version.

It is this careful editorial process that distinguishes the NIV translation procedure. Before any passage was finally approved, at least 25 to 30 translators had, over a period of time, examined it for its faithfulness to the original and for its English style. An estimated 200,000 man-hours of scholarly effort had been expended in the translation—about 170 man-hours per chapter.

Although the NIV is a fresh translation and not a revision of the KJV, the translators sought to retain the literary beauty that endeared the KJV to Christians for three and a half centuries. There was no straining after novelty for novelty's sake. Many passages of the NIV have a familiar ring to people who have grown up with the King James Version:

"He was pierced for our transgressions, he was crushed for our iniquities; the punishment that brought us peace was upon him, and by his wounds we are healed" (Isaiah 53:5).

"He died for all, that those who live should no longer live for themselves but for him who died for them and was raised again" (2 Corinthians 5:15).

"You are a chosen people, a royal priesthood, a holy nation, a people belonging to God, that you may declare the praises of him who called you out of darkness into his wonderful light" (1 Peter 2:9).

The New King James Version

Armin J. Panning

The publishers of the New King James Version (NKJV) state that this version is solidly committed to both of the elements included in its name. This version intentionally remains in the venerable King James tradition, while at the same time also adding enough new features to make it fresh and new and useable for contemporary English readers.

The New King James Version is largely the result of the impetus given to the project by Mr. Sam Moore, who in 1975 was the president of Thomas Nelson Publishers. In that year general meetings of conservative Bible scholars were held in Chicago, Nashville, and London. The result of these meetings was the determination to extend the useful life of the KJV through the production of a careful revision of this classic. Some 130 international Bible scholars, editors, and church leaders were commissioned for the project. All of those commissioned signed a statement of faith, declaring their belief that the Scriptures in their entirety are the inspired Word of God, free from error in the autographs (original writings). The overriding consideration that governed all phases of the committee's work was the determination to produce a Bible that would be both readable and reliable.

A core consideration for assuring reliability of the new version's content was the committee's decision to utilize the Greek text used in 1611, the so-called *textus receptus,* or Byzantine text. The NKJV committee's using the *textus receptus* was in conscious opposition to using the text favored by the translators of most modern versions, namely, the Alexandrian text, which generally has shorter readings than the *textus receptus.*

The text of 1 John 5:7, speaking of three heavenly witnesses, serves to illustrate the weakness of locking in on

381

one family of manuscripts and taking its reading, regardless of how little textual evidence there is for its being the original wording. The story is well known how Erasmus, the editor of the text that eventually came to be known as the *textus receptus,* did not include verse 7 in his first edition because it was not found in any of the Greek manuscripts he used. For years that verse had been in the Latin Vulgate. Hence it is not surprising that there were complaints about Erasmus' not including it. When challenged, Erasmus promised that he would include the verse if any Greek evidence for its inclusion could be found. Under conditions many view as suspect, one Greek manuscript turned up and Erasmus dutifully included the verse in his second edition. The result is that verse 7 found its way into the text used in 1611 and, hence, is reproduced also by the NJKV, despite the fact that the editors saw the necessity of adding a footnote that acknowledges, "Only four or five very late Greek manuscripts contain this verse."

There is nothing theologically wrong with what verse 7 says, and the Byzantine text throughout is a reliable text that does not mislead or introduce false doctrine. But that the shorter Alexandrian text must necessarily in every case be inferior to the Byzantine is a contention that needs to be proven. Rather than settling on either the Byzantine or the Alexandrian text as the only reliable one, the better approach would be to follow the principle observed in the church from early times, namely, looking at all the manuscript evidence and then choosing the reading that is best supported by virtue of being both ancient and widespread.

As was the case with the KJV, so also in the NKJV, the Old Testament messianic prophecies are well handled. For example, the translation of Isaiah 7:14 does not compromise the doctrine of the virgin birth by rendering the word in question as "young woman." Rather, it says clearly, "The virgin shall conceive and bear a Son." Similarly, New Testament renderings do not undercut the deity of Christ. Capitalization of pronouns referring to God makes this very clear.

In the area of readability, a conscious effort was made to change as little as necessary. The KJV word order and the rhythm and cadence of its sentences were retained wherever possible. In general, the unquestioned literary beauty of the KJV was very effectively preserved. Words that have changed meaning over the years were replaced. For example, in 1 Thessalonians 4:15, *prevent* was changed to *precede*. At Philemon 20 "refresh my bowels" became "refresh my heart." "Superfluity of naughtiness" (James 1:21) was changed to "overflow of wickedness." Undoubtedly the most noticeable change was the replacement of *thee* and *thou* with *you*. Archaic verb endings (doth, doest) were modernized. Punctuation was updated, for example, quotation marks were added.

One change that unfortunately was not made was reformatting the material into paragraphs. The verse-by-verse format is retained, with an indication of paragraph divisions attempted by using bold-faced verse numbers for paragraph beginnings. To some extent, however, the addition of subject headers into the body of the text offsets the lack of clear paragraph divisions.

One of the committee's editorial changes was immediately overruled by readership reaction. The KJV had indicated with italics those words that were not in the original Greek or Hebrew but were added to make a good English construction. When the New Testament edition of the NKJV was released in 1979, it did not have those supplied words indicated with italics. Public outcry led to the italics being restored when the complete Bible was issued after the Old Testament work had been completed in 1981.

The NKJV is a good addition to the list of modern translations that are available to the English Bible reader. Particularly for those who have grown up with the KJV and have come to love its reverent sound and its stately beauty, the NKJV fills a useful niche and is a welcome addition. With its close adherence to its predecessor, it is as reliable as the KJV that served well for so many years. It can therefore be recommended without reservation for general use.

Contemporary English Version

David P. Kuske

The Contemporary English Version (CEV), also known as *The Promise,* is a translation prepared by the American Bible Society and published by Thomas Nelson, Inc. in 1995. An earlier Bible produced by the American Bible Society is Today's English Version (TEV).

The introduction (page vii) gives this description of the translation process: "The drafts in their earliest stages were sent for review and comment to a number of biblical scholars, theologians, and educators representing a wide variety of church traditions. In addition, drafts were sent for review and comment to all English-speaking Bible Societies and to more than forty United Bible translation consultants around the world. Final approval of the text was given by the American Bible Society Board of Trustees on the recommendation of its Translation Subcommittee."

The introduction (page vi) also explains what the American Bible Society sees as unique about the CEV: "Traditional translations of the Bible count on the *reader's* ability to understand a *written* text. But the CEV differs from all other

English Bibles—past and present—in that it takes into consideration the needs of the hearer, as well as the reader, who may not be familiar with traditional biblical language. The CEV has been described as a 'user friendly' and a 'mission-driven' translation that can be read aloud without stumbling, *heard* without misunderstanding, and *listened to* with enjoyment and appreciation, because the language is contemporary and the style is lucid and lyrical."

The text appears in two columns in a paragraph format with bold-faced section headings. The translation carefully avoids unfortunate line breaks that might otherwise occur in poetry printed in double columns.

Like the TEV, the CEV prefaces each book of the Bible with an introduction and a brief outline of the contents. Though the introductions are generally helpful, some are faulty. The introduction to Isaiah fails to speak about the messianic message of the book. The introduction to Revelation presents a very questionable interpretation, saying that the fall of Babylon in this book refers to the destruction of the Roman Empire.

Some of the faults of the earlier TEV are eliminated. Genesis 1:1 states that God created the heavens and the earth. Genesis 3:15 can be understood as a messianic promise. Job 19:25-27 can be understood as a confession of hope in the resurrection. The word *blood* is not avoided in passages that speak about the Savior's work (Acts 20:28; Romans 3:25; Ephesians 1:7). "Turn back to God" (Matthew 3:2; 4:17) is better than "change your hearts and minds" or "turn away from your sins" as a way to express the concept of repentance when the context indicates that it means both a turning away from sin and unbelief and a turning to faith in the Savior.

Some of the faults of the TEV are retained. Genesis 6:2,4 still uses the translation "supernatural beings." Romans 9:5

weakens a clear statement about Jesus' divinity. The jarring note in 2 Timothy 4:8 remains when "a crown of righteousness" is translated as "a crown . . . for pleasing the Lord." John 3:6 misses the point that sinful human beings give birth to sinful human beings. The sinful nature we inherit from our parents at birth is not properly reflected in the translation "selfish desires" (Galatians 5:16; 6:8; Romans 7:18). Psalm 51:5 loses the thought that we are sinners even before we are born. Matthew 18:18 ("God in heaven will allow whatever you allow on earth") is not an improvement on the TEV. Titus 3:5 eliminates any reference to Baptism ("God washed us by the power of the Holy Spirit"). First Corinthians 11:29 ("you fail to understand that you are the body of the Lord") adds words that remove a reference to the real presence in the Lord's Supper.

Some new faults are added to those of the TEV. One is the substitution of *accept* in CEV for *justify, righteous* in TEV. The Greek means "a judge making an official declaration that a person's legal status is completely cleared of any wrongdoing." It is true that *justify* and *righteous* do not convey this meaning to the contemporary Bible reader, especially one who is not well acquainted with Christianity. Also, to use two different words to translate one Greek word isn't good. But the translation "accept" (Romans 3:22; 4:3; Galatians 3:8; 5:5) limps badly in attempting to give the reader the sense of one of the most important words in Scripture. Although acquit is not used as commonly today as *accept,* it would reflect the meaning of the Greek word much better.

An even more serious problem is the frequent substitution of the phrase "because of faith" in the CEV for "by faith" in the TEV. "Because of faith" leads the reader to think that our faith is a reason why God acquits us, along with Jesus' saving work. To suggest that anything we do contributes to God's declaring our sins forgiven destroys the gospel. Our salvation is no longer a free gift of God if there is even one thing we do to merit it. What complicates the problem is combining "because of faith" with "accept" to say that God accepts people because of their faith (Romans 3:22; Galatians 3:8; 5:5).

All these observations demonstrate that the CEV, or *The Promise,* is not a very good translation to use for careful study of doctrine. However, it is very readable and could serve as a "first reader" for those who are not familiar with the Bible.

God's Word

David P. Kuske

God's Word (GW) is a translation prepared by the God's Word to the Nations Bible Society of Cleveland, Ohio. It was published by World Publishing, Inc., of Grand Rapids, Michigan, in 1995.

The translation was done by a half dozen full-time Lutheran employees and two full-time English editorial reviewers. The translation process is described in the Preface (page ix): "The [translation] theory followed by the . . . translators is closest natural equivalent translation. The first consideration for the translators . . . was to find equivalent English ways of expressing the meaning of the original text. . . . The next consideration was readability. The meaning is expressed in natural American English. . . . The third consideration was to choose the natural equivalent that most reflects the style of the Hebrew, Aramaic, or Greek text."

In regard to theological terms, the policy was to avoid "terms that have little, if any, meaning for most nontheologically trained readers" and to substitute "words that carry the same meaning in common English. . . . Examples include *covenant, grace, justify, repent,* and *righteousness*" (page xiv).

The layout of *God's Word* is an open, single-column format with the text broken into paragraphs and topical headings for longer sections. The translators also used line indentation to indicate the relationship of one line to others in the same context, especially in Hebrew poetry. Long, complicated sentences were studiously avoided.

The GW is available in both hardcover and paperback editions. Special editions are available, such as one for teens, a daily Bible reading edition, and a pocket book New Testament and Psalms. Most editions include an "Application Index," which lists appropriate readings for 60 topics: sickness, marriage, discouragement, difficult times, etc.

The translators at times flattened the text by eliminating cultural references or figures of speech. In Psalm 120 "red-hot coals" is used instead of "burning coals of the broom tree." In Psalm 121 "I lift my eyes up toward the mountains" is flattened to "I look up toward the mountains." Such translations eliminate some wordiness that may cause some readers to pause, but they also eliminate some of the color and the vividness of the text. There is also the even greater consideration of whether translators have the right to simply eliminate something just because they feel that doing so makes the text a bit easier to read.

Of more serious consequence is the way this translation handles some of the concepts that are at the very heart of the Christian faith. In some cases the substitution is a good one as in "the payment that freed you" for *redeem* (1 Peter 1:19). What Christians mean by the word *redeem* is not the same as what the contemporary non-Christian understands by this word.

However, replacing the words *justify* and *righteous* with *approve* or *approval* is questionable. Granted the translation "approve" or "approval" (Romans 3:20-22; Galatians 3:11) has the advantage of using only one word as the Greek does instead using two different terms. Granted also that what was said about redeem in the previous paragraph also applies to *justify* and *righteous*. Yet the translation "approval" falls short of what the Greek word means and so fails to convey to the reader the full meaning of a key concept of the Christian faith. The Greek word has the legal sense of a person being fully acquitted by a judge. "Approve, approval" doesn't say this. Why not use the legal term acquit or acquittal, which commonly appears in newspapers today?

Another key scriptural concept is "law." Using the translation "Moses' Teachings" instead of "law" (Romans 3:19-21,31; 4:13-16) is at times misleading. Sometimes in Scripture the word *law* refers to the five books of Moses. In other places *law* means the Mosaic Law given at Mount Sinai, which applied only to God's chosen people, Israel. When the word *law* refers to either of these two, "Moses' Teachings" could be an acceptable translation. But often the word *law* refers to God's moral law that applies to all people of all time. To translate the word *law* as "Moses' Teachings" in these instances can mislead the reader by implying that the Mosaic Law is still in effect and applies to all people.

Even more serious is the use of "because of faith" and "change the way of thinking and acting" instead of "by faith" and "repent." The concepts faith and repentance are pivotal for understanding God's free gift of salvation. Any hint of introducing works into passages that speak about how we are saved can be disastrous for the reader. Unfortunately, that is what is done in GW.

Most English readers will read "because of faith" as implying that faith is what we do to merit God's acquittal. Apparently objections to this particular phrase have caused the editors to consider changing "because of faith" to "by faith" in some places. A complete elimination of all "because of faith" phrases would have been best.

The word *repentance* is often a synonym for conversion (Acts 5:31; 11:18). In these instances, the GW translation "change the way they think and act" makes the gift of God sound like something sinners accomplish by the way they live.

God's Word does make Scripture easy to read, and a reader can learn to know the way of salvation from this translation. But its handling of some key concepts about the way of salvation is faulty. This means that one cannot use this translation to instruct people more fully in Christian doctrine in order to show them the truth, in contrast to all false teachings, about God's free gift of salvation.

The New Living Translation

Richard P. Balge

This translation is published by Tyndale House Publishers of Wheaton, Illinois. The first edition appeared in 1996. The translators compared the original Hebrew and Greek with Kenneth B. Taylor's 1971 *Living Bible* (LV) and the American Revised Version of 1901. Their aim was to update Kenneth B. Taylor's *Living Bible*. The translating team was made up of 90 evangelical scholars, from various theological backgrounds and denominations

Helpful features include a "Bible Verse Finder," with listings from "abortion" to "worship." "Millennium" is not included. At "rapture" the reader is referred to "second coming," where the selection of verses is "objective" or "neutral." There are 12 map plates, including maps of Israel and the Middle East today, and a timeline of biblical events.

The New Living Translation (NLT) has tried to preserve the simple style and readability that makes the *Living Bible* popular. As accurately as possible, the NLT has converted ancient weights and measures into modern counterparts. It treats Hebrew dates and ancient designations for times of day in a similar manner. Where the original language uses unfamiliar metaphors, the NLT translators strove for understandable equivalents. Footnotes indicate what a literal translation would be.

In their effort to produce a readable translation, the team tried to produce a thought-for-thought rather than a word-for-word translation, "dynamic equivalence" rather than "literal equivalence." That included using gender-appropriate (not gender-inclusive) language where it does not violate the clear intention of the original. Examples would be *descendants* rather than *sons,* and *people* rather than *men* where the author intended to include both men and women.

Often thought-for-thought translation results in an interpretive paraphrase, which may either be helpful or do violence to the original meaning. An example of a helpful paraphrase is seen at Galatians 6:5: "For we are each responsible for our own conduct." At Galatians 6:15, the NLT signals which word for "new" the Greek uses when it translates "new *and different* people." In its context, the statement "but God is one" at Galatians 3:20 requires some interpretation. The NLT provides it with "but God acted on his own when he made his promise to Abraham."

Especially commendable is the interpretive paraphrase at Galatians 4:23, where the birth of Ishmael and the birth of Isaac are contrasted. In the Greek text, "according to the flesh" and "through the promise" are clearly contrasted, just as "slave woman" and "free woman" are. Most modern versions treat "according to the flesh" along the lines of "born in the usual way." The NLT, taking into account the history of the event, the context of Galatians, and the distinction between flesh and promise interprets "according to the flesh" as "in a human attempt to bring about the fulfillment of God's promise."

Regrettably, at John 3:6 both the NLT and the LB treat "flesh" as simply "what is human." The NLT reads: "Humans can reproduce only human life, but the Holy Spirit gives new life from heaven." This does not take into account that Jesus' words are part of his dialogue with Nicodemus on the need to be born again of water and the Spirit (John 3:5). The contrast between flesh and spirit (or Spirit) is very frequently used in the New Testament to contrast sinful human nature with what is spiritual. Much preferred is the NIV's "Jesus answered, 'I tell you the truth, no one can enter the kingdom of God unless he is born of water and the Spirit. Flesh gives birth to flesh, but the Spirit gives birth to spirit.'"

Also of the less helpful variety are a number of other paraphrases. At Luke 3:3 the NLT reads "preaching that people should be baptized to show that they had turned from their sins and turned to God to be forgiven." It provides a literal and correct rendering in its footnote: "Greek *preaching a baptism of repentance for the forgiveness of sins.*" Unfortunately, many readers do not refer to footnotes. At Acts 5:31, the original Greek clearly says that God exalted Jesus "in order to give repentance and forgiveness of sins to Israel." The NLT reads, "He did this *to give . . . an opportunity* to turn from their sins and turn to God so their sins would be forgiven." Thus God's gracious *gift* of repentance and forgiveness is turned into an *opportunity* to have that gift. Something similar occurs at Acts 11:18, where both the LB and the NLT read, ". . . the privilege of turning . . . and receiving eternal life." The Greek original knows nothing about a "privilege," but only an outright gift. Such translating seems to reflect the Arminian orientation of the Evangelical translation team. Arminianism fosters a doctrine of free will in unregenerate sinners that allows them to make a choice once the Holy Spirit grants an "opportunity" or bestows a "privilege."

A related problem is that the NLT consistently makes faith a cause of justification. Instead of "by faith," it regularly translates "because of faith."

In the Old Testament, the NLT improves on the LB in the very first verse of the Bible. The translators relegate the LB's "When God began to create" to a footnote and translate as the KJV and NIV do: "In the beginning God created . . ." (Genesis 1:1). Not necessarily in error, but unnecessarily, the NLT adds the footnote "Or *young woman*" after translating "virgin" at Isaiah 7:14. Unfortunately, NLT retains the LB's interpretation of Genesis 6:2-4. Neither version treats the account as though the "sons of God" were believers and the "daughters of men," unbelievers. The NLT improves on the LB by translating literally, "sons of God" rather than "beings from the spirit world." Regrettably, however, it interprets "daughters of men" as "women of the human race" (verse 2) and "human women" (verse 4). This interpretation introduces an idea into the narrative that has no support elsewhere in Scripture.

At Mark 16:9-20 the NLT shows its preference for the shorter ending by footnoting, "The most reliable early manuscripts conclude the Gospel of Mark at verse 8." While it is possible that the evangelist Mark did conclude at verse 8, there are reputable scholars who do not accept the idea that those manuscripts that omit verses 9 to 19 are the most reliable.

One should not expect a thought-for-thought translation to serve as a study Bible for literal translation. This version, however, is not useful for careful study of doctrine either. Too often the NLT evidences the theological viewpoint of the translators, and then it becomes a sectarian commentary. It is certainly readable, but too often it is not reliable.

Topical

Numbers refer to sections.

difference 174.
harmony of 166.
relation 175.
Goths, Visigoths 292.
Guericke 247.
Guilt-offerings 19.

Hades 296.
Hagiographa 7.
Hamites 130.
Harmony of Gospels 166.
Hasmoneans 127.
Hebrew language 6, 120, 170, 172, 180, 244.
Hebrew poetry 49ff.
Heliand 294.
Hermas 280.
High priest 19, 67, 137, 138, 278.
Hilarius 290.
Hippo (city) 169.
Homologumena 241, 246, 250.

Ignatius 166, 280.
India, Gospel in 180, 277.
Inspiration 2, 44, 72, 120, 165, 169.
Irenaeus 166.
Itala 168, 289.

James the Elder 247, 277.
James, son of Alphaeus 140, 247, 277.
Japhetites 130.
Jeremiah 35.
Jerome 86, 103, 180, 247, 289.
Jesus Sirach 120, 125.
John, Apostle 164, 190, 255, 256, 259.
John, Presbyter 256, 259.
Joseph, husband of Mary 275, 281.
Jubilee, year of 18.
Judaists 215, 225.
Judas, Barsabas 257.
  Iscariot 277.

Lebbaeus 277.
  son of James 257, 281.
Judith 122.
Justin Martyr 166, 280.

King James's Bible 296.
Kings, Persian 40, 45, 47, 136.
Kyria 256.

Lamentations of Jeremiah 82, 83.
Language, sacred of Old Testament 6, 120, 170.
Language, sacred of New Testament 171, 172.
Laodicea 199, 225, 264 (note).
Lebbaeus 277.
Lectors 8, 284.
Lepton 159.
Levitic worship 17, 19, 37, 243.
Luke 164, 174, 175, 186, 195, 203.
Luther quoted 22, 46, 54, 85, 96, 106, 108, 119, 122, 123, 124, 126, 127, 128, 196, 208, 242, 246, 250, 255, 259, 295.
Luther's Bible version 39 (note), 54, 88, 119, 121, 126, 281, 286, 295.

Maccabees 120, 127, 138.
Magi 87.
Magnificat 56.
Majuscules 284.
Manuscripts, Old Testament 8, 282.
Manuscripts, New Testament 282-284.
Marcion 166, 281.
Mark 164, 173ff., 181, 203.
Mary, feasts of 274.
  mother of Jesus, 274.
  Queen of England, 296.
Matthew 164, 173ff., 177.
Matthias 277.

INDEX TWO

Scriptural

(Note—This list omits all passages referred to in the sections treating the biblical books to which they belong; thus, Genesis texts mentioned in the section on Genesis are not listed here, etc.)
Numbers refer to sections.